Preface

When I began writing the first edition more than 10 years ago, we were in the midst of a debate about the role, function, and contribution of phonics in learning to read. Phonics is still a hot button. While most educators agree that children need to learn how our alphabetic writing system works, the bone of contention is how much time and energy teachers should put into phonics.

The perspective I take in this book is that we cannot afford not to teach phonics, but we cannot afford to overdo it either. Phonics is a means to an end, not an end in and of itself. Children learn phonics so they can read and learn new words and, in so doing, build a large fluent reading vocabulary. The goal of all approaches to teaching reading is for children to become independent readers. Phonics is a necessary tool in achieving this universal goal.

Core Beliefs About What Makes a Good Phonics Teacher

From my perspective, a good phonics teacher knows how the letter patterns of phonics match the sounds in words. A good teacher understands and knows how to teach the prefixes, suffixes, syllables, and other multiletter groups in the structure of long words. Also important for good teaching is understanding how children develop competence in reading new words, and the strategies children use at different stages in their development as readers. A good teacher understands that a balanced classroom reading program provides phonics instruction in proportion to children's needs.

Who Will Benefit From Reading This Book: This book is for kindergarten through fifth-grade teachers getting ready to enter the classroom for the first time, and for practicing teachers who already have classroom experience. This book offers a comprehensive, easy-to-understand explanation of what children do when they first begin to pay attention to print, how children learn and use the letter-sounds of phonics, and the contribution that knowledge of the prefixes, suffixes, and syllables in word structure makes to building a large reading vocabulary. It offers a theory-based, developmental perspective on teaching word identification, and describes teaching activities that are consistent with this theoretical perspective.

What Principles Guide Phonics Teachers: The first guiding principle is that learning to read new words unfolds in a predictable developmental sequence that begins long before children ever pay attention to the specific words in books, and ends when children rapidly, accurately, and effortlessly recognize all the words in everyday reading. The second guiding principle is that we teach children how our writing system works so that they can develop a large fluent reading vocabulary and, ultimately, become independent readers. Children may begin kindergarten with only the foggiest knowledge of our writing system, but they leave fifth grade with a wide and rich body of words that they recognize quickly, accurately and effortlessly. A third and final principle is that ultimately successful teaching is measured by children's ability to learn new words on their own, to read independently, to easily recognize many different words, and to focus their attention on comprehension.

New in This Edition

Each bulleted item describes a new few feature for this third edition.

- We have learned a good deal more about how to effectively teach word identification in kindergarten through fifth grade since the last edition, and so this edition includes a section in chapters solely devoted to best practices.
- New teaching activities have been added to help teachers implement best practices in their classrooms, and the explanations of the teaching activities have been refined to make them easy to apply in any classroom setting.
- Also new in this edition are descriptions of the different ways in which children show their teachers that they are aware of the rhymes and sounds in language.
- And because word identification is successful only when children identify words that fit the reading context, chapter 4 includes a new section on how to help children cross-check, self-monitor, and self-correct when reading new words.

What the Reader of This Book Will Learn About Teaching Word Identification

Readers of this book will learn about the different word identification strategies children use to read new words and also how to effectively teach these strategies. Chapter 1 considers the proper place of phonics in a balanced reading program, the cues children use to read new words, and the stages for learning new words and spelling. Chapter 2 explains the sequence in which phonemic awareness develops, best teaching practices, 14 activities to teach rhyme awareness, 17 activities to teach phonemic awareness, and tests for assessing children's phonemic awareness.

Chapter 3 explains the very first strategies children use when reading new words, and best practices for teaching children who are progressing through the first two word-learning stages. Chapter 4 explores how children use the letter patterns in known words to read unknown words; how to help children cross-check, self-monitor, and self-correct; 6 research-based best teaching practices; and 20 activities for teaching rimes and onsets. Chapter 5 describes the letter-sound strategy, the letter-sound patterns of phonics, a sequence for teaching letter-sound patterns, the proper way to use decodable books, 10 best teaching practices, and 23 easy and effective activities for developing knowledge of letter and sound relationships. Chapter 6 explains the multiletter groups readers use to identify long words; best practices for teaching prefixes, suffixes, and syllables; and 22 activities for developing knowledge of multiletter chunks in the structure of words. The last chapter, chapter 7, focuses on children who may benefit from extra help and consideration because they are not yet successful at reading new words on their own or because they speak a language other than English at home.

This book is a ready reference for teachers in every elementary grade. In taking a developmental approach to word identification, it gives teachers the information they need to match what is taught to what children need to learn. I hope that the cross-grade developmental perspective combined with the new additions to this revision will support effective teaching in every grade. The ultimate objectives are, after all, developing children's ability to read new words and enabling their steady progress toward becoming accomplished readers who instantly recognize all the words they read in everyday text.

ACKNOWLEDGMENTS

I am indebted to the many teachers who welcomed me into their classrooms, to the children who were willing readers and eager participants in the activities their teachers shared, and to the principals who encouraged and supported their teachers. Without them this book could not have been written. Of the teachers I visited and who shared their classrooms with me, I would like to especially thank: Elo Goodman of Cary Elementary School; Judy Goodnight, Supervisor, and Tamara Jones and Traci Ashbaugh of the Kannapolis City Schools; Christine Greene of Holly Springs Elementary School; Judy Skroch of Effie Green; Joan Perry of Emma Conn; Sarah Rodgers of Fox Road School; Denise Rhodes, principal, and David Wall of Franklinton Elementary; William Abel, principal, and Amy Stone of Immaculata Catholic School; Donna Dysert, Donna Kocur, and Karen Royall of Lacy Elementary; Helen Collier, principal, Gail Ace, and Marilyn Gray of Penny Road School; Moria O'Connor, principal, Carolyn Banks, Diana Callaghan, Debbie Faulkner, Pat Lemmons, and Gail Walker of Poe International Magnet School; Pam Bridges, principal, Judy Honeycutt and Patricia Gonzales of Willow Springs; JoAnn Everson; and Ronald Honeycutt. A special thanks to Catherine Clements for her good advice, to Celia Jolley for her helpful words, and to Elizabeth Beecher for her wise counsel. Thanks also to the reviewers of this text: Beth C. Anderson, Moorhead State University; Diane E. Bushner, Salem State College; Patricia P. Kelly, Virginia Tech University; and Thomas Gunning, Central Connecticut State University. William S. O'Bruba, Bloomsburg University; I. LaVerne Raine, TA&MU Commerce; Grace Nunn, Eastern Illinois University; and Hazel A. Brauer, University of San Francisco. Finally, thanks to Linda Montgomery, my editor at Merrill, for her guidance and vision.

Educator Learning Center: An Invaluable Online Resource

Merrill Education and the Association for Supervision and Curriculum Development (ASCD) invite you to take advantage of a new online resource, one that provides access to the top research and proven strategies associated with ASCD and Merrill—the Educator Learning Center. At **www.EducatorLearningCenter.com** you will find resources that will enhance your students' understanding of course topics and of current educational issues, in addition to being invaluable for further research.

How the Educator Learning Center will help your students become better teachers

With the combined resources of Merrill Education and ASCD, you and your students will find a wealth of tools and materials to better prepare them for the classroom.

Research

- More than 600 articles from the ASCD journal *Educational Leadership* discuss everyday issues faced by practicing teachers.
- A direct link on the site to Research Navigator™ gives students access to many of the leading education journals, as well as extensive content detailing the research process.
- Excerpts from Merrill Education texts give your students insights on important topics of instructional methods, diverse populations, assessment, classroom management, technology, and refining classroom practice.

Classroom Practice

- Hundreds of lesson plans and teaching strategies are categorized by content area and age range.
- Case studies and classroom video footage provide virtual field experience for student reflection.
- Computer simulations and other electronic tools keep your students abreast of today's classrooms and current technologies.

Look into the value of Educator Learning Center yourself

Preview the value of this educational environment by visiting **www.EducatorLearningCenter.com** and clicking on "Demo." For a free 4-month subscription to the Educator Learning Center in conjunction with this text, simply contact your Merrill/Prentice Hall sales representative.

Word Identification Strategies

Phonics from a New Perspective

Third Edition

Barbara J. Fox
North Carolina State University

PEARSON

Merrill
Prentice Hall

Upper Saddle River, New Jersey
Columbus, Ohio

Library of Congress Cataloging-in-Publication Data

Fox, Barbara J.
    Word identification strategies: phonics from a new perspective / Barbara J. Fox.–3rd ed.
      p. cm.
    Includes bibliographical references and index.
    ISBN 0-13-110099-8 (pbk.)
    1. Word recognition. 2. Reading—Phonetic method. 3. Reading (Elementary) I. Title.

LB1573.6.F69 2004
372.4'145—dc21   2003044156

Vice President and Executive Publisher: Jeffery W. Johnston
Senior Editor: Linda Ashe Montgomery
Production Editor: Mary M. Irvin
Design Coordinator: Diane C. Lorenzo
Text Design and Production Coordination: Carlisle Publishers Services
Cover Designer: Ali Mohrman
Cover Image: Stock Illstration Source
Production Manager: Pamela D. Bennett
Director of Marketing: Ann Castel Davis
Marketing Manager: Darcy Betts Prybella
Marketing Coordinator: Tyra Poole

This book was set in Palatino by Carlisle Communications, Ltd., and was printed and bound by R. R. Donnelley & Sons Company. The cover was printed by Phoenix Color Corp.

10 9 8 7
ISBN 0-13-110099-8

Discover the Companion Website Accompanying This Book

The Prentice Hall Companion Website: A Virtual Learning Environment

Technology is a constantly growing and changing aspect of our field that is creating a need for content and resources. To address this emerging need, Prentice Hall has developed an online learning environment for students and professors alike—Companion Websites—to support our textbooks.

In creating a Companion Website, our goal is to build on and enhance what the textbook already offers. For this reason, the content for each user-friendly website is organized by topic and provides the professor and student with a variety of meaningful resources. Common features of a Companion Website include:

For the Professor—

Every Companion Website integrates **Syllabus Manager™,** an online syllabus creation and management utility.

- **Syllabus Manager™** provides you, the instructor, with an easy, step-by-step process to create and revise syllabi, with direct links into Companion Website and other online content without having to learn HTML.

- Students may log on to your syllabus during any study session. All they need to know is the web address for the Companion Website and the password you've assigned to your syllabus.
- After you have created a syllabus using **Syllabus Manager**™, students may enter the syllabus for their course section from any point in the Companion Website.
- Clicking on a date, the student is shown the list of activities for the assignment. The activities for each assignment are linked directly to actual content, saving time for students.
- Adding assignments consists of clicking on the desired due date, then filling in the details of the assignment—name of the assignment, instructions, and whether or not it is a one-time or repeating assignment.
- In addition, links to other activities can be created easily. If the activity is online, a URL can be entered in the space provided, and it will be linked automatically in the final syllabus.
- Your completed syllabus is hosted on our servers, allowing convenient updates from any computer on the Internet. Changes you make to your syllabus are immediately available to your students at their next logon.

For the Student—

- **Topic Overviews**—Outline key concepts in topic areas.
- **Strategies**—These websites provide suggestions and information on how to implement instructional strategies and activities for each topic. The Assessment topic also contains Practice Case Studies as well.
- **Web Links**—A wide range of websites that allow the students to access current information on everything from rationales for specific types of instruction, to research on related topics, to compilations of useful articles and more.
- **Electronic Bluebook**—Send homework or essays directly to your instructor's email with this paperless form.
- **Message Board**—Virtual bulletin board to post or respond to questions or comments from a national audience.
- **Chat**—Real-time chat with anyone who is using the text anywhere in the country—ideal for discussion and study groups, class projects, etc.

To take advantage of these and other resources, please visit the *Word Identification Strategies*, Third Edition, Companion Website at

www.prenhall.com/fox

Contents

CHAPTER 1

Word Identification in a Balanced Reading Program 1

CHAPTER 2

Phonemic Awareness: Becoming Aware of the Sounds of Language   21

CHAPTER 3

Early Word Identification Strategies: Using Logos, Pictures, Word Configuration, and One or Two Letter-Sound Associations to Read New Words   61

CHAPTER 4

The Analogy Strategy: Using Parts of Familiar Words to Read New Words   77

CHAPTER 5

The Letter-Sound Strategy: Using Letters and Sounds to Read New Words   111

CHAPTER 6

The Multiletter Chunk Strategy: Using the Multiletter Groups in Word Structure to Read New Long Words   153

CHAPTER 7

Children Who Need Extra Help   195

APPENDIX A

APPENDIX B

APPENDIX C

APPENDIX D

CHAPTER 1

Word Identification in a Balanced Reading Program

This chapter explains the proper place of word identification in a balanced classroom reading program. You will learn about five approaches to teaching phonics and how to determine the most appropriate balance between word identification and other components of the reading program. You also will learn how children use syntactic, semantic, and graphophonic cues to read unfamiliar words; the stages of word learning; and why understanding these stages is important for teaching children to read unfamiliar words.

KEY IDEAS

➤ In balanced reading programs, the emphasis on word identification is in proportion to children's individual needs.
➤ Phonics is a shortcut for learning words; helps children develop rich, fluent reading vocabularies; and contributes to reading independence.
➤ Readers use graphophonic, syntactic, and semantic cues to read new words.
➤ In understanding how word reading develops in stages, you can teach exactly what children need to know to add new words to their reading vocabularies.

KEY VOCABULARY

Alphabetic principle

Analogy-based phonics

Analytic phonics

Consonants

Embedded phonics

Fluent reading vocabulary

Graphophonic cues

Linguistic approach

Metacognitive awareness

Phonics

Semantic cues

Syntactic cues

Synthetic phonics

Vowels

Word fluency

You automatically recognize all the words you commonly encounter when reading. Instead of figuring out words, you focus on comprehension. This is exactly as it should be. But consider what it is like for young readers who come across many unfamiliar words. Meeting a large number of new words is a major impediment to comprehension, and so it is not surprising that these children concentrate on developing their reading vocabularies. One way to do this is to use the cues in the reading context, including cues from our alphabetic writing system, to figure out the identity of words that have never been seen before.

Consider the note in Figure 1–1 written by Maria. If you speak and read Spanish, Maria's message is crystal clear. The words are easy to recognize, the sentences are well formed, and you know why the picture and the message are a perfect match. Suppose instead that you speak Spanish but cannot read it. Now the format of the note and Maria's drawing are the only reliable clues to meaning. You might make an educated guess based on information gleaned from the picture and your

Querida Señora Saracho,
    Ustedes una maestra
magnífica. Yo estoy
aprendiendo cosas nuevas
todos los días. Yo espero
que usted pueda
enseñar el próximo año.
Usted es la más linda
maestra del quinto grando.
        Con cariño,
        Maria

Figure 1-1 Maria's note: Can you get the message?

own background knowledge. From the heart-shaped drawing, you might logically infer that this is either a Valentine or a love letter. But unless you recognize the words Maria wrote, your grasp of meaning is limited, and your comprehension is at best an approximation of Maria's message.

To go beyond supposition, you must learn the same things beginning readers learn—how to use phonics and the multiletter groups, or chunks, in word structure (the -er in sharper) to read new words. Just recognizing words is not enough, however. You must also know the meaning of the words Maria wrote, understand the sentence structure, have a specific purpose for reading it, and appreciate the social context in which notes such as this are written and read. (See the translation of Maria's note at the end of this chapter.)

What Is Phonics, Who Teaches It and Why?

Our written language is based on the *alphabetic principle*. This is the principle of using letters to represent sounds. In a perfect alphabet, only one letter represents only one sound, and so readers can pronounce any written word by simply associating sounds with letters. *Phonics* consists of the relationship between the letters and sounds and approaches for teaching these relationships. Letter-sound relationships are a set of visual directions—a map, if you will—telling readers how to pronounce words they have never seen before. You teach phonics when you demonstrate that the letter *b* represents the sound heard at the beginning of /banana/[1], /boat/, and /bubble/. In helping children compare and contrast the sounds represented by the letters in *hid* and *hide*, you are teaching phonics. When you challenge readers to think about a word that begins with *c*, ends with *t*, and makes sense in the sentence *Mark's _____ eats tuna fish*, you are a teacher of phonics. And when you encourage writers to spell a word "the way it sounds," you help children think about and analyze our alphabetic writing system, which is what you do when you teach phonics.

All teachers—whether advocates of basal, whole language, language experience, literature-based, integrated language arts, technology-based, or skills-based instruction—include word identification in their classroom reading program. They do this for three reasons:

1. **Phonics is a short cut to word learning.** With a relatively small amount of information, readers can identify a large number of words. For instance, the children in your class who know the sounds that *t* and *ur* represent can figure out the pronunciation of words that share these letters, such as *turn, hurt,* and *turtle.*

2. **Knowing phonics helps children develop a large *fluent reading vocabulary.*** The words in children's fluent reading vocabularies are recognized accurately, effortlessly, and instantly—within a second of seeing them (Ehri, 1997). These words are "on the tip of the tongue," always ready and instantly available anytime children see them.

3. **Phonics helps children become independent readers.** Children who know now to use phonics can identify many new words in text. Consequently, they can read any book at any time in any place. They do not have to rely on their teachers to tell them words; they read independently. Children who are good at word identification are good readers (National Reading Panel, 2000). These children have better attitudes toward reading and better self-concepts of their ability to succeed in school than children who do not use word identification strategies (Tunmer & Chapman, 2002). Your classroom word identification program will be successful when you teach phonics early, systematically, directly, and meaningfully, and when children have many opportunities to use their letter-sound knowledge in reading and writing. By early, we mean beginning in kindergarten or first grade, well before children are independent readers (National Reading Panel, 2000). As for systematically, there is no research-based sequence in which letter-sound associations should be taught, as explained in chapter 5. This said, it is important to have an overall plan for teaching letter-sounds, to teach them in a logical sequence, to make sure that the plan is implemented, and to assure that all children have an equal opportunity to learn useful letter-sound relationships. In well-planned direct instruction, teachers explain, model, and demonstrate phonics knowledge and how to use

---

1 In this book, for simplicity, rather than using a standard system of phonetic symbols, letters that typically stand for sounds are used and placed between slashes (/ /). Single vowels represent short vowel sounds, while long vowel sounds are either described as such or indicated by the use of a macron (¯).

it when reading and writing (Warton-McDonald et al., 1997). Phonics instruction also needs to be meaningful; that is, we want to teach phonics within the context of words that not only illustrate certain phonics letter-sound relationships, but also are important for everyday reading and writing. And, of course, we want to give children much needed practice using letter-sound relationships, and many opportunities to use this knowledge when reading and writing every day (Armbruster, Lehr, & Osborn, 2001). It is also important to consider what children need to know to be better readers and then to provide instruction in proportion to children's needs, which brings us to the topic of balance in your classroom program.

Phonics in a Balanced Reading Program

When something is balanced, it is in proportion. The United States will achieve a balance of trade when the nation's exports are in proportion to its imports. Your classroom reading program is in balance when all components are in proportion to children's needs at a given time in their reading development. Teachers and administrators alike value a balanced perspective that includes systematic phonics instruction in literature-rich classrooms (Bauman, Hoffman, Duffy-Hester, & Ro, 2000).

Let us consider what we mean when we say that our classroom reading programs are balanced. A balanced program includes many approaches and materials, all in proportion to children's individual needs. A balanced classroom program is not a single "approach" to reading as is, say, a basal reader or a whole language approach. Rather, balance occurs when you select just the right approach, just the right materials, and just the right emphasis to develop the reading potential in every child.

The things children need to know to improve their reading achievement change as their reading ability develops. As a consequence, the role of phonics in a balanced reading program in first grade is quite different from its proper place in a fourth-grade classroom. Yet the goal of phonics—to give children the tools they need to develop a large fluent reading vocabulary—remains the same across grades. We want children to be independent readers who use phonics to teach themselves new words and develop the ability to automatically read all the words they see in everyday text.

In a balanced program, children learn to identify words by letter-sound patterns, which is the traditional grist of phonics (chapter 5). However, in this book we will also include in a balanced classroom reading program the teaching of analogous groups of shared letters (chapter 4), such as the *at* in *hat* and *fat*, and large multiletter groups, or chunks, in the structure of words (chapter 6), such as prefixes (the *re-* in *rerun*) and suffixes (the *-ed* in *jumped*). And, of course, balanced programs ensure that children have frequent, meaningful opportunities to use their knowledge of phonics, analogous letter groups, and multiletter chunks in word structure when they read and spell.

The International Reading Association's (1997) position is that teachers should ask *when, how, how much,* and *under what circumstances* to teach phonics. We can see from this statement that phonics is not an all-or-nothing curriculum component. Rather, it is a portion of the curriculum that complements other reading and writing activities, and enables children to read and spell independently.

When Do We Teach Phonics?

The answer to *when* depends on the level of children's development as readers. For children to develop *word fluency* (fast, accurate, and effortless word identification) and reading independence, a balanced reading program dedicates a significant amount of time to phonics in the early grades. This is what happens in practice, for more than half the first-grade teachers in a nationwide survey said they spend significant time teaching phonics, while only a handful of fourth- and fifth-grade teachers reported doing so (Bauman, Hoffman, Moon, & Duffy-Hester, 1998). Because children in the fourth grade and above already know how to use letter-sound associations, a balanced program for these children focuses on the multiletter chunks in word structure (prefixes, suffixes, contractions, base words, syllables, and root words, including Greek and Latin roots) as well as advanced comprehension strategies and study skills. Thus, the answer to the question of *when* to teach phonics is that it should be taught in the first few grades (National Reading Panel, 2000; Snow, Burns, & Griffin, 1998). This brings us to the next point—*how* to teach phonics.

How Do We Teach Phonics?

A plethora of phonics teaching materials are available, but phonics instruction can be distilled into a choice among (a) synthetic, (b) analytic, (c) linguistic, (d) analogy-based, and (e) embedded phonics (Armbruster et al., 2001; Stahl, Duffy-Hester, & Stahl, 1998; Vacca et al., 2003).

1. *Synthetic phonics* is part-to-whole instruction. Synthetic phonics starts with letter-sounds. Children "sound out" new words by associating letters with sounds and then blending the sounds together (Armbruster et al., 2001; Vacca et al., 2003). For example, children first learn that the letter *s* represents /s/, *i* represents /i/ and *t* represents /t/. Then children blend these three sounds together to pronounce /sit/ and, in hearing a familiar word, read the word *sit*.

2. *Analytic phonics* is whole-to-part-to-whole instruction. This approach begins with whole words. Children first learn to read words with certain letter-sound correspondences and then later are taught, or encouraged to discover, which sounds go with which letters. For example, children learn to read many different words with a short /a/ letter-sound, as in *cat*. Then the teacher writes a known word, *cat*, on a chart, and asks children to pay special attention to the short /a/ sound. The teacher now writes other short *a* words the children already know how to read, such as *fan, mad, Sam, bad, ham,* and *map.* Everyone studies the word list and draws the conclusion that a single *a* in a short word stands for /a/. Children do not pronounce isolated sounds in the analytic ap-

proach (Armbruster et al., 2001); sounds are pronounced only within the context of whole words.

   3. In a *linguistic approach,* children read sentences with words that have predictable letter-sound patterns, such as *The man can fan. The van cannot fan. The man and the fan are in the van.* The assumption is that young readers will learn letter-sound associations by reading words with highly predictable letter patterns. Unfortunately, the text makes little sense, is difficult to read silently or aloud, and may bog readers down in a morass of similar looking and similar sounding words. This approach was popular in the 1960s and is still found in the Merrill Linguistic Reading Program (1986) and Programmed Reading (Phoenix Learning Resources, 1994).

   4. Like the linguistic approach to phonics, *analogy-based phonics* focuses on predictable letter patterns in words. But unlike the linguistic approach, the analogy-based approach groups words with the same patterns into word families (the *it* family, for example, consists of *sit, fit,* and *lit*), teaches children how to pronounce and spell the families, and emphasizes wide-range reading and writing. Here the teacher helps children learn the basis for a family, such as *it,* saying something like, "*It* says /it/. Words with *it* belong to the *it* family." The teacher and children then participate in activities that call attention to *it* family words. You will learn more about this approach in chapter 4.

   5. In *embedded phonics,* children learn the letter-sound associations they need to decode the new words they see in text. Phonics is taught "as needed"—that is, teachers teach only those letter-sound associations that children need to decode words in the books they are reading. Because each book has a different set of words, and since many of these words are likely to contain different letter-sound patterns, embedded phonics does not systematically teach the letter-sound relationships (Armbruster et al., 2001). Consequently, as children move from kindergarten to the first and second grades, they may well bring to text a highly personal, and therefore highly individualistic, storehouse of phonics knowledge.

How Much Time Should We Spend Teaching Phonics?

How much time and energy to spend on phonics depends on children's knowledge of the alphabetic principle, and their ability to use this knowledge when reading and writing. To strike the right balance in your classroom, consider children's needs and then select the intensity (how much) that is the best match for the individuals and groups you teach. Greg and Sharon illustrate how beginning readers from the same first-grade class have different levels of phonics knowledge. As illustrated in Figure 1–2, Greg fluently recognizes only a few words, relies almost entirely on pictures to guess at meaning, inconsistently uses beginning and ending letter-sounds to identify words, and forgets words from one day to the next. He does not always separate words with white spaces when he writes, and does not consistently use letters to represent sounds.

   Sharon, whose work can be seen in Figure 1–3, understands what she reads, uses phonics and context cues to read new words, and uses letter-sound relationships when spelling. Her fluent reading vocabulary is growing rapidly, and

Figure 1–2 At the end of the first grade, Greg knows only a handful of words. He will benefit from explicit instruction in all aspects of reading, including phonics, and from opportunities to use letter and sound relationships when reading and spelling.

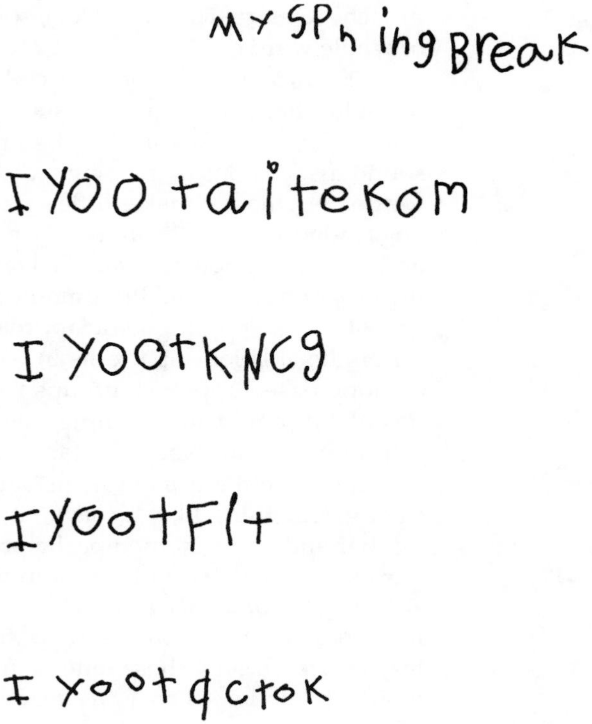

MY SPhing BReaK

IYOO taiteKom

I YOOtKNCg

IYOOtFIt

I xootdcroK

Figure 1–3 While Sharon, Greg's first-grade classmate, will benefit from learning more about how letters represent sounds, she knows and uses many more letter-sound associations when she reads and writes than Greg. An appropriate classroom balance would include less concentration on phonics for Sharon than it would for Greg.

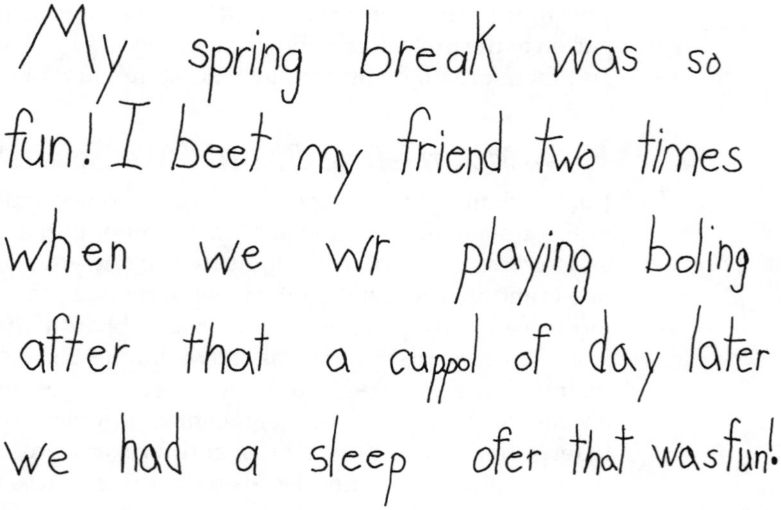

My spring break was so fun! I beet my friend two times when we wr playing boling after that a cuppol of day later we had a sleep ofer that was fun!

she is developing reading independence. We can see from her writing that Sharon correctly spells many words in her fluent reading vocabulary, understands the sounds most consonants represent, and is learning how vowels represent sounds. The letters in our alphabet are divided into consonants and vowels. From the perspective of teaching children to read, the *vowels* consist of *a, e, i, o,* and *u,* and *y* when it comes in the middle (*cycle*) or at the end of a syllable or short word (*try*). All the other letters are *consonants.* While both Greg and Sharon will benefit from more phonics knowledge, Greg has far more to learn than Sharon. For this reason, an appropriate classroom balance would include more phonics instruction for Greg than it would for Sharon. So, we see that the answer to *how much* phonics to teach depends on children's understanding of letter-sound relationships and on their ability to use these relationships in everyday reading and writing.

Under What Circumstances Should We Teach Phonics?

The answer to *under what circumstances* depends on how teachers differentiate instruction. In balanced classrooms, children may learn (a) all together in one large group, (b) in small groups, (c) in flexible skill groups, or (d) individually. Large groups typically include everyone, or nearly everyone, in the class, while small groups include a handful of children who are reading on or near the same level. Another kind of group, a flexible skill group, consists of children reading at vastly different levels who need to know more about specific letter-sound associations, specific reading strategies, or specific reading skills. These groups are disbanded once children know and apply the information and strategies when reading. And last, children may be taught individually. According to the National Reading Panel (2000), all types—large groups, small groups, and whole classes of children—are effective, provided that instruction is systematic.

You will find that different teachers in your school conceptualize balance differently. Naturally, when teachers' views differ, so too does the emphasis they place on phonics (Freppon & Dahl, 1998). Many factors go into finding the right balance among phonics and other components of your classroom reading program—the grade you teach, children's ability to use letter-sound relationships when reading and writing, and the size and growth of children's fluent reading vocabulary, to name a few. A well-balanced program for a child like Greg, who brings less phonics knowledge to reading and writing, looks quite different from a well-balanced program for a child like Sharon, who has more phonics knowledge. Even though the individual teachers in your school may not agree on the answers to when, how, how much, and under what circumstances to teach phonics in a balanced program, they all teach children how to use syntactic, semantic, and graphophonics cues to read new words in text, which is the topic of the next section.

Three Cues for Reading New Words

Good readers bring to print a deep understanding of the word order, meaning, and sounds of the spoken language. Information about grammar, meaning, and letter-sound relationships are three types of information—or cueing systems—that support readers as they make sense of authors' messages. Syntax is the grammatical arrangement of words in phrases, sentences, and paragraphs. *Syntactic cues* are the basis on which readers decide whether an author's word order is consistent with English grammar. Syntactic cues help readers predict words in phrases and sentences. For instance, in *The little* _____ *chewed on a bone,* readers know that the word following *little* is a person or an animal (a noun). Likewise, readers know that the word following *dog* in *The little dog* _____ *on a bone* is an action word (a verb). Syntactic cues also give readers insight into the meaning of sentences. Readers who use these cues know that the meaning of phrases, sentences, and paragraphs may change when words are sequenced in different ways, for example, *The little dog chewed on a bone* versus *The dog chewed on a little bone.* Though the first sentence refers to a small dog and the other to a small bone, both conform to the structure of English. But the sentence *The chewed on a dog bone little* makes no sense at all. The word order is not consistent with English structure, so the sentence is not meaningful language. Hence, when readers use syntactic cues, they ask themselves, "Does this seem like language?"

Semantic cues, a second source of information, are the meaningful relationships among words in phrases, sentences, and paragraphs. This is the basis on which readers decide whether an author's message is logical and represents real-world events, relationships, and phenomena. Readers draw on their knowledge of the meaningful relationships among words and on their prior knowledge of the topic they are reading about. In so doing, readers look for meaning that is consistent with both the text and their experiences. For example, readers use semantic cues to determine that the relationship among words in *The little dog chewed on the bone* is meaningful and that the relationship among the words in *The little bone chewed on the dog* is not. Hence, when readers use semantic context cues, they ask themselves, "Does this make sense?"

Syntactic and semantic cues, together with the overall conditions under which materials are read, create a rich base on which word identification and reading comprehension rest. When readers use the reading context, they draw on all the cues available to them, selecting and combining information to construct authors' messages. Brian's note, seen in Figure 1–4, illustrates how syntactic and semantic context cues work together. You, the reader, automatically recognize all the words as belonging to your fluent reading vocabulary except one: *spreencler.* If you were to try to decode this word without thinking about context, it would be difficult to figure out what Brian meant to say. However, *spreencler* is surrounded by other words that contribute valuable clues to its identity.

From syntactic cues, you infer that *spreencler* is a noun, not a verb, adverb, or adjective. From semantic cues, you surmise that this unknown object is something children play with, which rules out such things as spoons or spigots. If you know the

Figure 1–4 Brian's note: How do you figure out the meaning?

types of activities Brian and Mike enjoy, and if you also know the types of things Mike has to play with, you can use this prior knowledge to narrow your choices even further. For many readers, this information is enough to deduce the identity of *spreencler.*

Though the syntactic cues and semantic cues are rich, if you want to be absolutely certain about the word, you will turn your attention to cues that are a combination of how words look and sound. Goodman (1996) coined the term *graphophonic* for these cues and other visual cues indicated by punctuation. *Graphophonic cues,* in this example the letter-sound cues in *spreencler,* help you further narrow the field of possible words. When readers use graphophonic cues, they ask themselves, "Does this word sound and look right?"

When using syntactic, semantic, and graphophonic cues to identify words, readers think about words that make sense in passages, and hence keep the focus on meaning. Given the unconventional way Brian spelled *spreencler,* simple letter-sound cues might help you approximate pronunciation. The easiest way to combine graphophonic letter and sound cues with syntactic and semantic context cues is to ask yourself, "What word begins with *spr,* ends with *er,* and makes sense in Brian's message?" With this combination of cues, your chance of making an educated guess increases substantially because graphophonic cues help you narrow the field of possible words. If the guess you make is sensible, you discontinue decoding, confident that you understand Brian's message.

If the beginning and ending letter and sound cues in *spreencler,* as well as the syntactic cues and semantic cues are not enough to figure out this word's identity, then you consider all the letters in spelling. Should you choose to do this, you would probably sound out *spreencler* letter-sound by letter-sound. But, having sounded out *spreencler,* you still have not pronounced a recognizable word. Brian's spelling is unconventional, and so the outcome of sounding out is a nonsense word. Yet this nonsense word is quite similar in sound to a meaningful word in your speaking vocabulary that fits nicely into the overall reading context.

There is a curious and very interesting phenomenon at work here: In using graphophonic cues, readers do not always have to perfectly pronounce the words they are figuring out. Pronunciation need only sound enough like a real word to trigger recognition. By combining information from different cues, you know without a shadow of a doubt that Brian intended to write that he is playing in Mike's *sprinkler.*

While use of all types of cues contributes to understanding messages like Brian's, this does not imply that every cue is equally helpful in every reading situation. Children's reasons for reading affect the importance they assign to accurate word identification. For example, a fifth grader who reads her science textbook for information needs to pay close attention to the words the author wrote. A second grader who is reading an article in a children's magazine is more likely to be concerned with the overall ideas in the article, not with detailed information. Correct identification of nearly all words is far more important for understanding the information in science textbooks than it is for enjoying magazine articles.

Insofar as Brian's note is concerned, if your reason for reading is to find out who Brian is playing with, you might make an educated guess for *spreencler,* having found out that Brian is in Mike's company. Conversely, if you are concerned with knowing precisely what Brian is doing, you will analyze *spreencler* to determine exactly what type of play Brian is engaged in. All in all, the amount of mental attention you allot to word identification depends on how concerned you are about absolute understanding. Your concern for understanding is, in turn, determined in part by the reason you are reading Brian's note in the first place.

Over-relying on any one cue is inefficient, time-consuming, and likely to result in poor comprehension. Good readers know this and hence balance syntactic, semantic, and graphophonic cues with the type of text they are reading, the reading environment, their own reasons for reading, and their own background knowledge. Although it is not necessary to distribute attention equally to all cues, it is necessary to be able to take maximum advantage of the information cues provide, should reading situations call for it. When all is said and done, the strategic use of the reading context hinges on taking advantage of syntactic, semantic, and graphophonic cues. And, of course, the reasons for reading and the prior knowledge readers bring to text help determine how much attention readers choose to pay to the cues available to them.

Developing Metacognitive Awareness

Unlike the Greek goddess Athena who sprang fully grown from Zeus's head, word identification strategies do not emerge fully formed from a few incidental experiences with print. Strategies are systematic, organized procedures for identifying words and as such require careful nurturing and a supportive environment in which to develop. This does not mean a drill-and-kill approach to learning where readers memorize isolated letter-sound combinations. Rather, it means giving readers many opportunities to understand how our alphabetic writing system works, and many chances to strategically use this information as they read and write every day. Your role as the teacher is to demonstrate and explain how letters represent sound, to guide children, to model and demonstrate strategies, and to discuss with children the strategies they use.

To develop and apply word identification strategies, readers need to become metacognitively aware of their own strategy use and how letters represent sound. *Metacognitive awareness* is the self-conscious understanding of our own knowledge, skills, and strategies. From a word identification perspective, metacognitive awareness is knowing how, when, and why to use different word identification strategies. It is the self-awareness, or personal insight, into what an individual reader knows about letters and sounds, why this knowledge is important, and how and when to use certain strategies. Children who are metacognitively aware monitor their own word identification while reading, cross-check to make sure that the words they read make sense, and correct their own miscues. (This is explained further in chapter 4.)

Thinking analytically and critically helps children become conscious—metacognitively aware—of their own strategy use and in so doing gain greater control over word identification strategies. When children explain in their own words what they know about how our alphabetic writing system works and give reasons for using the strategies they do, they develop a self-conscious awareness of their own knowledge, as well as an appreciation of why and when to use different strategies. To help children become aware of what they know about letters and sounds, and how and when to use word identification strategies, ask questions such as these:

1. When would you use this same way to figure out another word?
2. What other kinds of words can be figured out just the way you figured out this one?
3. What do you do when you come to a word you do not know?
4. How did you know that _____ (pointing to a letter or letter group) makes the _____ (indicating the sound or describing the sounds, such as the long vowel sound) in _____ (the word the child correctly read)?
5. When you see a _____ (describing a particular phonics pattern, such as a *vowel-consonant-e,* as in *home*), what sound should you try first?
6. If the first try doesn't make a real word, what sound(s) could you try next? (This question helps children develop flexibility in decoding.)
7. How would you write _____ (a word with a letter-sound association children are learning in your classroom)? Then follow up with the question: "Why did you write it this way?"
8. What did you learn today that will help you be a better reader?

As children answer questions like these, they organize observations, form generalizations, change or alter information and ideas, and, perhaps most important, become sensitive to how the use of word identification strategies supports comprehension.

Four Ways to Read Words

There are four ways children might read words: (a) fluently, (b) by analogy, (c) by associating letters with sounds, or (d) by identifying multiletter chunks in word structure. Familiar words are automatically read. In reading words, children may take advantage of all the cues in text, including semantic and syntactic cues. They may also look at pictures for cues to meaning, and bring their own real-world experiences to bear on deciding which words authors are likely to use to express ideas. All these sources of information—semantic cues, syntactic cues, picture cues, prior knowledge cues—help readers narrow word choices. However, even with these rich sources of information, readers still must look inside *new* words to identify them; that is, readers must pay attention to the letters in words and to the sounds those letters represent. Whereas readers pay attention to the letters and the sounds they represent in new words, the words in readers' fluent reading vocabulary do not require sustained attention to identify them.

We already have learned that children's fluent reading vocabulary consists of all the words that they recognize quickly, accurately, and effortlessly. These *known* words are read or spelled from memory (Ehri, 2000). On reading words over and over, children eventually remember how words sound, what they mean, and how they look. All this information is stored together in children's memory. On seeing known words, children draw on this memory to instantly read them.

Word fluency—fast, accurate, and effortless word identification—is a bedrock of fluent reading (Wolf & Katzir-Cohen, 2001). Fluent oral reading is smooth and expressive and sounds like talk. Fluent readers concentrate on comprehension, read in logical phrases, and read with expression. Stumbling over hard words or making excessive miscues disrupts the natural flow of oral reading. Skipping over hard words and misidentifying words when reading silently results in weak comprehension and, for children in the upper elementary grades, reduced ability to use reading as a tool in content subjects. Fluent readers concentrate their energy on understanding the meaning, not on figuring out word identity. When readers automatically recognize words, they can allocate attention to comprehension and, additionally, they can effortlessly read words aloud. And so we see that word fluency contributes to smooth, expressive oral reading and also supports comprehension when readers pay attention to meaning rather than to word identification.

In addition, children may read *new* words by analogy. In reading new words by analogy, children use the letter groups in known words to read unknown words. For example, on seeing the new word *hat*, readers realize that *at* also is in *sat*, a known word. Readers then use the analogous information (*at*) to read *hat*. When spelling, children realize that the /at/ in /hat/ also is in /sat/, a word they already know how to spell. On remembering that /at/ in /sat/ is spelled *at*, spellers then use this analogous information in combination with the beginning letter-sound (/h/ = *h*) to spell *hat*.

Third, in reading new words by associating letters and sounds, readers say the sounds that the letters represent and then blend all the sounds together to pronounce a word that they recognize in speech. For example, on seeing *hat* for the first time, readers would associate the /h/ sound with the letter *h*, the /a/ with *a*, and the /t/ with *t*. Having now pronounced each sound individually, readers then blend these sounds together to say the whole word, /hat/. On hearing /hat/, readers recognize it as a word in their speaking vocabulary and, therefore, associate both meaning and sound with *hat*. When spelling, writers associate letters with the sounds they hear in a word, and then write those letters. For instance, children who wish to spell *hat* listen for the sounds in /hat/ (/h/, /a/, /t/), associate a letter with each individual sound (/h/ = *h*, /a/ = *a*, /t/ = *t*), and then write the letters (*hat*).

Fourth, in using the multiletter chunks in word structure to read new words, readers bring to reading a thorough knowledge of how to pronounce large letter groups and, when appropriate, what the large multiletter chunks mean. For example, on seeing the new word *precooked*, readers look for familiar multiletter chunks in word structure. In this example, readers would notice the *pre-*, meaning before, and the *-ed*, indicating past tense. This leaves the word *cook*, which the readers recognize as a word in their fluent reading vocabulary. By associating sound and meaning with the large multiletter chunks in word structure, readers understand how the new word sounds and what it means.

The strategy readers choose to use for reading new words—analogy, letter-sound, or analyzing the multiletter chunks in word structure—depends on the reading context; whether the word is long or short; and what readers know about letters, sounds, and word structure. Children move through different word learning stages as they become more and more skilled at reading new words. Each stage is associated with the ability to use different word identification strategies, as you will learn in the next section.

The Five Stages of Movement Toward Word Fluency

Children move through four word identification stages—prealphabetic, partial alphabetic, alphabetic, and consolidated—on their way to the fifth stage, the automatic recognition of all the words in text, as shown in Table 1–1 (Ehri, 2000). As children enter each new stage, they use a new strategy. Strategies develop in a reasonably predictable sequence that begins long before children read storybooks and long before they go to school. Though the exact order in which strategies develop is not completely understood, we do know that readers use some strategies before others. The earliest strategies are used when children are in the prealphabetic stage.

Prealphabetic Stage

The prealphabetic stage begins in preschool and usually ends some time during kindergarten. Children in this stage may not understand that words are separated by white spaces, and that one written word matches one spoken word. Children know few, if any, letter names, and do not yet know how letters represent sounds. The earliest strategies do not call for paying attention to the letters and sounds in words. Children associate meaning with pictures in familiar books, recognize

TABLE 1–1   *Stages of Movement Toward Word Fluency*

Stages of Movement Toward Word Fluency	What Children Know and How They Use Their Knowledge
Prealphabetic	Children do not yet understand the alphabetic principle. *Children are able to* (a) memorize text, (b) associate meaning with pictures, (c) associate meaning with environmental print, and (d) identify words by their unique configuration. *Children are learning* (a) how print is oriented on the page, (b) how to match written words with spoken words, (c) letter names or letter-sounds, and (d) how to identify beginning sounds and rhymes in words. *When writing, children use* (a) scribbles, (b) mock letters, (c) letter strings, and (d) pictures. Children do not use letters to represent sounds in words.
Partial Alphabetic	Children understand the alphabetic principle. Children's reading vocabulary slowly increases. *Children are able to* (a) give the names and sounds of most letters, (b) match spoken and written words, (c) find words in sentences, (d) find letters in words, (e) automatically recognize a few words, (f) use one or two letter-sounds or letter names to read new words, and (g) associate meaning with picture cues. *Children are learning to* (a) combine picture cues with beginning letter-sound cues to read new words, (b) find letters that represent rhyming sounds (the rime), such as the *at* in *hat* and *sat,* and (c) use parts of known words to read unknown words. *When writing, children use* one or more consonants to spell words (*dg = dog*).
Alphabetic	Children's reading vocabulary rapidly increases. *Children are able to* (a) use the analogy strategy to read new words, (b) sound out new words with the letter-sound strategy, (c) separate spoken words into sounds and blend sounds into words, (d) use semantic, syntactic, and graphophonic cues in words, (e) cross-check, self-monitor, and self-correct during reading, (f) read some text independently, (g) read some text fluently, and (h) teach themselves new words through reading and writing. *When writing, children* (a) conventionally spell known words, (b) invent the spelling of unfamiliar words, and (c) write a least one letter for every sound in a word.
Consolidated	Children's reading vocabulary rapidly increases. *Children are able to* (a) use the multiletter chunks in word structure to read new words, (b) read long words, (c) teach themselves new words through reading and writing, and (d) focus most all of their attention on comprehension. *When writing, children* (a) correctly spell most words and (b) use alternative spellings to represent some sounds (*naim* for *name*).
Automatic	Children's fluent reading vocabulary is very large and continues to grow. *Children are able to* (a) automatically recognize all the words they see in print, (b) teach themselves new words through reading and writing, (c) recognize more words in print than they use in conversation, (d) read independently, and (e) focus entirely on comprehension while reading.

words by their familiar everyday surroundings, or recognize words because of their unique shapes, as explained in chapter 3. We cannot read what children write because there is no association among letters and sounds. In writing, children may scribble, draw pictures, make mock letters, or randomly string letters together.

Partial Alphabetic Stage

Children enter the second stage, the partial alphabetic stage, sometime in kindergarten or at the beginning of first grade, as described in chapter 3. These children know most, if not all, letter names. Children also know the sounds of most consonants, and some children are learning some vowel sounds, usually short vowel sounds as heard in *bad, bet, bit, hot,* and *hut.* Children read a few words from memory, and recognize new words by associating one, maybe two, letter sounds with them. Children may also use letter names to recognize words, provided that the letter names contain a portion of the letter-sounds. In spelling, children use one or more letters, usually consonants, to write whole words (*k* for *kat; dg* for *dog*). Children's fluent reading vocabulary is growing, but only slowly and with a great deal of repetition in reading and writing.

Alphabetic Stage

The third stage, the alphabetic stage, begins when children pay attention to and learn about vowel letter-sounds. Children usually enter this stage in late kindergarten or early first grade. Children in the alphabetic stage pay attention to vowel letters when reading and spelling new words. These children also pay attention to the beginning, middle, and ending letters in the new words they read. Children in the alphabetic stage sound out new words, discussed in chapter 5, or read new words by analogy, discussed in chapter 4. When children spell, they include a letter for every sound heard, although not always in a conventional way (*truk* for *truck*). Children's fluent reading vocabulary grows rapidly; they learn words on their own through reading and writing; and they are becoming independent readers and spellers.

Consolidated Stage

Toward the end of second grade, and most certainly before fourth grade, children enter the consolidated stage. Children have had enough experience reading and writing to recognize large multiletter chunks in word structure, including prefixes, suffixes, syllables, base words, and root words. The strategy of analyzing word structure (described in chapter 6) is a streamlined approach to reading and spelling new words. And, not surprisingly, children's fluent reading vocabulary grows rapidly, and children learn many new words on their own through reading and writing. Children now read books independently, without the help of their teachers.

Automatic Stage

Children reach the automatic stage when they instantly recognize all, or nearly all, the words they see in text. Words are read rapidly, accurately, and effortlessly. Readers pay full attention to comprehension because they do not need to spend energy on word identification. At this point in their development as readers, children recognize more words in print than they use in conversation. Now, at last, the size of the reading vocabulary surpasses the size of the speaking vocabulary. And because readers automatically recognize words, reading is pleasurable, rapid, and fluent.

Movement toward word fluency is gradual. Children seem to move from one stage to another, slowly learning and using more complex information and strategies. When children begin using a new strategy, their ability to apply the strategy and their understanding of print and speech relationships is immature. But with instruction, and ample reading and writing experiences, children's knowledge gradually matures and their ability to use the new word identification strategy improves. Then, when children are relatively comfortable using a certain strategy and have a good understanding of the print and speech relationships that support it, they gradually move into the next higher stage, which calls for using a more efficient strategy based on a more elaborate understanding of print and speech relationships.

As is to be expected with any complex learning process, sometimes children will use strategies to read and spell words that are characteristic of more than one stage. For instance, in reading a short storybook, a child may use letter-sound relationships to sound out the new word *made* (a strategy consistent with the alphabetic stage), and then on the next page use only the beginning and ending letters to read the new word *duck* (a strategy consistent with the partial alphabetic stage). Gradually, however, the strategies from earlier stages fade away so that, whenever possible, readers use their most streamlined strategy to read and spell words.

When you, the teacher, are familiar with the stages and understand the knowledge and abilities that underpin the use of strategies in the different stages, you can make decisions that will help children move from one stage to the next. A good word identification program is balanced with other components of the literacy curriculum, to be sure, but it is also related to children's stages of movement toward word fluency and conventional spelling. In understanding the stages of word learning and the strategies that children in various stages use to read and spell new words, you have the information you need to relate what you teach to what children need to know to move to the next word learning stage. You can use this knowledge to select just the right material to match the skills and abilities of children, and challenge children to develop new and more effective strategies. You become a more effective teacher because you are teaching exactly what children need to know to become better at reading and spelling the new words that may stand in the way of understanding text.

Our goals are to develop readers who have such large fluent reading vocabularies that they seldom see words they do not already know how to read and produce writers who correctly spell nearly all of the words in their fluent reading vocabularies. Instant word recognition takes readers' attention away from word identification and completely shifts it to comprehension, which is exactly what we expect of accomplished readers. When all is said and done, word identification is not *the* goal of reading instruction. Rather, it is a means to an end, a way to help children learn new words on their own and, in the process, become confident readers who focus their attention on understanding text, on learning from text, and on enjoying reading as a leisure activity throughout their lives.

Translation of Figure 1–1, Maria's Valentine
Dear Mrs. Saracho,
        You are a great teacher. I am learning new things every day. I hope that you will be able to teach here next year. You are the nicest teacher in fifth grade.
Love,
Maria

REFERENCES

Armbruster, B. B., Lehr, F., & Osborn, J. (2001). *Put reading first: The research building blocks for teaching children to read kindergarten through grade 3.* Washington, DC: National Institute for Literacy.

Bauman, J. F., Hoffman, J. V., Duffy-Hester, A. M., & Ro, J. M. (2000). The first R yesterday and today: U.S. elementary reading instruction practices reported by teachers and administrators. *Reading Research Quarterly, 35,* 338–377.

Bauman, J. F., Hoffman, J. V., Moon, J., & Duffy-Hester, A. M. (1998). Where are teachers' voices in the phonics/whole language debate? Results from a survey of U.S. elementary classroom teachers. *The Reading Teacher, 51,* 636–650.

Ehri, L. C. (1997). Sight word learning in normal readers and dyslexics. In B. Blachman (Ed.), *Foundations of reading acquisition and dyslexia* (pp. 163–189). Mahwah, NJ: Erlbaum.

Ehri, L. C. (2000). Learning to read and learning to spell: Two sides of a coin. *Topics in Language Disorders, 20,* 19–36.

Freppon, P. A., & Dahl, K. I. (1998). Theory and research into practice: Balanced instruction: Insights and considerations. *Reading Research Quarterly, 33,* 240–251.

Goodman, K. (1996). *On reading: A common-sense look at the nature of language and the science of reading.* Portsmouth, NH: Heinemann.

International Reading Association. (1997). *The role of phonics in reading instruction: A position statement of the International Reading Association* [Brochure]. Newark, DE: Author.

Merrill Linguistic Reading Program. (1986). (4th ed.). Upper Saddle River, NJ: Merrill/Prentice Hall.

National Reading Panel. (2000). *Teaching children to read: An evidence-based assessment of the scientific research literature on reading and its implications for reading instruction: Reports of the subgroups* (NIH Publication No. 00-4754). Washington, DC: U.S. Government Printing Office.

Programmed Reading. (1994). (3rd ed.). New York: Phoenix Learning Resources.

Snow, C. E., Burns, M. S., & Griffin, P. (1998). *Preventing reading difficulties in young children.* Washington, DC: National Academy Press.

Stahl, S. A., Duffy-Hester, A. M., & Stahl, K. A. D. (1998). Everything you wanted to know about phonics (but were afraid to ask). *Reading Research Quarterly, 33,* 338–355.

Tunmer, W. E., & Chapman, J. E. (2002). The relation of beginning readers' reported word identification strategies to reading achievement, reading-related skills, and academic self-perceptions. *Reading and Writing: An Interdisciplinary Journal, 15,* 341–358.

Vacca, J. A. L., Vacca, R. T., Gove, M. K., Burkey, L., Lenhart, L. A., & McKeon, C. (2003). *Reading and learning to read* (5th ed.). Boston: Allyn & Bacon.

Warton-McDonald, R., Pressley, M., Rankin, J., Mistretta, J., Yokoi, L., & Ettenberger, S. (1997). Effective primary-grades literacy instruction = Balanced literacy instruction. *The Reading Teacher, 50*(6) 518–521.

Wolf, M., & Katzir-Cohen, T. (2001). Reading fluency and its intervention. *Scientific Studies in Reading, 5,* 211–239.

CHAPTER 2

Phonemic Awareness

Becoming Aware of the Sounds of Language

This chapter describes how children develop insight into the sounds of language. You will learn about the different types of language awareness children bring to your classroom, the importance of language awareness, and tests to determine children's insight into the sounds in words. You also will find 11 research-based best practices for teaching phonemic awareness, 14 activities to develop rhyme awareness, and 17 activities to develop sound awareness.

KEY IDEAS

➤ Phonemic awareness is the ability to think analytically about the sounds in words, and the ability to act on the basis of this analysis to separate words into sounds and blend sounds into words.
➤ Phonological awareness is a more general term that refers to the ability to purposefully manipulate the words, syllables, rhymes, and sounds of language.
➤ Awareness of the words, rhymes, and sounds of language develops in a relatively predictable sequence that begins with word awareness and ends with sound awareness.
➤ Children with high phonemic awareness are better word learners, better readers, and better spellers than children with low awareness.

KEY VOCABULARY

Adding sounds	Isolating sounds	Rhyme awareness
Blending sounds	Phoneme	Segmenting sounds
Categorizing sounds	Phonemic awareness	Sound awareness
Deleting sounds	Phonological awareness	Substituting sounds
Identifying sounds		

The language children bring to school serves many purposes. First and foremost, it gives children a way to interact with others so as to exert some measure of control over their lives and their environment. As long as children carry on everyday conversations, they concentrate on communication, not on the individual sounds from which the words are created. All this changes when children begin to learn to read. As they move toward literacy, children begin to think about spoken language in a totally different way: They stand back from the meaning of language in order to analyze speech. As they do this, children discover that the words they use in everyday conversation consist of individual sounds.

Nadia is discovering the individual sounds in spoken words, and learning how letters go with sounds. When Nadia writes, as in the note in Figure 2–1, she thinks about the sounds in the words she wishes to spell, and then associates letters with them. When Nadia reads, she looks for familiar letter patterns in unfamiliar words, considers the reading context, and then reads a word that fits both

Figure 2–1 Nadia uses her emerging awareness of the sounds in words and her developing knowledge of letter-sound patterns to write: I went to Sue's and ate pizza.

the reading context and the sounds that the letters represent. Unlike Nadia, Marty is not aware of the sounds in words, and does not know how letters represent sounds. Yet Marty does know that writing is important, and that writing goes from left-to-right (see his writing in Figure 2–2). Marty experiments as he writes a few recognizable letters, uses some mock letters, and simulates cursive writing with scribble writing (the long wavy line traversing the page). As Marty becomes aware of the sounds in words and as he learns how letters go with sounds, he will begin to use letters to represent the sounds in the words he wishes to spell and, consequently, we will be able to read his writing.

What Is Phonemic Awareness?

The word *phonemic* comes to us from the French who borrowed it from the Greek language. A *phoneme* is the smallest sound that differentiates one word from another. For example, the phonemes /s/ and /r/ differentiate /sat/ from /rat/. While a few English words have only one phoneme, most consist of two or more phonemes. For example, /be/ consists of two phonemes (/b/, /e/), *fish* has three phonemes (/f/, /i/, /sh/), *frog* has four (/f/, /r/, /o/, /g/), and *zebra* has five (/z/, /e/, /b/, /r/, /a/). The *-ic* is Greek for pertaining to; hence, *phonemic* means pertaining to phonemes.

Figure 2–2   Marty, a kindergartner, is not yet aware of the individual sounds in words and how letters represent sounds. He uses a few real letters, mock letters, and scribbles as he experiments with writing.

Phonemic awareness is the ability to think analytically about the sounds in words, and the ability to act on the basis of this analysis to separate words into sounds and to blend sounds into words. Children with well-developed phonemic awareness can arrange, rearrange, add, and delete sounds in words, and can blend individual phonemes into words. For example, these children will tell you, their teacher, that /man/ consists of /m/-/a/-/n/; that /a/ is the middle sound in /man/; that taking the /m/ away leaves /an/; and that the sounds /m/ + /a/ + /n/ blend together to make /man/. In the absence of phonemic awareness, children perceive speech as a continuous, undivided stream and therefore do not understand the principle of alphabetic writing—that print represents speech at the sound level. Children who are phonemically aware are aware of sounds, and, therefore, will use the terms *sound awareness* and *phonemic awareness* when referring to insight into the sounds of language.

What Is Phonological Awareness?

The *phon-* in *phonological* is of Greek origin, meaning *sound* or *voice*, as in *telephone*. *Logy* also comes to us from the Greek language, and means the *study of*. Phonological, then, pertains to the study of sound. When applied to the teaching of reading, *phonological awareness* refers to awareness of the words, syllables, rhymes, and sounds in language, and to the ability to blend individual sounds into words. Later in this chapter we will explore rhyme awareness, a phonological awareness skill taught in many preschool and kindergarten classrooms. Children with good phonological awareness know that (a) sentences consist of individual words, (b) words consist of syllables, (c) some words rhyme while others do not, (d) words consist of individual sounds, and (e) blending individual sounds together produces meaningful spoken words.

The Connection Between Phonemic Awareness and Phonics

Phonemic awareness and phonics are different. Phonemic awareness pertains to awareness of the sounds in spoken language, while phonics pertains to the relationship among letters and sounds and to approaches for teaching these relationships. Phonemic awareness and phonics develop reciprocally as children learn to read; that is, getting better in one results in improvement in the other. As children learn how letters represent sounds, they develop greater awareness of the sounds in words. And as children develop greater phonemic awareness, they become better able to use letter-sound patterns to read new words. For instance, learning that the letter *t* represents /t/ may help children become aware of the /t/ sound in words like *top* and *tiger*. The reciprocal relationship also works in the other direction; that is, knowing that the spoken words /top/ and /tiger/ begin with the /t/ sound may help children associate the /t/ sound with the letter *t* in *top* and *tiger*. Children need phonemic awareness to make sense of the principle of alphabetic writing; they need phonics to identify new words, develop a large fluent reading vocabulary, and spell new words when writing.

Phonemic Awareness Develops in a Sequence

Phonemic awareness develops in a relatively predictable sequence in which children first become aware of large language segments and then become aware of increasingly smaller ones. Awareness of the words in everyday conversations develops first. While some children may discover words as early as age 3, many become aware of words at about age 4. Most children begin kindergarten with word awareness. These children can separate sentences and phrases into individual words. For example, a word-aware child can tell you that /John ate dinner/ consists of /John/, /ate/, and /dinner/.

Rhyme and syllable awareness are generally thought to develop after word awareness (Bradley & Bryant, 1978), although there is not universal agreement on this sequence (Macmillan, 2002). Generally speaking, most 4-year-olds can divide long words into syllables, and by ages 4 and 5, most children can identify rhyming words and beginning sounds (Juel & Minden-Cupp, 2000). Children who are aware of rhyme can identify words that do and do not rhyme (/wag/ and /tag/ rhyme, but /wag/ and /sit/ do not), and can think of their own rhyming words (/mad/, /sad/, /bad/). As children develop awareness of rhyming words, they also become aware of beginning sounds. Some children find rhymes easier to identify than beginning sounds (Cardoso-Martins, Michalick, & Pollo, 2002), while others become aware of beginning sounds before they are aware of rhyme (Walton & Walton, 2002). Beginning sound awareness (/mop/ begins with /m/) and rhyme awareness (/mop/ and /hop/ rhyme) are thought to be one single level of language awareness (Armbruster, Lehr, & Osborn, 2001). Therefore, you can expect children to become aware of beginning sounds and rhyming sounds at approximately the same time or at least within a relatively short period of time.

Identifying individual sounds in words is more difficult than identifying rhyme (Cardoso-Martins, Michalick, & Pollo, 2002). To identify the individual phonemes in words, children must (a) recognize that sounds are nonmeaningful portions of words, (b) understand that words consist of sounds, (c) be able to say each of the sounds in words, and (d) be able to blend disconnected sounds into complete, meaningful words. Sound awareness is, therefore, far more demanding than rhyme awareness. The sounds in words are much smaller than rhymes and, not coincidentally, the sounds themselves last only a very short time. Typically developing children become aware of sounds sometime in kindergarten or early first grade as they learn to read and write. Children then increase their sound awareness through direct instruction in phonemic awareness, instruction in the letter-sounds of phonics, and opportunities to use letter-sound knowledge when reading and spelling.

Rhyme Awareness

Children as young as 3 may be sensitive to rhyme (MacLean, Bryant, & Bradley, 1987). Kindergartners who have experience with poetry and rhyming language games are generally quite good at identifying rhyming words (Treiman & Zukowski, 1991). Kindergartners with good *rhyme awareness* are better readers later in school than kindergartners who are not sensitive to rhyme (Bradley & Bryant, 1978). Justin, who was aware of rhyming language as a kindergartner, demonstrates rhyme awareness in a poem he wrote after his first-grade class had shared the book *Ten Apples Up on Top!* (LeSieg, 1961). This book, which tells the rhyming story of animals balancing apples and being chased by an angry bear with a mop, clearly influenced Justin's thinking as he composed. Notice in Figure 2–3

Figure 2–3 Justin's rhyming poem, "Apples," shows that he has developed an awareness of rhyming sounds in language.

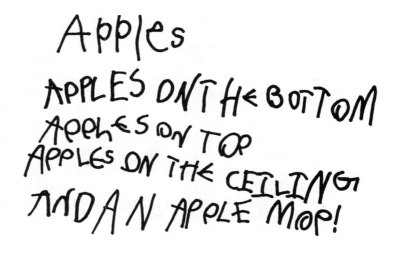

how Justin uses two of the rhyming words from the storybook—*top* and *mop*—to create his own special poetic mood, message, and expression.

　　There are two ways rhyme awareness may help Justin as he learns to read: First, rhyme awareness may act as a scaffold to help Justin identify the sounds in words (Goswami, 2001). And second, rhyme awareness may prime Justin to look for the letters in written words (*mop* and *top*) that represent the rhyme /op/ in spoken words (Goswami, 2001). Children like Justin who are aware of rhyme (/mop/ and /top/) may think of the rhyme (/op/) as one category of sound, and the beginning sounds (/m/ and /t/, in this example) as another category. In so doing, children separate the beginning sound (/m/ or /t/) from the rhyming sound (/op/). These children may then be able to learn to substitute one beginning sound for another (Norris & Hoffman, 2002). For instance, Justin might begin by saying the word with /mop/ and then substitute an /h/ for an /m/ to pronounce /hop/. Substituting, or swapping, one sound for another is important for reading new words by analogy, as explained in chapter 4.

Three Ways Children Demonstrate Rhyme Awareness

Children show us that they understand the rhyme in language when they identify rhyme, produce rhyme, and separate words into beginning sounds and rhyming sounds (Armbruster et al., 2001). Let us take a closer look at each of these skills:

　　1. Identifying rhyme. In identifying rhyme, children say which words rhyme and which do not.

This is the easiest of the three rhyming skills. Children who can identify rhyme will say that /pig/ and /big/ rhyme, but that /big/ and /cat/ do not. To help children learn to identify rhyme, ask questions like: "Does /man/ rhyme with /can/?" "Does /man/ rhyme with /rat/?" "Which words rhyme—/box/-/car/-/fox/?"

2. **Producing rhyme.** When children produce rhyme, they think of their own rhyming words. Help children produce rhyme by asking them to, "Say a word that rhymes with /cat/. With /man/. With /dog/."

3. **Separating words into beginning sounds and rhyming sounds.** This is the most difficult of the three rhyme skills. Children split words into two parts: the beginning sound and the rhyming sound. Help children pay attention to beginning sounds by asking, "Say the first sound in /mop/." Help them pay attention to the rhyme by asking, "Say the rhyming sound in /mop/ and /top/." And help them split a word into its beginning sound and rhyme by asking them to, "Say /mop/. Say the first sound in mop." /m/ "Now say the rhyming sound in mop." /op/ (See chapter 4 for teaching activities to encourage and support children as they apply this skill to reading and writing words.)

Fourteen Easy and Effective Rhyme Awareness Activities

Although children are naturally drawn to rhyming language, they may not develop rhyme awareness by simply participating in normal classroom activities (Layton, Deeny, Tall, & Upton, 1996). It is important, therefore, to support those children in your classroom who are not yet aware of rhyming language. Activities that ask children to produce their own rhyming words have been shown to improve children's rhyme awareness, even when those activities are brief, lasting only 4 minutes or so (Majsterek, Shorr, & Erion, 2000). Therefore, even relatively short activities, when consistently and repeatedly used with children like Nadia (see Figure 2–1) and Marty (Figure 2–2), help children develop rhyme awareness. While the focus is on rhyming language, many activities can be easily adapted to develop beginning sound awareness.

 Six Ways for Everyone in a Small Group to Identify Rhyme

Skills: Identifying Rhymes or Beginning Sounds

All the children in a small group respond to questions about rhyme or beginning sounds, which helps you quickly spot children who do and do not recognize rhyming words or beginning sounds.

Things You'll Need: Nothing special.

Directions: Children listen to rhyming (/mop/ - /top/) or nonrhyming (/top/ - /cat/) words, decide which pairs rhyme and which do not, and then respond as a group. To develop beginning sound awareness, pronounce two words (/mop/ - /man/ or /mop/ - /big/) and ask children to decide which words have the same beginning sound. For variety, you may wish to vary the way that children respond:

A. *Hands-up*   Children hold up their hands when they hear rhyming words (/sat/ - /fat/) or words that begin alike.
B. *Stand-up*   Children stand for rhyming words or words that begin with the same sound.
C. *Pencils-up*   Children hold their pencils up when they hear two rhyming words or words that begin alike.
D. *Clap*   Children clap once for each pair of rhyming words or for each pair of words that begin alike.
E. *Thumbs-up*   Children put their thumbs up for two rhyming words (or words that begin alike) and put their thumbs down when words do not rhyme (or do not begin alike).
F. *Smiley Faces*   Children hold up smiley faces for rhyming words or for words that begin with the same sound.

Children who respond right away, without looking at their neighbors, are aware of rhyming words or beginning sounds. Those who copy their neighbors need more exposure to and experience with rhyme or beginning sounds. Extend this activity to written language by writing rhyming words (or words that begin alike) on the board, asking children to read the words, and pointing out the letters in words that represent spoken rhyme (or the beginning letter-sound).

Predicting Rhyme

Skill: Producing Spoken Rhymes

Children in small groups predict familiar rhyming words in often-read poems.

Things You'll Need: Poems on large charts; sticky notes.

Directions: Write a poem on a large chart. Cover up one or more rhyming words with sticky notes. Read the poem together with the children in chorus; and ask children to supply the hidden rhyming words.

Reading Rhyming Poems and Books

Skill: Identifying Rhymes

In listening to you read rhyming poems and books, children enjoy language and have opportunities to become sensitive to rhyme.

Things You'll Need: Rhyming poems and books.

Directions: Read and reread rhyming poetry and books written in verse. Point out rhyming words and ask children to listen for rhyming words. Make lists of rhyming words.

Choral Rhyme and Word Matching

Skill: Identifying Rhymes

Children in small groups read familiar poems aloud and then point to rhyming words.

Things You'll Need: Rhyming poems on laminated charts; laminated rhyming word cards with Velcro® on the back.

Directions: Have the children read poems and jingles together in chorus. As children read together, track words by moving your hand under words as they are read to focus children's attention on the print and to demonstrate left-to-right orientation and the connection between spoken words and written words. Give children rhyming word cards with Velcro® on the back. Ask children to put the rhyming cards on (or next to) the rhyming words in the poem.

Framing Rhyming Words

Skill: Identifying Rhymes

Framing words is an easy way to call children's attention to rhyming language.

Things You'll Need: Rhyming poems on large charts; a piece of oak tag with a window cut out of the middle.

Directions: Read rhyming poems. Call attention to rhyming words by framing them (cupping your hands around words). Alternatively, you might wish to use a word window—a piece of oak tag with a "window" or hole in the middle—to frame words. Ask children to come to the chart and use their hands or the word window to frame the rhyming words.

Rhyming Picture Bookmark

Skill: Identifying Rhymes or Beginning Sounds

Children make a handy bookmark with this small group or center activity.

Things You'll Need: A bookmark pattern on sturdy paper with a picture in the top square, as seen in Figure 2–4; pictures that do and do not rhyme with the top picture (or pictures that do and do not begin like the top picture); scissors; glue.

Figure 2–4 Making
rhyming picture bookmarks is
fun, gives children extra
practice recognizing rhyming
words, and results in a handy
place marker for the books
children enjoy at school or at
home.

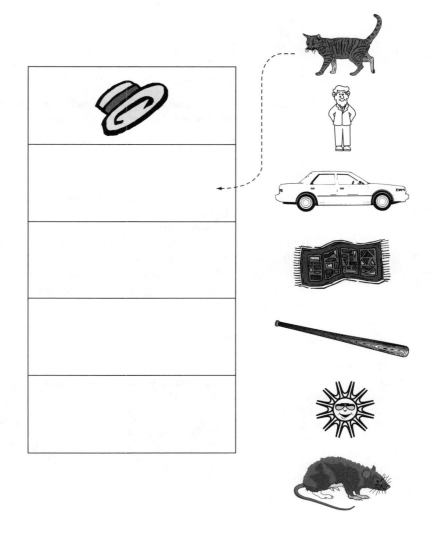

Directions: Have the children cut out pictures that rhyme with the picture at the
top of the bookmark pattern and glue the rhyming pictures in the bookmark
squares. Extend this activity to written language by having children watch as you
write the words under the pictures on their bookmarks. Or, you might ask
children to join you in interactively spelling one or two words. Laminate finished
bookmarks.To develop sensitivity to beginning sounds, ask children to cut out
and glue pictures with the same beginning sound, thereby making a beginning
sound bookmark.

Rhyming Picture Sack Sort

Skill: Identifying Rhymes or Beginning Sounds

Children work with partners, individually, or in learning centers to sort rhyming pictures (or pictures that begin with the same sound) into paper sacks.

Things You'll Need: Pictures taped to two or three lunch sacks for each child or set of learning partners; rhyming pictures (or pictures that begin alike) on 3-inch-by-5-inch cards.

Directions: Discuss rhyming words or words that begin alike; show children the picture-cards; have them name each picture. Ask children to sort the picture-cards by putting them into sacks that have a rhyming picture on them, as shown in Figure 2–5, or by putting pictures that begin alike into sacks. If you place this sorting activity in a learning center, ask children to fold over the top of the sack when they finish sorting and to write their names on the back. This way you have a record of the learning center activity, and you know who sorted correctly and who did not.

Figure 2–5 Sorting rhyming pictures into paper lunch sacks gives children an opportunity to analyze the rhyme in words and to differentiate one set of rhyming sounds from another.

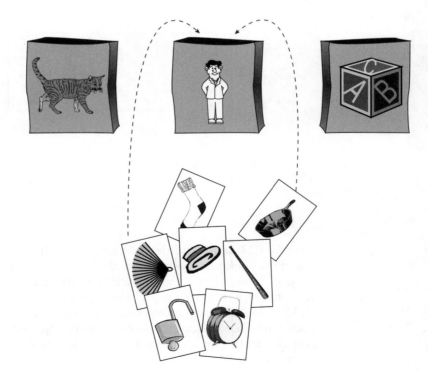

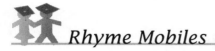

Rhyme Mobiles

Skill: Identifying Rhymes or Beginning Sounds

Children in small groups make mobiles that feature pictures and words that either rhyme or begin with the same sound.

Things You'll Need: Old magazines and catalogs; scissors; colorful construction paper cut into geometric shapes; glue; colorful yarn cut into different lengths; coat hangers to hang the mobiles.

Directions: Have the children cut out pictures with names that either rhyme or begin alike, and then paste the pictures onto one side of colored pieces of construction paper. Write the word for the picture on the opposite side. Punch a hole in the top of each geometric shape, thread a colorful strand of yarn through the hole, then tie the yarn to a coat hanger (see Figure 2–6). Integrate this activity with mathematics by discussing the circles, triangles, squares, and rectangles that adorn the mobiles.

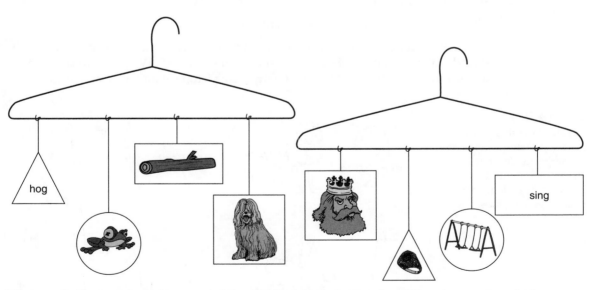

Figure 2–6 In making rhyming mobiles, children think about and read rhyming words and, if construction paper is cut into circles, triangles, squares, and rectangles, you have an opportunity to integrate language arts and mathematics.

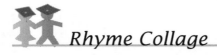 *Rhyme Collage*

Skill: Identifying Rhymes or Beginning Sounds

Small groups make collages of rhyming pictures or pictures that begin with the same sound.

Things You'll Need: Lots of pictures; oak tag; tape or glue.

Directions: Give children a group of pictures, some that rhyme and some that do not. Or, if focusing on beginning sounds, some that begin alike and some that do not. Have children select rhyming pictures or pictures with the same beginning sound, and then glue or tape them onto a large sheet of paper. When the collage is finished, have the children say the picture names in chorus. Extend this activity to written language by writing words on cards and asking children to match the words with the pictures on the collage.

 Drawing Rhyming Pictures

Skill: Producing Rhymes

Children draw pictures that rhyme and share them with their classmates in this small group, individual, or learning center activity.

Things You'll Need: Paper folded in half; crayons.

Directions: Have children draw two rhyming pictures, one picture on one side of the folded paper and one on the other, as shown in Figure 2–7. Write the words under the pictures. Ask children to share the rhyming pictures with their classmates.

Figure 2–7 After Gerald drew this pair of rhyming pictures, his kindergarten teacher shared them with the class. The rhyming pictures are: bat-cat; goose-moose; mouse-house.

Picture-Rhyme Memory Game

Skill: Producing Rhymes or Beginning Sounds

This is a rhyming or beginning sound picture version of the ever-popular Concentration®, and is a good game for children to play with a partner or while visiting the centers in your classroom.

Things You'll Need: A deck of cards with pairs of rhyming picture-word cards, as shown in Figure 2–8, or pictures of words that begin alike.

Directions: Have children put the rhyming (or beginning sound) pictures face down on a table, and take turns flipping up two picture-word cards. Children keep pairs of picture-word cards that rhyme or begin with the same sound. Cards that do not rhyme or begin with the same sound are turned face down again. The player with the most cards wins.

 Rhyme Puppet

Skill: Producing Rhymes or Beginning Sounds

Puppets are great teaching tools for large and small groups. This is one of the ways I use my own puppet, whom I call Tacoma.

Things You'll Need: A wonderful puppet with a very large mouth that opens and closes.

Directions: The puppet says two (or more) words and children decide if the words rhyme or begin alike. For instance, the puppet might say *"bag-rag"* or *"bag-nose."* Children put their thumbs up for rhyming or begin-alike words, down for nonrhyming words or words that begin differently. When the puppet's words do not rhyme or begin alike, the puppet asks the children to suggest rhyming words or words that do begin alike. An additional option is to write on the board or on a chart the rhyming or begin-alike words the puppet says. If you do this, be sure that the rhyming words you write both sound and look alike (*bed-red*, not *bed-head*).

 Shoe Box Rhymes

Skill: Producing Rhymes or Beginning Sounds

Small groups or individuals say words that rhyme with or begin with the same sound as pictures or objects that you have hidden in a shoe box.

Things You'll Need: A shoe box; an assortment of small objects or pictures.

Figure 2–8 A rhyming picture-word memory game. Recognizing pairs of rhyming picture-word cards reinforces sensitivity to, and awareness of, rhyme in spoken and written language.

Directions: Place objects or pictures in a shoe box; do not let the children watch as you do this. Put your hand in the shoe box and grab an object or picture. Show it to the children. Ask the children to think of a word that rhymes with the name of the object or picture, or to think of a word that begins with the same sound. Set that object aside and take another from the shoe box. You might also want to write the words that children suggest, thereby connecting spoken words with written words.

Shower Curtain Rhyme Toss

Skill: Producing Rhymes or Beginning Sounds

In this large muscle activity, small groups toss a beanbag onto a shower curtain with pictures taped on it, and then say a word that rhymes with or begins with the same sound as the picture-name.

Things You'll Need: Plastic shower curtain; beanbag; pictures; tape.

Directions: Tape pictures to a shower curtain, and put the shower curtain on the floor. Children stand around the curtain and take turns tossing a beanbag onto (or near) a picture. Children say the picture-name and then say a word that rhymes with it or that begins with the same sound.

Sound Awareness

At 6 years old, Melanie already knows how letters represent sounds. Look at Figure 2–9 and the clever way she writes sn-snow balls, ch-chillier, ch-ch-ch-chilly,

Figure 2–9 Melanie demonstrates sound awareness when she separates the beginning sounds from words in her story to help her readers experience the sensation of being cold.

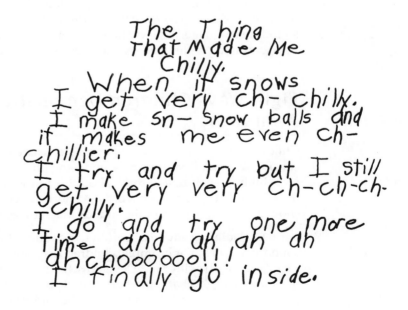

and ah ah ah ahchoooooo! She literally separates language into sounds before her readers' eyes. Melanie can separate words into sounds, and she can blend individual sounds into meaningful words. Children like Melanie who begin school with high phonemic awareness make faster reading progress than children with low phonemic awareness (Dufva, Niemi, & Voeten, 2001; National Reading Panel, 2000). The positive relationship between phonemic awareness and reading achievement is evident whether children who grow up in economically advantaged families (Nicholson, 1997) or speak English as their second language (Muter & Diethelm, 2001). What's more, children with more phonemic awareness typically have larger fluent reading vocabularies than the children with less awareness (Whitehurst, & Lonigan, 2001). Although children with low phonemic awareness do poorly when they must use letter-sound associations (Juel, Griffith, & Gough, 1986), when these children improve their phonemic awareness, they successfully use phonics to read new words (Ehri et al, 2001; Fox & Routh, 1984).

Not surprisingly, children with good phonemic awareness are better spellers than children with poor awareness (Caravolas, Hulme, & Snowling, 2001; Frost, 2001; Kroese, Hynd, Knight, Hiemenz, & Hall, 2000). The positive relationship between phonemic awareness and spelling may be explained by the ability of high-awareness children to identify the sounds that need to be matched with letters in the words they wish to spell. We would expect the effect of phonemic awareness to be evident in the early grades before children have memorized the spellings of many different words. It makes sense, then, that the words that first and second graders correctly separate into sounds are spelled with greater accuracy than the words children incorrectly separate into sounds (Foorman, Jenkins, & Francis, 1993). Hence, phonemic awareness is linked to both reading and spelling. All things considered, if some of the children whom you teach have not discovered the sounds in language, they will benefit from activities that increase phonemic awareness, becoming better readers and better spellers as a consequence.

Eight Ways Children Demonstrate Sound Awareness

Children with good sound awareness step aside from the meaning of language to consider the smallest units of sound—the phonemes—in our language. In so doing, children analyze and think about the individual sounds in words, and blend these sounds to pronounce words. Armbruster et al. (2001) explains that children show us they are aware of the sounds in language by:

1. Isolating sounds. Children pronounce the beginning, ending, or middle sound in a word. For example, children may say that /man/ begins with /m/ or that /sun/ ends with /n/. Develop sensitivity to the sounds in words by asking questions like, "What's the first sound in /soap/?" "What's the last sound in /cat/?" "What sound do you hear in the middle of /boat/?"

2. **Identifying sounds.** Children recognize the same sound in different words. For example, children will tell you that /toy/ and /tail/ begin alike or that /rain/ and /man/ end alike. To develop the ability to identify sounds, ask children questions like, "Do /mop/ and /moon/ begin with the same sound?" "Do /pill/ and /tail/ end alike?" "Do /nail/ and /tame/ have the same middle sound?" Another way to help children identify sound is to ask them if they hear a particular sound in different words: "Do you hear /s/ in /sun/ or /dog/?" "Do you hear /s/ in /mouse/ or /truck/?" "Do you hear /s/ in /easel/ or /paper/?"

3. **Categorizing sounds.** Children decide which of three or four words does not share a common sound. This calls for detecting the "odd" word. You might ask children the following questions: "Which word does not belong—/mile/ - /mop/ - /bike/?" "Which word has a different ending sound—/mad/ - /top/ - /hid/?" "Which word has a different middle sound—/hat/ - /big/ - /sad/?"

4. **Segmenting sounds.** Children pronounce each phoneme in the same order in which it occurs in a word. Develop segmenting by asking, "What sounds do you hear in /rain/?" Or you might ask children to "Say all the sounds in /soap/." Also ask children to count sounds in words. In sound counting, children identify each sound to decide how many sounds they hear.

5. **Adding sounds.** Children add a new sound to a word or syllable. For instance, children might add /r/ to the beginning of /at/ to pronounce /rat/, or /t/ to the end of /bee/ to say /beet/. Develop the ability to add sounds by asking, "What word do we get when we add /r/ to /at/?" Or you might ask children to, "Start with /an/. Add a /t/ to the end of /an/. What is the word?"

6. **Deleting sounds.** Children remove a sound from a word or syllable. For example, children might take the /s/ from /sat/ to pronounce /at/, or the /m/ from /seem/ to say /see/. Develop the ability to delete beginning sounds by asking children to "Say /meat/ without the /m/." You also might ask children to "Say /meat/. Now say it again without the /t/." Another way to phrase sound-deletion questions is to ask, "What is left when we take /m/ away from /meat/?"

7. **Substituting sounds.** Children delete a sound from a word, and then add another in its place to make a different word. For example, children might substitute the /t/ in /sat/ with a /d/ to pronounce /sad/. Help children develop the ability to substitute beginning sounds by asking them to "Say /cat/. Now say /r/ instead of /c/." Or you might have children "Say /cat/. Say it again, but now say /n/ instead of /t/." Encourage children to substitute middle sounds by asking them to "Say /pan/. Change the /a/ to /i/."

8. **Blending sounds.** Children combine phonemes to pronounce a whole word. Children might, for example, blend /sh/ + /ip/ to pronounce /ship/, or they might blend /sh/ + /i/ + /p/ to say /ship/. In both cases, children must fold sounds together. In so doing, the sounds themselves are somewhat altered. Children cannot simply "say it fast" because this essentially results in saying one isolated sound after another in close succession. In successful blending, sounds overlap somewhat, something like the shingles on a roof.

Eleven Best Practices for Teaching Phonemic Awareness

You can expect the children whom you teach to develop greater sensitivity to the sounds in words when you include phonemic awareness in your balanced class-room reading program (Ehri et al., 2001; Foorman & Torgesen, 2001). In following these 11 best practices, you ensure that phonemic awareness instruction is effective and in proportion to children's needs:

1. **Begin with short, two-sound words** (Uhry & Ehri, 1999). It is easier to separate short, two-sound words into phonemes (/be/ = /b/ - /e/) than to segment three- and four-sound words. What's more, two-sound words that begin with a vowel, such as /ape/, /it/ and /eat/, are easier to segment into individual sounds than words that begin with a consonant, such as /be/, /tie/ and /to/ Introduce three- and four-sound words when children can segment and blend two-sound words.

2. **Teach awareness of beginning sounds, followed by awareness of ending sounds, and then awareness of middle sounds** (Foorman et al., 1993). This is the sequence in which sound awareness develops in most children.

3. **Teach phonemic awareness and phonics together** (Ehri et al., 2001; Stuart, 1999). Teaching phonemic awareness along with letter-names and letter-sounds is more effective than teaching phonemic awareness alone. Whereas the phonemes in language are fleeting, letters stay fixed on the page. Children can point to letters that represent sounds; find letters in words; look for letters in alphabet books and on the word wall. Recognizing letters and associating sounds with them encourages children to think of sounds as separate entities. This, in turn, enhances phonemic awareness. Better sound awareness then helps children use the letter-sound patterns of phonics when reading new words.

4. **Only teach one or two skills at a time.** Teaching one or two phonemic awareness skills is twice as effective as teaching many skills at once (Ehri et al., 2001; National Reading Panel, 2000). Perhaps children do not really master skills when many different skills are taught at the same time, or perhaps children become confused about how to apply the skills. So, when you teach phonemic awareness, focus on only one or two skills at a time. When children have mastered those skills, move on to one or two other skills, all in proportion to children's needs, of course.

5. **Teach phonemic awareness early, in kindergarten and first grade.** Becoming aware of the sounds in language is important for understanding the alphabetic principle in the kindergarten (Ehri et al., 2001), and necessary for using phonics to read and spell new words in first grade.

6. **Teach in small groups.** Teaching small groups of children is more effective than teaching large groups of children (National Reading Panel, 2000). Children in small groups may have more opportunities to personally respond to you, their teacher. And you may have more opportunities to observe the effects of instruction when you teach small groups of children.

7. **Differentiate instruction** (Ehri et al., 2001). Children differ in the level of sound awareness they bring to your classroom. Consistent with a balanced view

of instruction, spend more time teaching phonemic awareness to children with low awareness, and move high-awareness children on to other reading and writing activities.

8. Demonstrate how to use phonemic awareness when reading and writing new words (Juel & Minden-Cupp, 2000). We cannot assume that children will automatically infer how to use their developing phonemic awareness skills when they read and spell. Therefore, you will be a more effective teacher when you model how to use phonemic awareness to read and spell new words, and when you give children opportunities to practice, under your guidance, the phonemic awareness skills they are learning.

9. Set aside no more than 20 hours for teaching phonemic awareness (National Reading Panel, 2000). The most effective programs range from 5 to 18 hours of instruction. The amount of time spent teaching individual children will vary, of course, depending on their levels of sound awareness. Whereas children with low sound awareness may benefit from 18 to 20 hours of instruction, children with good sound awareness will need little, if any, instruction other than that which naturally occurs as you teach them letter names, letter-sounds, and how to use phonics to read new words.

10. Encourage children to finger-point read (Uhry, 2002). When children finger-point read, they point to each word as it is read. Finger-point reading is significantly related to phonemic awareness, particularly when children point to words as they read text from memory. Children who are good at finger-point reading are aware of words in speech, may be aware of the beginning sounds in words, and, additionally, may have some letter-sound knowledge. In finger-point reading, children not only attend to words, but also have opportunities to notice beginning letter-sound associations and to use those associations to match printed words with spoken words.

11. Clearly differentiate between speech sounds and letter names. When referring to the sounds in a word, pronounce the sounds you wish to emphasize, not the letter names. Say something like, "Monkey begins with /m/ (the sound)." If you wish to call children's attention to the letter name, you might say, "Monkey begins with the letter *m* (the name)."

Seventeen Easy and Effective Activities for Teaching Phonemic Awareness

The 17 activities in this section develop awareness of the sounds in words and blending. They are useful for children who do not yet have enough phonemic awareness to independently read new words. Consistent with best practice, we find these activities to be most effective when we teach in small groups. By and large, you will want to use these activities with younger children, say kindergartners or first graders, or older children who lack sound awareness and, therefore, have difficulty using phonics to read new words. In addition to these activities, you may wish to modify some of the rhyme awareness activities to use them to develop sound awareness.

As you use these sound awareness activities, call attention to the sounds in words by rubber banding (or stretching) words when you pronounce them. Say words slowly, keeping the sounds connected while at the same time stretching them out, much as you pull a rubber band. For instance, in rubber banding /man/ you would stretch the word to pronounce something like, "/mmmaaannn/." Some sounds are easier to stretch than others. For example, the /n/ in /pan/ is easily stretched, while the /p/ is not. When we interrupt airflow to make a sound, as in the /p/ and /d/ phonemes, is it difficult to make the sound last. Therefore, you may want to say sounds like these several times, in quick succession. For instance, in rubber banding /pan/, you might say something like, "/p/-/p/-/p/-/aaannn/. An alternative to saying sounds in a quick staccato is to emphasize the difficult-to-stretch sounds by saying these sounds somewhat louder and slightly separating them from the rest of the word, /P/-/aaannn/. Modify these activities to suit your own teaching style, and use them along with the letter and sound activities in chapters 4 and 5.

 Sound Awareness Activities
Three Ways to Use Sound Squares

Skills: Identifying Sounds

    Segmenting Sounds

    Adding Sounds

    Deleting Sounds

    Substituting Sounds

    Associating Letters and Sounds

Children in a small group line up a colored square for each sound in a word.

Things You'll Need: One-inch colored construction paper squares.

 A. *Sound Squares for Segmenting Sounds*

Skills: Identifying and Segmenting Sounds

Directions: Give each child three or four colored squares. Say a word slowly, rubber banding it to clearly pronounce all the sounds. Children move one colored square for each sound heard. Then have children point to individual squares that represent specific sounds in the word. For instance, if children have lined up three squares for the sounds in /fun/, you could ask them to, "Point to the square for the first sound in /fun/." Or you might phrase the same question somewhat differently, asking, "What's the first sound in /fun/? Point to that square." Another option is to ask children to "Point to the /f/." Similar questions might be asked for middle and ending sounds. Extend this activity to written language by writing letters on the squares after children have moved them into a line. This increases awareness of the connections between the sounds in spoken words and the letters in written words, and helps introduce children to letter-sound relationships.

B. *Sound Squares for Adding and Deleting Sounds*

Skills: Adding and Deleting Sounds

Directions: Children line up squares for the sounds in a word, as described in the previous activity. Now, if adding sounds, ask children to add an extra square to represent a new sound; if deleting sounds, ask children to remove a square to take a sound away. For purposes of illustration, let us assume that children have moved two squares side by side to represent /an/. To add a sound, pronounce a new word, such as /pan/. Ask children to listen to the new word, identify the sound at the beginning, and put a new square in front of the two squares already on the table, thereby showing the three sounds in /pan/. In deleting a sound, have the children move three squares into a row to represent the phonemes in /pan/. Then pronounce /an/. Ask the children to identify the missing sound and to remove that square, thus leaving only two squares, one for /a/ and one for /n/. Write the letters on squares, and then refer to the word wall to find examples of other words that begin or end with the letters on the squares.

C. *Sound Squares for Substituting Sounds*

Skill: Substituting Sounds

In substituting sounds, children must remove a sound and replace it with another. Sound substitution is much more difficult than identifying, segmenting, adding, and deleting sounds. Therefore, you will want to use this version of sound squares with children who have developed enough phonemic awareness to separate short words into their individual phonemes.

Directions: Repeat steps 1 and 3 in activity A. Begin by asking children to substitute beginning sounds, then ask them to substitute ending sounds. When children are comfortable substituting beginning and ending sounds, you also may want to ask them to substitute middle sounds. Let's assume that children have moved three squares to represent the sounds in /pan/. To swap one beginning sound for another, you would say /pan/ and then tell children you are going to say another word that has a different beginning sound, such as /man/. Have children identify the new beginning sound, /m/, remove the colored square that represents the /p/, and replace it with a different color square to represent the /p/ in /pan/. Follow the same procedure for substituting ending sounds (/pan/ changed into /pat/) and middle sounds (/pat/ changed into /pot/). Write the letters on the squares, either before or after children have identified sounds, to demonstrate the sounds in words that go with the letters in words.

 Counting Sounds

Skill: Segmenting Sounds

Children in small groups count sounds in words, and then hold up cards with numerals that correspond to the number of sounds heard.

Things You'll Need: A set of 5-inch-by-8-inch cards with the numerals 2, 3, or 4 on them.

Directions: Give each child index cards with the numerals 2, 3, or 4. (Distribute cards with 2 and 3 if you plan on pronouncing only two- and three-sound words.) Slowly pronounce a word, rubber banding it so that each sound is clearly heard. Children listen to the word and count the number of sounds they hear. Children then hold up a card that shows the number of sounds heard. Carefully watch to see who responds quickly, who hesitates, and who waits for a neighbor to select a card. Anyone who hesitates or copies from a neighbor needs more practice.

Three Ways to Use Sound Boxes

Skills: Isolating Sounds

Segmenting Sounds

Sound Blending

Associating Letters and Sounds

Sound boxes are connected boxes where each box represents a sound in a word. Variations of this activity have been used since the 1970s when a Soviet researcher, Elkonin, developed a method in which children move tokens for the sounds in words. Today, a similar technique is used in Reading Recovery lessons (Clay, 1985). There are three versions of this activity, one with pictures, one without pictures, and one with letters written in the boxes. All may be used when working with small groups or with individual children.

A. *Sound Boxes With Pictures*

Skill: Segmenting Sounds

Pictures help children remember the words they are separating into sounds. This activity is appropriate for children who are just beginning to pay attention to the sounds in words.

Things You'll Need: Sound boxes, as shown in Figure 2–10; tokens; pictures with two-, three-, or four-sound names.

Directions: Give each child a piece of paper with several pictures and sets of sound boxes. The number of connected boxes below each picture should equal the number of sounds in the picture's name. Call attention to the picture and slowly say its name, rubber banding the sounds. Children push a token into a box for each sound heard (sound segmenting). Have children count the boxes. Talk about the idea that each box represents only one sound. Ask children to say together in chorus the individual sounds in the word by pointing to each box as they say the sound. Last, have children blend sounds to pronounce the whole word, tracking (sweeping) their fingers under boxes as they say the sounds.

Figure 2–10 Sound awareness increases when children move tokens into boxes for the sounds they hear in words and point to the tokens that represent beginning, middle, and ending sounds.

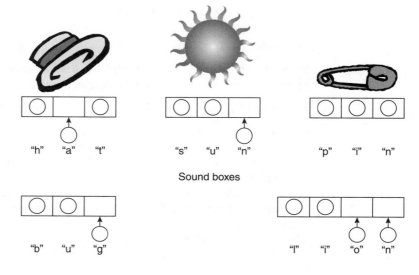

Sound boxes

B. *Sound Boxes Without Pictures*

Skills: Segmenting Sounds

Isolating Sounds

Children remember words on their own, without the help of pictures. This version is appropriate for children who have some experience listening for sounds in words.

Things You'll Need: Sound boxes (see Figure 2–10); tokens.

Directions: Once children have moved a token for each sound heard, ask children to point to the box that represents a single sound, and to tell the sound's position—beginning, middle, end—in the word (isolating sounds). For example, you might say, "Point to the box that stands for the /b/ in /boat/." Then ask, "Does /b/ come at the beginning, middle, or end of /boat/?"

C. *Sound Boxes With Letters*

Skills: Segmenting Sounds

Associating Letters and Sounds

Children remember the sounds in words and associate them with letters you have already written in the boxes.

Things You'll Need: Sound boxes with letter written in them.

Directions: As children move tokens into each box, you call their attention to the letter written inside the box. After all the tokens are moved into boxes, pronounce the whole word. Ask the children to say the sounds one at a time. Have the children move the token in each box to reveal the letter. (Children need only slide the token just below the boxes.) Ask children to identify each letter as they (or you) identify the sound. Talk about the letters that go with the sounds.

Popcorn Sounds

Skill: Identifying Sounds

In this fast moving activity, children in a small group take turns saying the beginning, middle, or ending sound in picture names.

Things You'll Need: Cards with pictures and words on them.

Directions: Show children who are sitting around a table a selection of picture-word cards. Point to a card and say, "Popcorn," followed by a child's name, and the position of the sound the child is to identify (beginning, middle, end) in the picture name. For example, in pointing to a picture of a *pig* you might say, "Popcorn: Annaleise. Beginning sound." Annaleise then says the beginning sound, /p/. Annaleise now passes her turn to another child by pointing to a different picture-word card, saying a child's name and asking for a beginning (middle or ending) sound. The activity continues until everyone has had a turn or until all of the beginning (middle or ending) sounds are identified.

Sound Graphing

Skill: Segmenting Sounds

Working in small groups or with a partner, children make a graph showing words with two, three, or four sounds.

Things You'll Need: Pictures; tape; a large piece of newsprint. Beforehand draw two, three, and four connected boxes at the top of the newsprint, spacing boxes fairly far apart. Fasten the newsprint to a bulletin board.

Directions: Children count the sounds in picture names. Children then tape the pictures below the connected boxes that match the number of sounds in the names. When finished, children have a giant graph that shows words with different numbers of sounds similar to the graph in Figure 2–11. Integrate this activity with mathematics by adding up the words under each group of connected boxes, as well as the total number of words found. Talk about distribution and proportion (most, least).

Two Ways to Sort Sounds

Skills: Identifying Sounds

Isolating Sounds

Associating Letters With Sounds

Figure 2–11 Graphing sounds gives children practice identifying the number of sounds in words, and the finished graph is a wonderful resource for integrating language arts with mathematics.

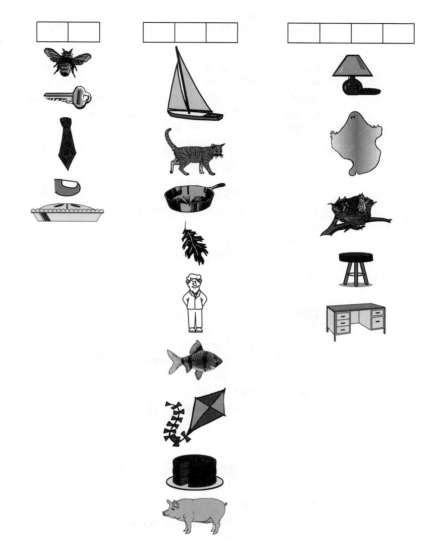

Children working individually, with a partner, or in a learning center sort pictures according to beginning, middle, or ending sounds.

  A. *Sack Sorting*

Skill: Identifying Sounds

Children sort pictures by putting them into paper sacks according to shared sounds.

Things You'll Need: Two or more sacks for each individual or set of partners; pictures on cards. Tape a picture to each sack. The pictures on cards should have a beginning, middle, or ending sound in common with one of the pictures on each sack.

Directions: Children sort pictures by putting them into the sack that has a picture with a shared sound. For example, to sort for the same beginning sound, children would put pictures of a *bus, bee, bear, banana, bat,* and *balloon* in a sack with a picture of a *ball* in it, and pictures of a *doll, doughnut, duck,* and *drum* go in a sack with a *dog* on the front. Have children follow the same procedure when sorting for ending or middle sounds.

B. *Paper and Glue Sort*

Skills: Isolating Sounds

Associating Letters With Sounds

Children listen for sounds in picture names, associate them with letters, and glue pictures with sounds in columns.

Things You'll Need: Papers divided into two or three columns with a letter at the top of each column.

Directions: Give children sorting papers, as shown in Figure 2–12. Children glue pictures in columns under letters that represent the beginning, ending, or middle sound. Figure 2–12 shows a paper for sorting pictures into groups that share the same ending letter-sound. When children finish sorting, talk about the sound (beginning, middle, or ending) that children hear in the picture names, and the letters that represent those sounds. Ask children to suggest other words that have the same beginning, middle, or ending letter-sounds. Make charts for these words.

 Interactive Spelling

Skill: Segmenting Sounds

Associating Letters With Sounds

Blending

Interactive spelling is a technique in which you, the teacher, ask children to join you in spelling words by listening for sounds and then associating letters with them.

Things You'll Need: Nothing special.

Directions: Begin by pronouncing a word slowly, rubber banding it so that all the sounds are clearly heard, yet connected together. Ask the children what sound they hear at the beginning and what letter goes with that sound. Write the letter on the board. Again pronounce the word, only this time emphasize the second sound as you rubber band the pronunciation. Have children tell you the letter that goes with that sound, and write that letter on the board. Continue rubber

Figure 2–12   Associating letters with sounds (picture, paper and glue sort) sorting pictures by beginning, ending, or middle letter-sounds gives children practice listening for sounds and associating letters with sounds.

banding and emphasizing the sounds children are to match with letters until the entire word is spelled. To give children practice blending sounds, read the word with them, sliding your finger under the letters as the sounds are pronounced. This technique helps children develop greater phonemic awareness, reinforces letter-sound knowledge and blending, and supports conventional spelling. Interactive spelling is most successful when used with phonetically regular words; that is, words that sound like they are spelled, such as *man, lime,* and *see*.

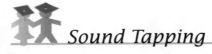
Sound Tapping

Skill: Segmenting Sounds

Children tap a pencil for every sound in a word.

Things You'll Need: Nothing special.

Directions: Say a word and have children tap a pencil once for each sound heard. Rubber banding and repeating words help children focus on the individual phonemes. Begin with two-sound words (/ape/). After children can tap the phonemes in two-sound words, introduce three- (/cap/) and then four-sound (/soda/) words.

I Spy

Skill: Isolating Sounds

This gamelike activity is excellent for those times when the class is getting ready to go to lunch, P.E., art, the library, or home for the day.

Things You'll Need: Nothing special.

Directions: Think of something in your room and say, "I spy something that begins with /_/ (a beginning sound)." Children then think of things in the room that begin with the same beginning sound. Focus attention on ending or middle sounds by asking children to find objects with names that either end with a certain sound or have a specified sound in the middle.

Class Roll

Skills: Identifying Sounds

   Letter Names

This activity also fits nicely into small bits of time when children are transitioning from one activity to the next. Class roll uses children's names to develop beginning sound awareness.

Things You'll Need: Nothing special.

Directions: Say something like, "I am thinking of someone in our class whose name begins with the same sounds as *bug* and *bear*. Who is it?" When children say, "Bobby," ask them what letter *Bobby* begins with. Write the upper and lower case letter on the chalkboard. Name the letter or ask a child to give the letter name. Use this activity, or your own personal adaptation of it, to line up children for lunch, for recess, or to go home at the end of the school day.

 Two Ways for a Robot to Talk

Skills: Segmenting Sounds

       Blending Sounds

Children learn to talk just like a robot (or any other appealing fictional or cartoon-like character) by saying the sounds in words slowly, one after the other. Alternatively, children may decode the sound-by-sound robot talk by blending individual phonemes into words. In so doing, children get practice segmenting or blending sounds, all in a gamelike activity. While we use a robot as a medium for pronouncing words, you may wish to use other props, such as puppets, toys from the latest science fiction movie, or cartoonlike figures.

Things You'll Need: An optional robot puppet made from a paper sack, or other fictional characters, such as stuffed animals, dolls, or action figures.

  A. *Robot Talk*

Skill: Segmenting Sounds

Directions: Show children the robot puppet or a toy, and explain that the robot speaks only in a special "robot language." The robot always says every word very slowly. Demonstrate by saying a whole word, such as /fan/. Then translate /fan/ to robot talk by either rubber banding (/fffaaannn/) or saying each sound separately: /f/ - /a/ - /n/. Ask the children to join the robot in either rubber banding words or saying the individual sounds in words. In doing this, you might say something like, "What is robot talk for /sun/?" Or, "How would the robot say /no/?" After children are comfortable following the robot's lead in rubber banding words or saying each sound separately, give individual children in the small group opportunities to talk for the robot.

  B. *Robot Talk*

Skill: Blending

Directions: Using a robot puppet or toy, explain that the robot talks only in sounds. For example, the robot might say, /m/ - /a/ - /n/. Ask the children to identify the word the robot said, /man/. Continue pronouncing words sound by sound, and asking the children to say the whole words. Once children are comfortable blending robot-spoken sounds into whole words, ask individuals in the small group to be the robot, to pretend to talk just like the robot, and to have their classmates say the real word the robot really intended to say.

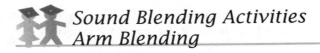

Sound Blending Activities
Arm Blending

Skill: Blending

Arm blending is a tactile, kinesthetic approach to blending that children can use on their own when reading all sorts of materials in all sorts of places.

Things You'll Need: Nothing special.

Directions: Have children imagine that they place sounds on their arms. For example, to blend /f/, /a/, /n/, children put their right hand on their left shoulder (reverse for left-handed children) and say /f/, their hand in the crook of their arm and say /a/, and their hand on their wrist and say /n/. Children blend by saying sounds as they slide their hands from shoulder to wrist. When finished, the children again pronounce the whole blended word. Mentally "placing" sounds on their arms helps children remember the right sounds in the right order. The motion of the sweeping hand sliding down the arm is a kind of tactile analog for what the voice does when sliding sounds together during blending.

 ### Two Ways to Finger Blend

Skill: Blending

Children use their fingers to anchor sounds in memory and to guide blending. Finger blending requires more dexterity than arm blending and is appropriate for children who easily can touch together the fingers on one hand.

A. *Five-Finger Blending*

Children use their forefinger (index finger), middle finger, ring finger, and little finger to blend by tapping these fingers to the thumb. Five-finger blending is useful for words with four sounds or less.

Directions: For the purposes of illustration, let's suppose that children are blending /b/, /e/, /l/, /t/ into /belt/. Children touch their forefinger to their thumb while saying /b/, their middle finger to the thumb saying /e/, their ring finger to the thumb while saying /l/, and their little finger to thumb saying /t/. To blend, children place each finger on their thumb as they pronounce sounds, thereby blending sounds into /belt/.

B. *Single-Finger Blending*

Children who feel self-conscious using four fingers to blend, prefer to single-finger blend, which is less obvious to onlookers.

Directions: Children use their right forefinger to place sounds on the knuckles of their left forefinger (reverse for left-handed children). To blend /ham/, children touch the innermost knuckle with their right forefinger while saying /h/, middle knuckle while saying /a/, outer most knuckle while saying /m/. In blending, children sweep their right finger over the left finger as they say sounds. For words with more than three sounds, distribute the sounds among knuckles.

Sounds on the Move

Skills: Blending

Associating Letters With Sounds

This is a kinesthetic, whole body approach to blending. Standing at arm's length, children wearing letters take turns rubber banding their own sound while moving closer to the partner until the whole word is pronounced.

Things You'll Need: Letters written on cards for each sound in a word.

Directions: Select words in which each letter represents a sound. Ask as many children as there are letters and sounds to come to the front. Give each child a letter and ask them to line up so that the word is spelled from left to right. Have children stand about an arm's length from one another. Children then take turns rubber banding their own sound. For example, suppose children are going to demonstrate how to blend /sun/. To begin, the children holding the letter *s* would rubber band the /ssss/ as the child slowly moves toward the child holding the letter *u*. When the child holding the letter *s* is shoulder to shoulder with the child holding the letter *u*, the child with the *u* begins to rubber band this sound, /uuu/. As the child rubber bands, saying /uuu/, the child moves closer to the child with the letter *n*. When the child with the *u* is shoulder to shoulder with the child holding the letter *n*, the child with the *n* begins to rubber band, saying /nnn/. The whole word, /sun/, is pronounced when the last child finishes rubber banding the /n/ phoneme. Now pronounce the whole word, /sun/, as a group. Repeat a couple of times to give children practice. To get everyone in the small group involved, ask onlookers to arm blend /sun/ while others are demonstrating sounds on the move.

Picture Blending

Skill: Blending

This activity uses pictures to develop the concept of blending (Catts & Vartiainen, 1993).

Things You'll Need: Large pictures of familiar objects; scissors.

Directions: Show children a picture and say the picture name. Cut the picture into as many parts as you wish to use for blending. For example, you might cut a picture of a *boat* into three equal parts, one for /b/, one for /oa/ (long o), and

Figure 2–13 Picture blending gives children a concrete visual reference to illustrate the idea of blending sounds into words.

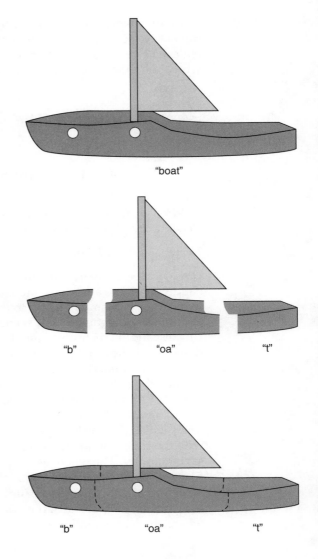

"boat"

"b"   "oa"   "t"

"b"   "oa"   "t"

one for /t/. A picture of a *bee* would be cut into two parts, one for /b/ and one for /ee/ (long e); a picture of a *book* into three pieces, one for /b/, one for /oo/, and one for /k/. Or you might cut a picture of a *pig* into two parts, one for /p/ and one for /ig/, and a picture of a *cat* into two pieces, one for /c/ and one for /at/. Point to each picture piece and say the sound it represents. For example, point to the first part of the *boat* picture while saying /b/, to the second part saying /oa/ (long o), and to the third when saying /t/. Explain that the pieces of the picture go together just like sounds go together to make a word. Demonstrate by moving the picture pieces together while you blend the sounds to pronounce /boat/. Ask the children to push the picture pieces together on their own while blending sounds. Figure 2–13 is an example of picture blending for the word

/boat/. Extend this activity to written language by writing the letters under each picture. After children blend, talk about the sounds in words and the letters the sounds represent.

 Sliding Sounds Together

Skills: Blending

   Associating Letters With Sounds

A picture of a slide depicts the blending process.

Things You'll Need: A picture of a slide drawn on the chalkboard as illustrated in Figure 2–14.

Directions: Draw a large slide on the chalkboard. Write a word on the slide, distributing letters from the top to near the bottom. Demonstrate blending by pronouncing each sound as you slide your hand under each letter, adding sounds one after the other until you reach the bottom. Ask children to say the whole word, and then write it at the bottom of the slide. Invite a child to be the slider—the person who moves his or her hand down the slide. Ask the whole group to blend the sounds as the "slider" slides toward the bottom. The slider pronounces the whole word when the slider's hand reaches the bottom.

Figure 2–14   The slide in the sliding sounds together activity gives learners a visual cue for blending. After sounds are blended, the whole word is written at the bottom of the slide.

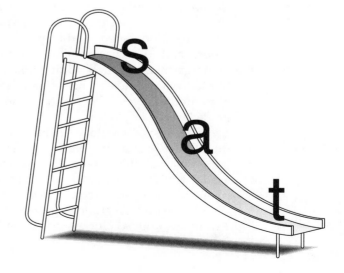

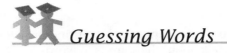 *Guessing Words*

Skills: Blending

Associating Letters With Sounds

The individual sounds in words give children clues to the identity of hidden objects.

Things You'll Need: One medium-size paper bag; many small items or pictures to put in the bag.

Directions: Put your hand in the bag and grab something, such as a small plastic *pig* or a picture of a *bike.* Keeping the object (or picture) hidden from view, say, "I have something. It is a /p/ - /i/ - /g/. What is it?" Show the *pig* when children say /pig/. Put the *pig* beside the bag and grab another object, perhaps a small, plastic *cat.* Generalize this activity to written language by writing the words children guess. Talk about the letters, say the sound that each letter or group of letters represents. This helps make the sounds visible in that children see the letters as visual representations of sounds. End by pointing to each letter or letter group, saying its sound, and blending the sounds into the word. This reinforces the idea that the letters in written words represent the sounds in spoken words.

Phonemic Awareness Tests

You now have many rhyme and phonemic awareness activities from which to choose. But before using these activities, you need to know which children in your class would benefit from increasing their rhyme or sound awareness. One way to find out about children's rhyme or sound awareness is to observe children as they read and write every day in your classroom. If you wish to go beyond classroom observation, you will want to use an assessment tool designed specifically to determine rhyme and sound awareness. There are a number of assessment tools from which to choose. With a single exception, all require that you assess children individually.

The Lindamood Auditory Conceptualization Test (LAC) (Lindamood & Lindamood, 1979) has been in use for nearly 30 years. This test is appropriate for kindergartners through adults, and requires that participants arrange colored blocks to show the sequence of sounds in nonsense words. The results are reported in minimum levels of performance for success reading and spelling at or above grade level.

The Test of Auditory Analysis Skills (Rosner, 1979) has 13 items that ask children to delete sounds from words. This test is suitable for children from kindergarten through third grade, and expected levels of performance are listed for each grade. Children whose performance is below expectation are candidates for phonemic awareness training, according to this tool.

If you prefer a group paper-and-pencil test, consider the Test of Phonological Awareness (TOPA) (Torgesen & Bryant, 1994). The kindergarten version assesses beginning sounds, while the first- and second-grade version assesses ending sounds. Percentile ranks and standard scores are reported.

The Phonological Abilities Test (Muter, Hulme, & Snowling, 1997), intended for children from 5 to 7 years old, assesses rhyme awareness, word completion with syllables and sounds, phoneme deletion, and letter knowledge.

The Comprehensive Test of Phonological Processes (CTOPP) (Wagner, Torgesen, & Rashotte, 1999) is a norm-referenced assessment of phoneme awareness, blending, memory, and rapid naming. Scores include percentile ranks, age and grade equivalents, and quotients for phoneme awareness, memory, and rapid naming. With its dual focus on phonemic awareness and rapid naming, this instrument is appropriate for assessing learning disabled and struggling readers.

The Yopp-Singer Test of Phoneme Segmentation (Yopp, 1995), intended for kindergartners and beginning first graders, has 22 items that measure children's ability to segment two- and three-sound words into phonemes.

The Roswell-Chall Auditory Blending Test (Roswell & Chall, 1997) assesses children's ability to blend from two to three sounds. First published in 1963, this test consists of 30 items and classifies blending as adequate or inadequate.

The Phonological Awareness Test (PAT) (Robertson & Salter, 1997) is intended for 5- through 9-year-olds, and includes rhyme awareness, sound segmentation, sound deletion, sound isolation, sound substitution, blending, phonics, decoding nonsense words, and invented spelling. The Phonological Awareness Profile (Robertson & Salter, 1995), a criterion-referenced test for children ages 5 through 8, assesses essentially the same areas as the PAT. The profile can be used as a pre- and post-teaching measure.

The Phonological Awareness Handbook for Kindergarten and Primary Teachers (Ericson & Juliebo, 1998) includes pre- and post-teaching measures for rhyme, blending, sound segmenting, and invented spelling. You will also find tests for classroom use in Phonemic Awareness for Young Children: A Classroom Curriculum (Adams, Foorman, Lundberg, & Beeler, 1998).

Teaching Phonemic Awareness in Your Balanced Classroom Reading Program

Rhyme and sound awareness are part of a balanced classroom program only when we provide instruction early and in proportion to children's needs. Phonemic awareness is important because it helps children develop insight into the alphabetic principle and, therefore, helps them understand the utility of letter and sound relationships. Use the activities in this chapter to support and develop phonemic awareness, and integrate language awareness into the normal learning activities in your classroom, such as shared reading and adding words to the word wall. In using these activities, bear in mind that phonemic awareness is a means to an end; it is a language-based conceptual understanding and related skills that support children as they use letter and sound associations to read and spell new words. Consequently, you will want to keep your focus on how children apply their developing language awareness and, additionally, you will want to emphasize the sounds in language as you use the types of letter and sound activities described in chapters 4 and 5 (Ehri et al., 2001).

When children first begin to approach text, they do not bring to reading an awareness of the sounds in words. Rather, phonemic awareness develops in most children as they play language games, and interact with language and print in school. In chapter 3 you will learn how emergent readers first approach written words by reading words in the environment, inferring meaning from pictures, and keying in on the unique visual features of words. You also will learn how, through reading experiences, writing experiences, and classroom instruction, children begin to use a few letter and sound associations to read and spell new words.

REFERENCES

Adams, M. J., Foorman, B. R., Lundberg, I., & Beeler, T. (1998). *Phonemic awareness in young children: A classroom curriculum.* Baltimore: Brooks Publishing.

Armbruster, B. B., Lehr, F., & Osborn, J. (2001). *Put reading first: The research building blocks for teaching children to read kindergarten through grade 3.* Washington, DC: National Institute for Literacy.

Bradley, L., & Bryant, P. E. (1978). Difficulties in auditory organization as a possible cause of reading backwardness. *Nature, 271,* 746–747.

Caravolas, M., Hulme, C., & Snowling, M. J. (2001). The foundations of spelling ability: Evidence from a 3-year longitudinal study. *Journal of Memory and Language, 45,* 751–774.

Cardoso-Martins, C., Michalick, M. F., & Pollo, T. C. (2002). Is sensitivity to rhyme a developmental precursor to sensitivity to phoneme?: Evidence from individuals with Down syndrome. *Reading and Writing: An Interdisciplinary Journal, 15,* 439–454.

Catts, H. W., & Vartiainen, T. (1993). *Sounds abound: Listening, rhyming and reading.* East Moline, IL: LinguiSystems.

Clay, M. M. (1985). *The early detection of reading difficulties* (3rd ed.). Portsmouth, NH: Heinemann.

Dufva, M., Niemi, P., & Voeten, M. J. M. (2001). The role of phonological memory, word recognition, and comprehension skills in reading development: From preschool to grade 2. *Reading and Writing: An Interdisciplinary Journal, 14,* 91–117.

Ehri, L. C., Nunes, S. R., Willows, D. M., Schuster, B. V., Yaghoub-Zadeh, Z., & Shanahan, T. (2001). Phonemic awareness instruction helps children learn to read: Evidence from the National Reading Panel's meta-analysis. *Reading Research Quarterly, 36,* 250–287.

Ericson, L., & Juliebo, M. F. (1998). *The phonological awareness handbook for kindergarten and primary teachers.* Newark, DE: International Reading Association.

Foorman, B. R., Jenkins, L., & Francis, D. J. (1993). Links among segmenting, spelling, and reading words in first and second grades. *Reading and Writing: An Interdisciplinary Journal, 5,* 1–15.

Foorman, B. R., & Torgesen, J. (2001). Critical elements of classroom and small-group instruction promote reading success in all children. *Learning Disabilities Research and Practice, 16,* 203–212.

Fox, B., & Routh, D. K. (1984). Phonemic analysis and synthesis as word attack skills: Revisited. *Journal of Educational Psychology, 76,* 1059–1064.

Frost, J. (2001). Phonemic awareness, spontaneous writing, and reading and spelling development from a preventive perspective. *Reading and Writing, 14,* 487–513.

Goswami, U. (2001). Early phonological development and the acquisition of literacy. In S. B. Neuman & D. K. Dickinson (Eds.), *Handbook of early literacy research* (pp. 111–125). New York: Guilford Press.

Juel, C., Griffith, P. L., & Gough, P. B. (1986). Acquisition of literacy: A longitudinal study of children in first and second grade. *Journal of Educational Psychology, 78,* 243–255.

Juel, C., & Minden-Cupp, C. (2000). Learning to read words: Linguistic units and instructional strategies. *Reading Research Quarterly, 35,* 458–492.

Kroese, J. M., Hynd, G. W., Knight, D. F., Hiemenz, J. R., & Hall, J. (2000). Clinical appraisal of spelling ability and its relationship to phonemic awareness (blending, segmenting, elision, and reversal), phonological memory, and reading in reading disabled, ADHD, and normal children. *Reading and Writing: An Interdisciplinary Journal, 13,* (1–2), 105–131.

Layton, L., Deeny, K., Tall, G., & Upton, G. (1996). Researching and promoting phonological awareness in the nursery class. *Journal of Research in Reading, 19,* 1–13.

LeSieg, T. (1961). *Ten apples up on top!* New York: Random House.

Lindamood, C. H., & Lindamood, P. C. (1979). *Lindamood auditory conceptualization test* (Rev. ed.). Austin, TX: Pro-Ed.

MacLean, M., Bryant, P., & Bradley, L. (1987). Rhymes, nursery rhymes, and reading in early childhood. *Merrill-Palmer Quarterly, 33,* 255–282.

Macmillan, B. M. (2002). Rhyme and reading: A critical review of the research methodology. *Journal of Research in Reading, 25,* 4–42.

Majsterek, D. J., Shorr, D. N., & Erion, V. L. (2000). Promoting early literacy through rhyme-detection activities during Head Start circle-time. *Child Study Journal, 30,* 143–151.

Muter, V., & Diethelm, K. (2001). The contribution of phonological skills and letter knowledge to early reading development in a multilingual population. *Language Learning, 51,* 187–219.

Muter, V., Hulme, C., & Snowling, M. (1997). *Phonological abilities test.* San Antonio, TX: The Psychological Corporation.

National Reading Panel. (2000). *Teaching children to read: An evidence-based assessment of the scientific research literature on reading and its implications for reading instruction: Reports of the subgroups* (NIH Publication No. 00-4754). Washington, DC: U.S. Government Printing Office.

Nicholson, T. (1997). Closing the gap on reading failure: Social background, phonemic awareness, and learning to read. In B. Blachman (Ed.), *Foundations of reading acquisition and dyslexia: Implications for early intervention* (pp. 381–407). Mahwah, NJ: Erlbaum.

Norris, A. N., & Hoffman, P. R. (2002). Phoneme awareness: A complex developmental process. *Topics in Language Disorders, 22,* 1–34.

Robertson, C., & Salter, W. (1995). *The phonological awareness profile.* East Moline, IL: LinguiSystems.

Robertson, C., & Salter, W. (1997). *The phonological awareness test.* East Moline, IL: LinguiSystems.

Rosner, J. (1979). *Test of auditory analysis skills.* Novato, CA: Academic Therapy Publications.

Roswell, F. G., & Chall, J. S. (1997). *Roswell-Chall auditory blending test.* Cambridge, MA: Educators Publishing Service.

Stuart, M. (1999). Getting ready for reading: Early phoneme awareness and phonics teaching improves reading and spelling in inner-city second language learners. *British Journal of Educational Psychology, 69,* 587–605.

Torgesen, J. K., & Bryant, B. R. (1994). *Test of phonological awareness.* Austin, TX: Pro-Ed.

Treiman, R., & Zukowski, A. (1991). Levels of phonological awareness. In S. A. Brady & D. P. Shankweiler (Eds.), *Phonological processes in literacy* (pp. 85–96). Hillsdale, NJ: Erlbaum.

Uhry, J. K., & Ehri, L. C. (1999). Ease of segmenting two- or three-phoneme words in kindergarten: Rime cohesion or vowel salience? *Journal of Educational Psychology, 91,* 594–603.

Uhry, J. K. (2002). Finger-point reading in kindergarten: The role of phonemic awareness, one-to-one correspondence, and rapid serial naming. *Scientific Studies of Reading, 6,* 319–341.

Wagner, R., Torgesen, J. K., & Rashotte, C. (1999). *Comprehensive test of phonological processes.* Austin, TX: Pro-Ed.

Walton, P. D., & Walton, L. M. (2002). Beginning reading by teaching in rime analogy: Effects on phonological skills, letters-sound knowledge, working memory, and word-reading strategies. *Scientific Studies of Reading, 6,* 79–115.

Whitehurst, G. J., & Lonigan, C. J. (2001). Emergent literacy: Development from prereaders to readers. In S. B. Neuman & D. K. Dickinson (Eds.), *Handbook of early literacy research* (pp. 11–29). New York: Guilford Press.

Yopp, H. K. (1995). A test for assessing phonemic awareness in young children. *The Reading Teacher, 49,* 20–29.

CHAPTER 3

Early Word Identification Strategies

Using Logos, Pictures, Word Configuration, and Letter-Sound Associations

This chapter describes four strategies that begin the development of a rich, fluent reading vocabulary. You will learn how emergent readers use cues in their environment and in pictures or recognize words by their unique configuration. You will find out how children use one- or two-letter names or sounds to read new words, and why this aids word fluency. You also will learn how these strategies correspond to development of a fluent reading vocabulary and conventional spelling and about seven research-based best practices for helping children begin to pay attention to print, and six best practices for teaching children to use one- or two-letter sounds to support word identification.

KEY IDEAS

➤ The earliest word identification strategies develop long before children go to school and long before they actually learn to read.

➤ Before children read words, they may associate meaning with cues in the environment, such as logos and product packages.

➤ Early in their journey toward literacy, children may infer meaning from illustrations, often "reading" by saying words that describe the pictures.

➤ As children begin to notice words, they may look for cues in a word's unique configuration, which consists of the word's shape and length, or an eye-catching letter.

➤ When children first pay attention to letters and sounds, they use the phonetic cue strategy in which they associate a letter-sound (or a letter name) with a whole written word.

KEY VOCABULARY

Configuration cues

Environmental cue strategy

Incidental cues

Partial alphabetic stage of movement toward word fluency

Phonetic cue strategy

Picture cue strategy

Prealphabetic stage of movement toward word fluency

Precommunicative spellers

Semiphonetic stage of spelling

The word identification strategies explained in this chapter develop before children go to school, when children are in kindergarten or, at the very latest, in early first grade. Identifying words with environmental, picture, and word configuration cues does not call for knowing anything whatsoever about the alphabetic principle or letter-sound relationships. When children do begin to consider letter- and sound-based cues, they focus on only one or two of these cues in an unfamiliar word, and hence take only minimal advantage of the alphabetic principle. Although these early strategies are not reliable ways to figure out the identity of unfamiliar words, emergent readers use them, and hence it is important for you to understand how they work. With insight into these early strategies, you are in a position to guide children as they move toward using more efficient and effective strategies for reading new words.

Environmental Cues: The Strategy of Associating Meaning With the Print in Our Everyday Surroundings

Children in prekindergarten and kindergarten often associate meaning with the signs, package labels, and logos in their everyday surroundings. This strategy, called the *environmental cue strategy*, is one of the first steps towards literacy. It is one of several strategies that 5-year-old John uses to make sense of print. When reading, John associates meaning with familiar signs and logos and, when writing, copies the words *California, October, no, stop,* and *soap* from the wall chart in his kindergarten classroom, as shown in Figure 3–1.

Associating meaning with familiar objects and signs in the environment gives preschoolers a measure of control over their lives. The preschooler who recognizes the box of Raisin Yum Yum cereal on the grocery shelf might be able to talk her mother into buying that particular breakfast food. Though she quickly recognizes the cereal box, this same child cannot read the word *raisin* on the package of raisins her mother buys for midday snacks. While this preschooler might not be able to tell what the writing *Raisin Yum Yum* actually "says," in all likelihood she can give an approximation that is both meaningful and contextually acceptable.

Figure 3–1 John enjoys copying the words he sees displayed in his kindergarten classroom.

Children give feasible approximations because they connect meaning with the everyday settings in which the print appears, not with the specific words in print. Although children do not read words when they are taken out of their familiar environmental contexts, the words from known logos and labels are easier for children to learn than words from unfamiliar environmental print (Cronin, Farrell, & Delaney, 1999). Additionally, by using the strategy of associating meaning with the environmental context in which print appears, children take an important step toward developing the concept that writing makes sense.

Picture Cues: The Strategy of Inferring Meaning From Illustrations

Like the print in children's everyday surroundings, the pictures in storybooks are an avenue to meaning that does not call for phonemic awareness, understanding the alphabetic principle, recognizing specific words, remembering letters, or knowing letter-sound associations. Long before children read storybooks on their own and well before they go to school, they read their favorite books by inferring and predicting meaning from pictures. For instance, 4-year-old Thomas used the *picture cue strategy* when he proudly held up a poster of a race car his father brought home from a business trip to Detroit, and announced that the poster said: "Gentlemen, start your engines." The fact that the words on the poster bore not the slightest resemblance to the message Thomas read was of little consequence to him; he focused entirely on the rich picture context.

Children who have been read to at home or in child care expect pictures to signal meaning. Turning the pages and cueing on pictures, these children say words that could have been written by the author but are not necessarily on the page. Children who use picture cues to "read" their favorite books may also use pictures when writing their own stories. Kesha, a beginning kindergartner, drew the picture story seen in Figure 3–2 after hearing her teacher read and reread *Arthur's Halloween* (Brown, 1982). Notice how Kesha faithfully renders the big scary house that is so prominent in *Arthur's Halloween,* including a smiley face on the door to show the house is not frightening. Kesha clearly understands the picture–meaning connection.

Kesha also knows that writing is an important feature of books, and therefore, in her picture story, she includes letters and a word copied from the print in her classroom. In some ways, the *Os* are part of Kesha's picture story. When Kesha read her picture story to her teacher, she described the house that she drew, and she described the events that she remembered from *Arthur's Halloween.* From Kesha's writing, we can infer that she is searching for a medium through which she might effectively communicate with her audience, as yet unaware of the manner in which our alphabetic writing system represents speech.

Figure 3–2   As children like
Kesha begin to pay attention to
written language, they may draw
pictures to represent the events in
familiar storybooks, and they may
include pictures, letters, and words
copied from their classroom.

Configuration: The Strategy of Using Word Length, Word Shape, or Eye-catching Letters to Read New Words

In their search for ways to bring meaning to print, children look beyond cues in the
environment and in pictures. In so doing, they move closer to print, discovering
and using the *configuration cues* in words. Configuration consists of a word's shape,
its length or, perhaps, an eye-catching letter. These cues are incidental to alphabetic
writing inasmuch as they do not call for connecting letters and sounds. This said,
the strategy of using *incidental cues* requires that children actively think about written words. Even though these cues essentially bypass the alphabetic principle, children who use them must be able to identify some letters and find words in print.
And, of course, to find words in print children must understand the purpose of the
white spaces between words and, if words are written in sentences, the left-to-right
and top-to-bottom orientation of print on the page. You can expect children to use
the incidental cues in word configuration before they use letter-sound cues. This is
so regardless of how easy or difficult words are to identify (Gough, 1993).

Jesse puts one letter after another across the page, as seen in Figure 3–3. He
writes his name and copies the words *yellow* and *me*, as well as the letters of the alphabet, from the print in his kindergarten classroom. He also includes numbers
and a picture. What Jesse does not do is link the letters in written words to the

Figure 3–3 Jesse knows that words and letters are important, and he explores written language by copying the many different types of print that he sees in his classroom.

sounds in spoken words. Jesse does not yet understand the basic premise on which alphabetic writing rests, and therefore he writes strings of random letters (when he is not copying). Jesse is interested in print, however, for his careful copying suggests that he attends to some of the words he sees in school, and is aware of the importance of the words in his classroom. As Jesse carefully notices the words that surround him in his kindergarten classroom, he looks at word configuration, and uses these cues to help him identify important words.

Word Shape

A word's shape is formed by letters that may be on, above, or below the line. The word *hat*, for example, has two ascending letters separated by a letter that stays on the line, so its shape looks like:

cat looks like:

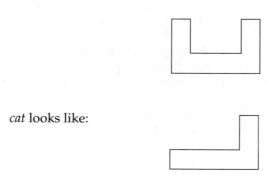

pat looks like:

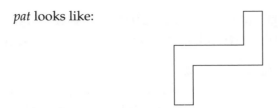

    While shape does not give readers cues to sound, it does provide some information for narrowing word choices, although this information is frequently unreliable. Because so many words have virtually identical patterns of upward and downward sloping letters (*pat, got, jet*), identifying words by their shape alone makes reading more difficult than it should be. Children who use shape to recognize the word *hat* are bound to be confused when they try to read other words that have the same shape, such as *bat, fit,* and *had.*

Word Length

Though *hand* and *homework* are the same shape (   ) a quick glance at word length tells us that *hand* and *homework* are different. It's not surprising, then, that sometimes children cue on word length alone. Length seems to be an important cue only when words differ considerably, such as the difference in length between *hand* and *homework,* or *elf* and *elephant* (Bastien-Toniazzo, & Jullien, 2001). Even without paying attention to letter and sound cues, children are far less likely to confuse *eat* with *elephant,* than they are to confuse *eat* with *elf.*

Letter Shape

In using letter shape, children pay attention to the circles, arcs, humps, and lines of the letters in words. Children might, for instance, remember the word *nail* because the letter *n* has one "hump"; *took* because the two circles look like eyes; *banana* because it begins with a stick and ball (the lowercase *b*). Only paying attention to circles, arcs, humps, and lines has the potential to create all sorts of confusion. Take *g* and *j*, as an example. Both *g* and *j* have "tails," so children may not think of *g* and *j* as different letters. Children who recognize *game* because it has a "tail" may misread *juice* because the letter *j* has a "tail," too.

    All things considered, the configuration cues that are so helpful in one reading condition are frequently not at all helpful in another condition. As long as there is an unusual characteristic like a distinctive shape, length, or letter, children may easily identify words. However, because configuration cues have no predictable, logical association with the sounds that letters represent, these cues are very fragile and often lead to misidentifications, as well as to confusion and frustration.

The Prealphabetic Stage of Movement Toward Word Fluency and the Precommunicative Stage of Spelling

The children in your classroom who use environmental, picture, and configuration cues to identify new words are in the *prealphabetic stage of movement toward word fluency* (Ehri, 2000). The prealphabetic stage begins in preschool and usually ends during kindergarten. Children in this stage cannot name the letters of the alphabet or, at best, can name only a few letters. They do not know the letter-sounds of phonics and lack phonemic awareness. Not surprisingly, these children seldom read words when they are outside familiar environmental contexts, when there are no picture cues, or when words do not have a distinct configuration. Also, not surprisingly, these children cannot read their own stories a day or so after writing them because children's writing does not systematically represent speech.

Children who are prealphabetic readers are also *precommunicative spellers.* The words they write have no relationship between sounds and letters (Gentry, 1987). Warren, a precommunicative speller, strings letters together, as seen in Figure 3–4, unaware of speech and print connections. You easily can recognize the precommunicative spellers in your classroom. Just look for writing with these five features:

1. No white spaces or inconsistent use of white spaces (Jesse, Figure 3–3).
2. Mock letters sprinkled among real letters (Warren, Figure 3–4).
3. Pictures that are at least as prominent as writing (James, Figure 2–1; Warren, Figure 3–4).
4. The same letter written over and over again (Kesha, Figure 3–2).
5. Writing that wanders randomly around the page (Jesse, Figure 3–3).

You will also observe that, although precommunicative spellers use uppercase and lowercase letters, they have a decided preference for writing in uppercase.

Seven Best Practices for Teaching Children in the Prealphabetic Stage of Movement Toward Word Fluency

From a word identification perspective, it is important for prealphabetic readers and precommunicative spellers to learn how to combine context cues with beginning and ending letter-sound cues when reading and writing new words. Effective teachers use these seven best practices:

1. **Teach phonemic awareness** (National Reading Panel, 2000). Use the activities in chapter 2 to develop awareness of the sounds in words and, when you teach phonemic awareness, also teach letter-names and letter-sounds. Teach-

Figure 3–4 A prealphabetic reader and precommunicative speller, Warren combines mock letters with real letters, stringing them across the page, unaware of speech and print connections.

ing phonemic awareness along with the names and sounds of letters makes phonemic awareness instruction more effective and this, in turn, means that children are likely to more quickly move through the prealphabetic stage and on to the next stage.

2. **Teach letter-names before letter-sounds** (Adams, 1990; Snow, Burns, & Griffin, 1998). In learning the letter-names, emergent readers discover how one letter differs from another. What's more, teaching letter-names can, with proper support from teachers, help children learn letter-sounds, provided that letter-sounds are partially present in letter-names (Cardoso-Martins, Resende, & Rodrigues, 2002). Generally speaking, it is easier to teach the letter-sounds if children already know the letter-names (Searfoss, Readence, & Mallette, 2001). Begin by teaching the names of easy-to-identify uppercase letters and then proceed to the more difficult-to-identify lowercase letters (Adams, 1990). When you teach letter-names, start out by teaching the names of the letters at the beginning of children's own names, followed by all the letters in children's names.

3. **Teach some of the letter-sounds, especially consonant letter-sounds** (Neuman, Copple, & Bredekamp, 2000; Snow et al., 1998). Teaching letter-sounds introduces emergent readers to the alphabetic principle, and, additionally, may encourage children to pay attention to the words in text. In teaching letter-sounds, begin with often-used consonant letters, as well as consonant letters with names

that include a portion of the letter-sound, such as *s* (/ess/), *l* (/ell/), and *m* (/emm/). Not only do most English words begin with consonants, but also consonant letters are more predictable in representing sound than vowel letters. This is significant because the beginning letter-sound in a word, when combined with the reading context, gives readers important insight into a word's identity.

4.   Give children opportunities to read a variety of easy, meaningful text   (Morrow, 2001; Neuman et al., 2000). Surround children with print in your classroom, and then use that print to engage children in reading. You might, for example, use shared reading with big books to familiarize children with words and letters, as well as to develop comprehension strategies. Or you could engage children in reading together in chorus the poems and stories you have written on large charts in your classroom. You also might have children tell you about their drawings, write under the pictures exactly what children say, and then ask children to read their dictated descriptions. Put labels in prominent places in your room (Neuman et al., 2000), and, as children become familiar with the labels, ask one child to bring you a label, and another child to put it back.

5.   Write every day in a variety of ways and for a variety of purposes (Morrow, 2001). Integrate writing into shared reading; ask small groups to dictate stories for wordless picture books—books that have only pictures, no words. Write language experience stories that describe shared experiences, and ask children to find words and letters in the familiar language experience stories. As children write, encourage then to spell by listening for sounds in words and then matching those sounds to letters. Also use interactive spelling to support children as they think of the sounds and letters in words (explained in chapter 2).

6.   Read aloud to children   (Morrow, 2001; Neuman et al., 2000). Reading aloud to children has a long-lasting, beneficial affect on reading achievement. Read to children every day and read a variety of genres. When you read aloud, pause occasionally to ask questions that prompt children to interact with the book by doing or saying something (Justice, Weber, Ezell, & Bakeman, 2002). You might, for instance, ask children to find words in text or to point to letters in familiar words, or you might engage children in discussing the structure of stories, including the setting, the characters, the problem, and the solution in the story.

7.   Point to words as you read them aloud   (Uhry, 2002). Pointing to words as they are read aloud not only draws children's attention to words, but also helps children match spoken words with written words. As you point to words, ask children to find the words in text. Emphasize the beginning sounds in words, and point out how the beginning letter goes with the beginning sound.

As children develop phonemic awareness, learn letter-names and letter-sounds, and have a variety of reading and writing experiences in your classroom, they will begin to identify words by connecting one or two letters with sounds. When children do this, they use the phonetic cue strategy to read new words, which is the next stage in movement toward word fluency.

Phonetic Cues: The Strategy of Using Letter-Names or One or Two Letter-Sounds to Read New Words

When children begin to use letter-sound cues, they typically take a rather simplistic route to word learning, the *phonetic cue strategy* (Ehri, 2000). Children connect a single letter-sound cue (maybe two) or a letter-name with the pronunciation of a whole word. For example, if a child sees the word *sandwich* in a storybook and if that child knows the sound associated with the letter *s*, the child may then identify *sandwich* by associating the letter *s* with the /s/ sound heard in /sandwich/. A letter-name may be used as a cue if the name includes a portion of the sound heard in the word (Cardoso-Martins et al., 2002). For example, the name of the letter *s*, /ess/, includes a portion of the sound the letter represents and, therefore, children may associate the name (/ess/) with the word *sandwich*.

Once emergent readers associate a letter-sound or a letter-name with a written word, they may assume that the same cue always represents the same word. As a consequence, children who recognize *sandwich* because they notice the letter *s*, are likely to read every word with an *s* as *sandwich*. Hence, *same* and *see* are read as /sandwich/ because each shares the same phonetic cue—the letter *s* that represents /s/.

At a *minimum*, children are aware of at least one sound in the spoken words they hear in everyday conversations, though their phonemic awareness may well be greater than this. You can expect these children to be aware of the beginning sounds in words, and to separate the beginning sound from the vowel and remaining consonants (Stahl & Murray, 1998). For instance, children can separate the /s/ from the /at/ in /sat/, and the /m/ from the /ap/ in /map/, as explained in chapter 2. Children also know the features that distinguish one letter from another, and therefore identify individual letters consistently and reliably. They know that written words consist of letters, and they also know the sounds or names of some of the letters.

Perhaps the greatest advantage of using the phonetic cue strategy is that children have opportunities to develop, test, and revise hypotheses about how the alphabet works. As children experiment with even a single letter-sound cue, they refine their phonemic awareness and extend their knowledge of how letters represent sounds. Though the phonetic cue strategy is relatively short-lived, it eases children into strategically using alphabetic writing, and as such is the precursor to the development of more advanced word identification strategies.

The Partial Alphabetic Stage of Movement Toward Word Fluency and the Semiphonetic Stage of Spelling

The *partial alphabetic stage of movement toward word fluency* emerges in kindergarten and, for some children, in early first grade (Ehri, 2000). Lexi, like other partial alphabetic readers, writes from left to right, uses white spaces to separate words, fluently recognizes a few often-used words, and can read and write her own name, as we can see in Figure 3–5. She approaches word identification systematically. In reading new words, Lexi uses letter-names when the names give sound clues, or she uses one, possibly two, letter-sound cues. Lexi might identify *father* because she hears the /eff/ in the name of the letter *f*; she might identify *monkey* because she knows the sound associated with the letter *m*. However, because Lexi does not pay attention to all the letters in words, she is likely to confuse words that begin and/or end alike. You will notice that partial alphabetic readers like Lexi misidentify and confuse words like *father, family,* and *funny* because these words all begin alike and, additionally, *family* and *funny* end alike.

Lexi knows more about letter-sounds and has more phonemic awareness than children like James, Jesse, and Warren who are in the prealphabetic stage. Lexi has enough phonemic awareness and knows enough about letter-names and letter-sounds to use one or two alphabetic cues when she reads. Although chil-

Figure 3–5 Lexi conventionally spells words in her fluent reading vocabulary and uses the beginning consonant to spell other words. Lexi often struggles when identifying new words, because she does not know enough letter-sound associations to fully translate words into speech. Her story reads: I want to go to the park. I want to swim. I want to play on the playground.

dren may know the sounds of frequently occurring single consonants, like *m, n, p,* and *s,* they do not have much, if any, knowledge of vowel letter patterns like the *oa* in *boat* or the *a* in *pat,* consonant clusters like *bl, tr,* and *st,* or consonant digraphs (two letters representing one sound), as *th, sh,* and *ch.* Lexi often struggles when reading new words because she does not know enough about letter-sounds and does not have enough phonemic awareness to associate sounds with all the letters in new words. Lexi and children like her frequently guess at words using the context cues, picture cues, and beginning and/or ending letter-sound cues. As long as context and picture cues are robust, these children may successfully read new words. Context has a strong effect on the word identification of these children: High context, especially text that tells a predictable story and uses excellent, descriptive pictures related to the story, is most conducive to accurate word identification; weak context and weak picture cues may result in guesses that do not make sense in the story.

Just as Lexi uses partial alphabetic cues when reading, so does she use partial alphabetic cues when spelling. She spells semiphonetically; that is, she uses letters to represent some, but not all, of the important sounds in words (Gentry, 1987). From Lexi's writing we observe that she uses consonant letters, such as *w* to represent *want* and *swim,* and *p* to represent *park.* Lexi conventionally spells words in her fluent reading vocabulary (*I, to, go, the, play*). Notice how she spells *playground: Play* is among the words she fluently recognizes. The portion of this compound word that is not fluent, *ground,* she represents with the letter *g,* resulting in *playg.*

Alecia has moved further than Lexi toward developing a rich fluent reading vocabulary. Alecia writes about her favorite things, as seen in Figure 3–6, using a blend of conventionally spelled words and semiphonetically spelled words that are not yet in her fluent reading vocabulary. In comparing Lexi and Alecia's writing, we see that Alecia has more known words in her story (*I, have, green, and, blue, a, my, is, love, dog, see*), and she typically uses two or three consonants for words she unconventionally spells (some examples are *bn* for *brown, sdr* for *sister,* and *lk* for *like*). Alecia's use of letters to represent some of the sounds in words (for example, *clr* for *color, fd* for *food,* and *rt* for *restaurant*) suggests that she is carefully thinking about letter-sound relationships. Further evidence comes from her use of the vowel letter *i* in *pink* (spelled *pik*). In contrast to Lexi who uses only beginning sounds to spell, Alecia frequently writes both beginning and ending sounds, and includes some middle sounds as well (*sdr* for *sister* and *clr* for *color*). We have additional evidence that Alecia is looking carefully at print in the way she uses hyphens to spell her favorite restaurant, Chick-Fil-A®—spelled as *C-F-a.* From her story we can infer that Alecia is phonemically aware of beginning and ending sounds, that she is developing awareness of the middle sounds in words, and that she is moving toward using more complex letter-sound relationships than simple phonetic cues.

Figure 3–6 Alecia is phonemically aware of beginning and ending sounds, and is developing awareness of middle sounds. She uses letters to represent the beginning and ending sounds, as well as some middle sounds in words. She is moving into the use of more sophisticated letter and sound relationships than simple phonetic cues. Her story reads: I have green and blue eyes. I have brown hair. I have a twin sister. My favorite color is pink. My favorite food is corn. My favorite restaurant is Chick-Fil-A®. I like to see my friends.

Six Best Practices for Teaching Children in the Partial Alphabetic Stage of Movement Toward Word Fluency

Children in the partial alphabetic stage will move farther toward word fluency when you follow these six best teaching practices:

1. **Teach phonemic awareness of all the sounds in words—first, middle, and last** (National Reading Panel, 2000). At this point in their development as readers, children have some awareness of the sounds in words, but lack sufficient awareness to separate words into each and every sound. Use the activities in chapter 2 to develop the ability to separate words into sounds and to blend sounds together. And, when teaching phonemic awareness, combine instruction with activities in chapter 5 that teach letter-sound patterns.

2. **Teach the sounds represented by consonant and vowel letters** (Armbruster, Lehr, & Osborn, 2001; National Reading Panel, 2000; Snow et al., 1998). While partial alphabetic readers and semiphonetic spellers are developing a working knowledge of single consonant letter-sounds, most children have little knowledge of vowel patterns. Vowels usually occur in the middle of English words, sandwiched between the consonants. Additionally, vowel letter-sound patterns are more complex than consonant letter-sound patterns, which makes vowels more challenging to learn. Since every English word contains at least one vowel sound, children cannot become expert readers and accom-

plished spellers without learning how vowel letter combinations represent sounds. In learning about both consonant and vowel letter-sound patterns, children will become capable of reading and spelling any new word that is spelled as it sounds.

   3.   Have children read every day   (Snow et al., 1998). Ask children to read books on instructional level—books that children can read with only moderate support from you (Cecil, 1999). Encourage children to read the small versions of big books, to read and reread familiar books with a buddy, and to read for pleasure. Keep a storehouse of books available, and encourage children to read them in their spare time, and to take books home to share with their families.

   4.   When reading books aloud, ask children questions that help them demonstrate and extend their knowledge of written language   (Justice et al., 2002). It is important at this stage of children's development to give them opportunities to demonstrate and extend their knowledge of written language and to actively participate in reading aloud. While reading aloud, ask children to use their word and letter knowledge to do things like find words, point to letters, and find letter-sound patterns in familiar words.

   5.   Engage children in activities to explore words   (Neuman et al., 2000). In exploring words with children, call attention to the vowel-consonant combinations at the end of words (the *op* in *hop, shop* and *drop*, explained in chapter 4) and to letter-sound relationships (explained in chapter 5). Make lists of rhyming words that share a similar spelling (*time-dime*, not *time-climb*), and lists of words with the same beginning, middle, or ending letter-sounds. Select some of these words to add to your classroom word wall; have children keep personal boxes of words they want to learn or words they need when writing; talk about how letters represent sounds in the words that children see on the word wall, in books, and in children's personal word boxes. You also might ask children to sort words according to particular letter-sound patterns, and to build words from the letter-sounds they know (as explained in chapter 5).

   6.   Encourage children to think about letters and sounds when they use invented spelling, and have children conventionally spell words in their fluent reading vocabularies   (Snow et al., 1998). Insist that children conventionally spell words they can fluently read. When children cannot conventionally spell a word they wish to write and cannot find the word on the word wall, encourage them to write letters that represent the sounds they hear in the word. This helps children focus on sound, which enhances phonemic awareness, and also helps children focus on letter-sound relationships, which enhances phonics knowledge.

   As children read and write in your classroom, they will pay more and more attention to words. Rather than looking at just one or two letters in words, children will begin to look at the unique letter combination in each word. In due course, children will begin to look for cues in unfamiliar words that are present in familiar words. When children do this, they use existing information to construct and acquire new knowledge. Using parts of known words to identify unknown words that share some of the same letters is the key to reading new words with the analogy strategy, which is the topic of the next chapter.

REFERENCES

Adams, M. (1990). *Beginning to read*. Cambridge, MA: MIT Press.

Armbruster, B. B., Lehr, F., & Osborn, J. (2001). *Put reading first: The research building blocks for teaching children to read kindergarten through grade 3*. Washington, DC: National Institute for Literacy.

Bastien-Toniazzo, M., & Jullien, S. (2001). Nature and importance of the logographic phase in learning to read. *Reading and Writing: An Interdisciplinary Journal, 14*, 119–143.

Brown, M. (1982). *Arthur's Halloween*. Boston: Little, Brown.

Cardoso-Martins, C., Resende, S. M., & Rodrigues, L. A. (2002). Letter-name knowledge and the ability to learn to read by processing letter-phoneme relations in words: Evidence from Brazilian Portuguese-speaking children. *Reading and Writing: An Interdisciplinary Journal, 15*, 409–432.

Cecil, N. L. (1999). *Striking a balance–positive practices for early literacy*. Scottsdale, AZ: Holcomb Hathaway.

Cronin, V., Farrell, D., & Delaney, M. (1999). Environmental print and word reading. *Journal of Research in Reading, 22*, 271–282.

Ehri, L. C. (2000). Learning to read and learning to spell: Two sides of a coin. *Topics in Language Disorders, 20*, 19–36.

Gentry, J. R. (1987). *Spel . . . is a four-letter word*. Portsmouth, NH: Heinemann.

Gough, P. B. (1993). The beginning of decoding. *Reading and Writing: An Interdisciplinary Journal, 5*, 181–192.

Justice, L. M., Weber, S. E., Ezell, H. K., & Bakeman, R. (2002). A sequential analysis of children's responsiveness to parental print references during shared book-reading interactions. *American Journal of Speech-Language Pathology, 11*, 30–40.

Morrow, L. M. (2001). *Literacy development in the early years: Helping children read and write* (4th ed.). Boston: Allyn & Bacon.

National Reading Panel. (2000). *Teaching children to read: An evidence-based assessment of the scientific research literature on reading and its implications for reading instruction: Reports of the subgroups* (NIH Publication No. 00-4754). Washington, DC: U.S. Government Printing Office.

Neuman, S. B., Copple, C., & Bredekamp, S. (2000). *Learning to read and write: Developmentally appropriate practices for young children*. Washington, DC: National Association for the Education of Young Children.

Searfoss, L. W., Readence, J. E., & Mallette, M. H. (2001). *Helping children learn to read: Creating a classroom literacy environment* (4th ed.). Needham Heights, MA: Allyn & Bacon.

Snow, C. E., Burns, M. S., & Griffin, P. (Eds.). (1998). *Preventing reading difficulties in young children*. Washington, DC: National Academy Press.

Stahl, S. A., & Murray, B. (1998). Spoken vocabulary growth and the segmental restructuring of lexical representations: Precursors to phonemic awareness and early reading ability. In J. L. Metsala & L. C. Ehri (Eds.), *Word recognition in beginning literacy* (pp. 65–87). Mahwah, NJ: Lawrence Erlbaum.

Uhry, J. K. (2002). Finger-point reading in kindergarten: The role of phonemic awareness, one-to-one correspondence, and rapid serial naming. *Scientific Studies of Reading, 6*, 319–341.

CHAPTER
4

The Analogy Strategy

Using Parts of Familiar Words to Read New Words

This chapter describes the analogy strategy for reading new words, and the cross-checking, self-monitoring, and self-correction strategies for making sure that identified words make sense in the reading context. As you read this chapter, you will learn how syllables consist of onsets and rimes, and how readers identify words by making analogies from known words to unknown words. You also will learn how to encourage readers to cross-check for meaning, monitor their own word identification, and correct their own miscues—and why this is important for successful word identification. And you will find 6 research-based teaching practices, and 20 activities for teaching the analogy strategy with onsets and rimes.

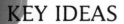

KEY IDEAS

➤ Syllables have a two-part structure, consisting of an onset, which is the consonant that comes before the vowel, and a rime, which is the vowel and all the letters thereafter.
➤ In analogy-based word identification, children use parts of familiar words to read unfamiliar words.
➤ The cross-checking strategy helps readers make sure that the words they identify fit the reading context.
➤ Readers monitor their own reading to detect probable word identification miscues.
➤ When readers realize that an identified word does not make sense, they use a self-correction strategy to fix their word identification miscue.
➤ Successful word identification depends on cross-checking, self-monitoring, and self-correcting, regardless of the strategy used to read new words.

KEY VOCABULARY

Cross-checking	Rime	Self-monitoring
Onset	Self-correcting	Word family
Phonogram		

Look at the following sets of words:

rain	dish	sore
train	swish	store
sprain	finish	before
explain	furnish	explore
maintain	astonish	pinafore

A quick glance is all it takes to realize that the same letter patterns occur in many different words. Once readers discover that the words in each of these three word mountains share a common letter pattern, they have a way to organize their thinking so as to use parts of known words to identify unknown words. When using the analogy strategy, readers find a shared letter pattern in words, such as the *ain* in *rain,* and then use this similarity to identify unfamiliar words with the same pattern, such as *train* and *sprain.*

Looking Inside Syllables

Lucy sets a decidedly lighthearted tone as she ruminates about school in the poem in Figure 4–1. Lucy repeats words and rhymes words—and what's more, all the words she uses have one syllable.

Looking inside the syllables in Lucy's poem reveals a two-part structure that consists of an onset and a rime (Goswami, 1997). *Onsets* are the consonants that come before the vowel in a syllable or one-syllable word, as the *sch* in *school*. Similarly, the *s* in *sit*, the *sl* in *slit*, and the *spl* in *split* are onsets. Onsets are always consonants, and there can be as many as three clustered together (*sch* and *spl*, for example).

Rimes are the vowel and everything after it. The *ool* in *school* is a rime. Correspondingly, the *ent* in *tent* is a rime consisting of the vowel (*e*) and the consonants that follow it (*nt*); the rime in *scream* is *eam*; in *black*, it is *ack*. We can see, then, that in dividing syllables and one-syllable words into onsets and rimes, we split the beginning sound(s) from the part of the word that begins with the vowel (*s - at; sl - at; spl - at*).

Rhyming words like *school* and *cool* share a rime, in this case the rime *ool*. When rime is common to two or more words, the words usually share a rhyming sound. This is not always the case, however, as we see in *know* and *now*, which share the *ow* pattern but do not rhyme. And, of course, sometimes rhyming words do not share a common letter pattern (*sheep* and *leap*). In this case, the words rhyme, but the rhyme is spelled differently (*eep* versus *eap*). In this chapter, we are interested in words that both rhyme (*sheep—deep*) and have the same vowel and ending letter pattern (*eep*). Table 4–1 shows the onset-rime structure of the one-syllable words in Lucy's poem.

Figure 4–1 Some of the one-syllable words in Lucy's poem consist of an onset and a rime; others consist of a rime only.

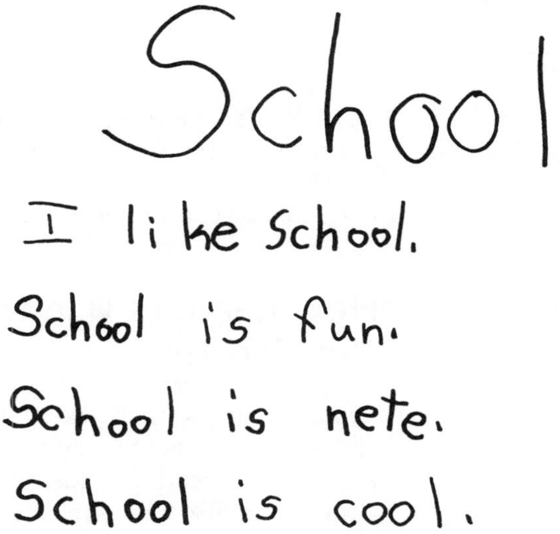

School

I like School.
School is fun.
School is nete.
School is cool.

TABLE 4–1   *Onsets and Rimes in Lucy's Poem*

Onset	+	Rime	=	One-Syllable Word
sch	+	ool	=	school
c	+	ool	=	cool
	+	is	=	is
l	+	ike	=	like
f	+	un	=	fun
n	+	eat	=	neat

TABLE 4–2   *Onsets and Rimes in Two-Syllable Words*

Onset	+	Rime	+	Onset	+	Rime	=	Word
p	+	ump	+	k	+	in	=	pumpkin
m	+	on	+	k	+	ey	=	monkey
spl	+	en	+	d	+	id	=	splendid
th	+	un	+	d	+	er	=	thunder
c	+	om	+	pl	+	ete	=	complete
pl	+	at	+	f	+	orm	=	platform
t	+	ur	+	k	+	ey	=	turkey
tr	+	in	+	k	+	et	=	trinket

Words with more than one syllable are analyzed the same way. The only difference is that syllables are combined, as shown in Table 4–2. When children learn the letter and sound patterns of onsets and rimes, the stage is set to move beyond the phonetic cue strategy and into using the analogy strategy.

How Readers Use the Analogy Strategy to Read New Words

Readers who use the analogy strategy connect onsets and rimes in the words they already know how to read with the same onsets and rimes in words they do not know how to read. The basic premise is that if words share onsets and rimes, then words must also have similar pronunciations. Children who use the analogy strategy can separate spoken words into beginning sounds (onsets) and rhyming sounds (rimes), and can blend beginning sounds and rhyming sounds together to pronounce meaningful words. It is not surprising, then, that awareness of the rhyming sounds in language is significantly related to the ability to use the analogy strategy (Goswami, 1998).

When generalizing the rime in one word (*m̲a̲p̲*) to the pronunciation of another word with the same rime (*c̲a̲p̲*), readers look for shared letter patterns. It turns out that even young readers are sensitive to the shared patterns, or the rimes, in written language, and use this knowledge to read new words (Goswami, 1997). Readers who remember the sounds associated with onsets and rimes will tell you, their teacher, that *ap* represents /ap/ in *map, tap,* and *nap.* Likewise, children will tell you that *m* represents /m/, *t* represents /t/, and *n* represents /n/. Since children make analogies from known to unknown words, the more words in children's fluent reading vocabularies, the more potential there is for children to use words they know to read words they do not know.

Suppose for the sake of illustration that Tamara, a first grader, does not automatically recognize the word *tent* in the sentence *Jane saw a large tent in the campground.* Suppose further that Tamara cannot figure out *tent* from picture cues, syntactic cues, semantic cues, or her own background knowledge. However, Tamara brings to reading the knowledge of onsets and rimes in words she already knows. Here is how Tamara uses the analogy strategy:

1. Tamara notices a familiar onset and a familiar rime in *tent*. She recalls that the *t* in *tell* (a familiar word) represents /t/, and that the *ent* in *went* (a familiar word) represents /ent/.
2. Tamara now substitutes (chapter 2) the /w/ in *went* for the /t/, which leaves /t/ + /ent/.
3. Tamara then blends /t/ + /ent/ to pronounce /tent/.
4. Last, Tamara checks to make sure that /tent/ is a good fit for the sentence. She asks herself: Does *tent* sound and look right? Does *tent* make sense in the passage? Do I know what the author means? If the answers to these questions are yes, Tamara continues reading. If the answers are no, Tamara tries once again to figure out *tent*.

Three Strategies for Keeping Word Identification Meaning Focused

Word identification works best when it serves comprehension. The new words children read absolutely must make sense in the reading context. So, in addition to using specific word identification strategies to read new words, children also use strategies to keep word identification meaning focused. There are three strategies children use to do this: cross-checking, self-monitoring and self-correcting. Readers use these three strategies to make sure that the new words they read are syntactically, semantically, and graphophonically consistent with passages.

Cross-Checking

In the example, the last thing Tamara did was to verify that *tent* made sense in the sentence. *Cross-checking* is the strategy readers use to make sure that the words they identify fit the reading context. In cross-checking, readers compare information from one cueing system with information from another. Readers use grapho-phonic, syntactic, and semantic information together to ensure that the identified word is consistent with the context. Cross-checking is a strategy all by itself, and the last step in word identification. Good readers always cross-check, regardless of whether they identify words with the analogy strategy or some other strategy.

Cross-checking ensures that word identification supports comprehension. When cross-checking, readers actively think about meaning, taking into account the overall sense of the surrounding phrases, sentences, and paragraphs, as well as sentence structure, letter and sound cues, and their personal reasons for reading. Cross-checking may involve rereading a phrase or sentence to accept or reject the identified word. Once satisfied that the newly identified word makes sense in the reading context, children immediately focus their attention back on reading and understanding the text.

Cross-checking gives readers valuable feedback on their own decoding efforts. Thus, one consequence of cross-checking is a metacognitive—or conscious—awareness of the success of word identification (*metacognition* is explained in chapter 1). Readers know whether an identified word is acceptable or unacceptable for the reading passage. An acceptable outcome is a real, meaningful word that makes sense in the context; an unacceptable outcome is either a nonsense word or a word that does not fit the context. The following prompts may help children develop and use the cross-checking strategy:

- "Reread it and think about what would make sense."
- "What's wrong with _____ (rereading what the child read)?"
- "Does _____ look right and sound right?"
- "Does what you just read sound like a real word?"
- "Try reading that again."
- "Could it be _____? What makes you think so?"
- "You read _____. Can we say it that way?"
- "Does _____ make sense?"
- After the child successfully cross-checks, ask, "How did you know this is _____?"

Readers who cross-check put only as much energy into word identification as is necessary to identify a word that is consistent with the author's message. These readers know when to stop word identification and proceed with textual reading, and when to give word identification another try. When a word makes sense, word identification stops and comprehension moves forward unimpeded by the confusion created by an unknown or misidentified word. On the other hand, if an identified word does not make sense, then cross-checking lets readers know that they have not constructed a meaningful message.

Readers who use the cross-checking strategy are guaranteed of a good fit between identified words and authors' messages. Readers who do not cross-check accept the results of word identification even if those results are nonsense. For these reasons, cross-checking is absolutely essential and must be used every time readers identify an unfamiliar word.

Self-Monitoring

Self-monitoring is the strategy of self-regulating one's own reading. Readers use self-monitoring to determine when they need to use the cross-checking strategy and when they do not. Self-monitoring assures that readers only stop to cross-check when an identified word does not fit the context. In monitoring their own reading, readers pay attention to comprehension, stopping to cross-check when they discover that text does not make sense. Use these prompts to encourage children to self-monitor:

- "Take another look at _____."
- "You read _____. Are you right?"
- "You made a mistake in this sentence (paragraph or page). Can you find it?"
- "Why did you stop?"
- "What's wrong with_____ ?"
- Pointing to the word, ask, "Could it be _____?"
- "You read _____. What did you notice?"
- "You read _____. Does it make sense?"

Self-Correcting

Self-correcting is the process of rereading to correct a miscue. Readers self-correct when, through cross-checking, they determine that the message does not make sense. Children go back into the text and reread to make the words fit the context. In so doing, children change or correct a misidentified word. Use these prompts to support readers as they self-correct:

- "What's the tricky part in this word?"
- "What is another word that begins with _____ (ends with _, or has _ in the middle) and makes sense?"
- "You were almost right. See if you can figure out what you need to fix."
- "You read _____. Try it again and think about _____."
- Pointing to the word, ask, "How did you know that was _____? Is there another way to tell?"
- Cover up all but the first letters and ask, "What would make sense that begins with _____?"

Encourage children to look at the letters, think of the context, and reread to confirm meaning. Then reinforce self-correcting, saying, "I like the way you went back to fix that word," or "You did a good job going back (rereading) to make sense."

When readers cross-check, self-monitor, and self-correct, they pay attention to meaning. Readers use self-monitoring to decide if they should cross-check. Readers cross-check to see if the identified word makes sense. If readers determine through cross-checking that an identified word does not fit the context, they self-correct their own miscue. Before returning to the text, readers once again cross-check to make sure that the self-corrected word makes sense in the reading context. If so, readers turn their attention back to reading and understanding the text. If not, then readers try once again to self-correct the miscue so as to recreate a meaningful message.

Rimes, Phonograms, and Word Families

Rimes, phonograms, and word families are related terms. Rimes and *phonograms* refer to the vowel and any consonant that comes after it in a syllable (the *at* in *cat*). *Word families* are word groups that share the same rime or phonogram (*cat, rat, fat, sat, bat*). Some popular teaching materials in the 1960s clustered words into "families" where every family member shared a common rime or phonogram. When these materials were first published, they were dubbed "linguistic" because their authors were linguists, not educators, and the materials were supposed to reflect linguistic principles. The Merrill Linguistic Reading Program (1986) and Programmed Reading (Phoenix Learning Resources, 1994) are contemporary examples of this approach. The sentences in linguistic materials are jam-packed with word family words like *The man has a tan pan in the van.* There is minimal variation among words, with many words differing only in the onset. Though the objective of linguistic materials is to teach word identification, children do not learn the "rules" of phonics. Words are taught by sight, not by sounding and blending as in traditional phonics programs. Readers abstract their own generalizations about letter-sound correspondences as a consequence of reading words from the same families.

Anna wrote the word list in Figure 4–2 when her teacher asked her to write as many words as she could in a short period of time. We can infer from Anna's list that she thinks about the rime in words, for the 20-word family words are made up of only four rimes, *op, ox, ad,* and *am.* Anna's teacher emphasizes phonograms, so it is no surprise that Anna thinks of word family words when she writes. Anna knows how to substitute onsets, or beginning consonants, to make new words, so we would expect that she will also be able to read and write words like *drop, stop, sad, lad, ram,* and *ham,* provided that she recognizes the *op, ad,* and *am* phonograms (or rimes).

Why Do Children Use Onsets and Rimes to Read New Words?

Identifying words by their analogous onsets and rimes is easier than decoding words letter-sound by letter-sound. First, learning that *ent* represents /ent/ is far less taxing than learning that the *e* represents the sound of /e/, *n* the sound of /n/,

Figure 4–2 When Anna's teacher asked her to write as many words as she could, Anna wrote 20 words using only four rimes—*op, ox, ad,* and *am.*

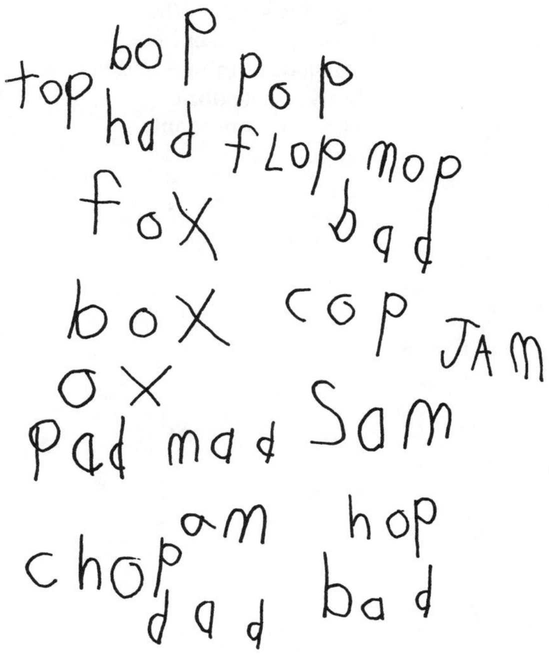

and *t* the sound of /t/. Second, blending onsets and rimes is much easier than blending individual sounds because with onsets and rimes there are only two items to blend. In the example of *tent,* analogy users would blend only /t/ + /ent/ in comparison with the four phonemes /t/ + /e/ + /n/ + /t/ associated with individual letters. Fewer items to blend, in turn, decreases the probability of reversing sounds, deleting sounds, or adding sounds during blending. Consequently, readers who might not be successful sounding out and blending *tent* as /t/ + /e/ + /n/ + /t/ may be able to read *tent* when it is divided into /t/ + /ent/.

As Lilly writes about her pet cat, see Figure 4–3, she conventionally spells words in her fluent reading vocabulary and spells other words by adding different onsets to the *at* rime. We can infer from her story that Lilly is thinking carefully about speech-to-print relationships, resourcefully combining her knowledge of onsets and rimes, her memory for known words, and her understanding of letter-sound associations. When Lilly reads, she uses frequently occurring rimes, as well as the letter-sound patterns of phonics, to identify new words.

It is quite typical for readers like Lilly to use both the analogy and the letter-sound decoding strategies (Walton, Walton, & Felton, 2001). Children like Lilly look for consistency in written and spoken language relationships. They learn and remember words by paying attention to recurring letter patterns, and hence they can write and read words that consist of onset-rime combinations they already know (*p* + *et* = *pet*), as well as the letter-sound patterns of phonics (*p* + *e* + *t* = *pet*). The beneficial effect of rimes may be more important in English than in other languages that have more consistent sound-letter matches (Booth & Perfetti, 2002).

Figure 4–3 When writing, Lilly uses her knowledge of rimes and her ability to substitute beginning consonants (onsets).

English does not match only one letter to only one sound. There are many more English sounds (43 or so) than English letters (26). The same sounds are represented by different letter patterns (the long /o/ in _toe_, _boat_ and _know_), and the same letters represent different sounds (the _e_ in _be_, _bet_ and _her_). In presenting readers with consistent sound-letter matches, rimes make our English spelling system somewhat simpler for beginning readers.

Onsets and rimes are reasonably dependable maps for sound, so readers can justifiably place a certain amount of confidence in them. Onsets consist exclusively of consonant letters. As it turns out, the consonant letters are far more reliable representations of sound than are the vowels. When combined with rich context cues, onsets give readers considerable insight into a word's identity. Upon seeing the word _track_ for the first time in the sentence _The train rolled down the track_, a reader who knows the onset, _tr_, and who is sensitive to context cues might logically assume that this never-seen-before word is _track_.

Though consonants are relatively dependable, this is not so for vowels. Each vowel represents more than one sound, as with the _a_ in _track, bake, saw,_ and _car._ Vowels are more easily remembered and decoded when learned as part of frequently recurring rimes (Goswami, 2001a). When syllables, in this example the one-syllable word _track_, are divided into onsets and rimes, the tricky vowels are not quite so troublesome. The explanation is that the vowels in rimes are learned as part of a chunk of letters and sounds. For this reason, readers who learn rimes do not have to understand why the *a* in *track* is pronounced one way and the *a* in *bake* another way. Instead, readers remember that the *ack* in *track* represents /ack/ and the *ake* in *bake* represents /ake/.

Remembering the rimes in word family words sidesteps the need to learn exceptions to the conventional way letters represent sounds in English words. Take the *old* in *told,* for example. The *o* in *told* should represent the same sound as the *o* in *rock*, since there is only one vowel (the *o*) in a short word followed by two consonants (*old - ock*). This is not so, of course. Children would be confused if they tried to read *told* as though the *o* represented the sound in /rock/. However, the sound represented by the *o* in *told* is not at all troublesome when remembered as part of the whole rime *old.* Children who know how to read the rime in *told* have a cue to the identification of any word in the *old* word family, for example, *gold, sold, cold,* and *fold.* The net effect is that even vowels that stand for a variety of sounds are more easily remembered and decoded when learned within the context of word family words. Therefore, it is not surprising that children who are taught to use analogous rimes are better at reading words that require attention to the rime, such as *sight* and *hold,* as compared with children taught only predictable letter-sound patterns, such as *bat* and *bit* (Walton, Walton, & Felton, 2001).

Six Best Practices for Teaching Children to Use the Analogy Strategy With Onsets and Rimes

If you teach children like Lilly, you can expect them to recognize and use the rimes in word family words when you directly teach the analogy strategy and when you provide reading and writing activities like those described later in this chapter. In helping children notice onsets and rimes in new words that are also part of familiar words, you help children use the analogy strategy. Suppose that a child sees the new word *tent* in a sentence in the text. You might guide the child in making an analogy to the rime in a familiar word, *went,* by saying, "Look at this word (pointing to *tent*). Now, look at this word (pointing to *went*). If this is /went/, what do you think this word might be (pointing to *tent*)?" Another way to guide readers as they apply the analogy strategy is to say, "Can you think of another word that ends with *ent?*" It is also important to help children develop a metacognitive, or conscious, awareness of their own ability to use the analogy strategy. Give children opportunities to reflect on their own strategy by asking, "What word do you already know that can help you figure out this new one?" Along with asking questions like these, use the following six best practices to ensure that instruction is effective and meets children's needs:

1.   Use word family clue words   (Goswami, 2001b). Readers are more inclined to use the analogy strategy when they learn clue words that contain rimes. A clue word is a familiar word that contains an often-used rime. Examples are: *cat* for the *at* word family; *pig* for the *ig* word family; *fan* for the *an* word family; *jet* for the *et* word family, *sun* for the *un* word family, and *night* for the *ight* family. Clue words like these help children remember the sounds and spellings of word family rimes. Once readers know clue words, make sure that readers can refer to them when reading new words (Muter, Snowling, & Taylor, 1994). Put word family clue words on the word wall, write them on charts, tape them to the tables where children read and write, and write them on the board.

2. **Show children how to use the analogy strategy**   (Nation, Allen, & Hulme, 2001). We cannot assume that children will naturally begin to use analogous onsets and rimes. Significantly, while some children may be able to figure out the identity of words with known onsets and rimes without their teachers' help, most children need guidance from their teachers and structure in learning (Goswami, 2001a; Savage, 2001). Teaching should be both explicit and systematic, and practice using the analogy strategy should be grounded in real reading and writing experiences. In showing children how to use the analogy strategy, think aloud as you demonstrate decoding. You might say something like, "I know the word *went*. The *ent* in *went* says /ent/. So to read this new word (pointing to *tent*), I will change the *w* (/w/) to a *t* (/t/), which makes /tent/. Now you try it with me."

3. **Teach onsets and beginning sound substitution before teaching the analogy strategy**   (Stahl, 2001). Children need to know how onsets—beginning consonant letter-sounds—represent sound and must be able to substitute one onset for another before they can use the analogy strategy. Consequently, it is important to teach children not only consonant letter-sounds, but also how to substitute the beginning sounds in words, as explained in chapter 2.

4. **Teach rimes from large, often-used word families**   Successful beginning readers can read more word family words with frequently occurring rimes than words with less-common rimes (Leslie & Calhoon, 1995; Wylie & Durrell, 1970). From a practical perspective, we want to teach children those rimes that are the most helpful; that is, the more common rimes that make up many different word family words. The rimes in appendix A are part of almost 500 words in books for beginning readers.

5. **Develop children's fluent reading vocabulary**   (Goswami, 2001a). Older, more skilled readers make more analogies when reading new words than do younger, less-skilled readers. The reason is that more skilled readers have larger fluent reading vocabularies, and hence have more words on which to base analogies (Strickland, 1998). For example, if readers do not have a word spelled with *ent* in their fluent reading vocabulary, such as *went*, then the analogy strategy is useless for reading a new word like *tent*. As a consequence, readers need a reasonably large pool of words in memory from which to make comparisons and analogies.

6. **Teach word family rimes along with the letter-sound relationships within rimes**   (Gaskins, Ehri, Cress, O'Hara, & Donnelly, 1996/1997; Juel & Minden-Cupp, 2000). Children who know the sounds that the individual letters in rimes represent are better able to use the analogy strategy than children who do not understand the letter-sound relationships within rimes. For example, the reader who knows that *at* represents /at/, and who also knows that the *a* in *at* represents /a/ (the short a) and the *t* represents /t/ is more likely to effectively use the analogy strategy than the child who knows only that *at* represents /at/. In fact, readers may need to know something about the manner in which individual letters represent sound before they can successfully use the analogy strategy (Ehri & Robbins, 1992).

Good readers use several word identification strategies, and change strategies, going between analogy and letter-sound decoding, depending on the reading circumstances (Walton, et al., 2001).

Twenty Easy and Effective Activities for Teaching the Analogy Strategy

The following activities help children learn the sounds that onsets and rimes represent, and how to use the analogy decoding strategy. You can use these activities to teach any rime you think beneficial for the children in your classroom. As with any activity in this book, adapt the activities so that they are compatible with your teaching style. Combine these activities with reading aloud books with rhyming words listed in appendix A. In addition to the following 20 activities, look in chapter 5 for activities to teach letter-sounds. Provide clue words to help children make analogies from known to unknown words, and include in your balanced classroom reading program a generous amount of time devoted to reading and writing, including the reading and writing of word family words.

 ## Word Family Word Building

Children build word family words by lining up small cards with onsets and rimes on them. This activity is suitable for children working in small groups, individually, or in learning centers.

Things You'll Need: One set of large 3-inch-by-5-inch onset and rime cards that combine to build often-seen and often-used word family words; sets of small onset and rime cards (or tiles); a pocket chart. Tiles are available commercially or if you wish to make your own, buy small tiles from a home improvement store and write on them in permanent ink the onsets and rimes children are learning in your classroom.

Directions: Use a pocket chart and the large onset and rime cards to demonstrate word building, as shown in Figure 4–4. Put an onset and a rime card side by side in a pocket chart (*s* and *at*, perhaps) and push the cards together to build a word family word (*sat*). Use a different onset and the same rime to build another word from the same family (*fat*, for instance). Line up word family words, thus creating opportunities to compare and contrast the rimes in words and to develop an understanding of how word family words sound alike and look alike. Give children onset-rime cards (or small onset-rime tiles), and ask them to work individually or with a partner to build the word family words you specify. Once children are familiar with word family word building, you may wish to ask them to build as many words as they can from the same set of onset-rime cards. Have children share the word family words they build, write the words on the board, and compare and contrast word family words.

Figure 4–4 The use of a pocket chart to build words helps readers gain insight into the sound that analogous onsets and rimes represent in word family words.

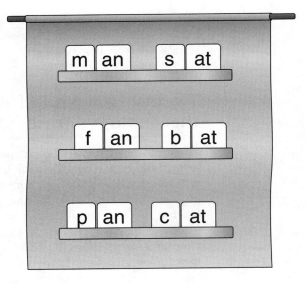

Paper Plate Word Family Words

Children working in centers combine onsets and rimes to build word family words, and write the words on word family paper plates, which then are put on the bulletin board and sent home for children to share with their families.

Things You'll Need: Sets of onset-rime cards; inexpensive paper plates.

Directions: Put onset-rimes cards and paper plates in a learning center. Children visiting the center combine onset-rime cards to build word family words. Children then write the word family words on the paper plates. Put the word family paper plates on the bulletin board, discuss the word families, and send the word family plates home with children to share with their own families. Table 4–3 has onsets and short vowel rime combinations for word family word building and other activities in this chapter.

Rewriting Familiar Poems

Children in small groups predict rhyming words in familiar poems, and then use their knowledge of word family rimes to add their own new and creative endings to the poems.

Things You'll Need: Sticky notes; familiar poems written on large charts. Only use poems with words that both rhyme and share a rime (*might—light*).

Directions: Use a sticky note to cover up one or more rhyming words in a familiar poem. Have children read the poem aloud and, when they come to a covered-up

TABLE 4–3 *Onsets and Short Vowel Rimes for Word Family Word Building and Other Activities*

Rimes				Onsets						
ap	at	ad	an	c	m	h	r	s	t	b
ed	en	et	ell	b	n	y	p	l	w	m
ig	id	in	ip	b	d	h	l	p	w	r
op	ob	og	ot	c	h	d	r	m	p	l
ug	um	un	ub	b	g	h	m	r	s	t
ap	ip	op	ot	s	t	l	n	c	m	d
ell	est	ill	in	b	f	p	w	t	s	d
ack	ash	ick	ock	s	t	l	p	r	st	sm

Word Family Words Built From the Onsets and Rimes

ap, at, ad, an
cap, map, rap, sap, tap
cat, mat, hat, rat, sat, bat
mad, had, sad, tad, bad
can, man, ran, tan, ban

ed, en, et, ell
bed, led, wed
yen, pen, men
bet, net, yet, pet, let, wet, met
bell, yell, well

ig, id, in, ip
big, dig, pig, wig, rig
bid, did, hid, lid, rid
bin, din, pin, win
dip, hip, lip, rip

op, ob, og, ot
cop, hop, mop, pop, lop
cob, rob, mob, lob
cog, hog, dog, log
cot, hot, dot, rot, pot, lot

ug, um, un, ub
bug, hug, mug, rug, tug
bum, gum, hum, mum, rum, sum
bun, gun, run, sun
hub, rub, sub, tub

ap, ip, op, ot
sap, tap, lap, nap, cap, map
sip, tip, lip, nip, dip
sop, top, lop, cop, mop
tot, lot, not, cot, dot

ell, est, ill, in
bell, fell, well, tell, sell, dell
best, pest, west, test
bill, fill, pill, will, till, sill, dill
bin, fin, pin, win, tin, sin, din

ack, ash, ick, ock
sack, tack, lack, pack, rack, stack, smack
sash, lash, rash, stash, smash
sick, tick, lick, pick, stick
sock, lock, rock, stock, smock

Figure 4–5 Writing new endings for familiar poems helps readers gain insight into words that share letter and sound patterns.

word, predict the word under the sticky note. Once children make their prediction, take off the sticky note to reveal the word family word. After children are thoroughly familiar with the poem, ask them to write their own versions by adding new endings. The endings in Figure 4–5 were written by first graders after their teacher shared the big book *Oh, A-Hunting We Will Go* (Langstaff, 1989). After children share their poems with the class, you may want to bind the poems together to make a class poetry book.

Figure 4–5 (continued)

Sticky-Note Word Family Word Books

Children working in small groups or in learning centers use sticky notes to make their own word family word books, such as those in Figure 4–6. To emphasize onsets, ask children to make sticky-note beginning letter-sound books.

Things You'll Need: Sticky notes; pencils; stapler.

Directions: Have children join you in making lists of word family words or, if the children are to make beginning sound books, lists of words that begin with the same letter-sound. Give each child a few sticky notes. Children write one word family word (or a word with the same beginning letter-sound) on each sticky note. Children put their sticky notes together to form a book; staple the pages to keep them together (Figure 4–6). Children then flip the pages to read their sticky-note word family word (or beginning letter-sound) books. Children then take the books home to read with their families.

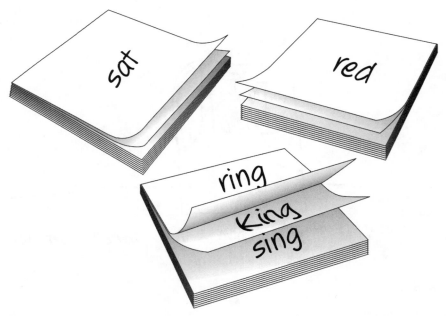

Figure 4–6   Sticky-Note Word Family Books. Children make sticky-note word family (or beginning letter-sound) word books and then flip the pages to read their books.

Onset-Rime Riddles

Small groups of first, second, and third graders use their knowledge of rimes and beginning letter-sounds to solve riddles, and then write their answers on small white boards. In writing solutions to riddles, children think about how to spell words and cross-check for accuracy, which help children remember the words.

Things You'll Need: As many small white boards (or small chalk boards) as there are children in a small group; dry-erase markers (or chalk); paper towels for erasers.

Directions: Begin by demonstrating how to solve riddles. Write two clue words on the board, *rice* and *bug*, perhaps. Explain that children are to use the clue words to solve a riddle. For example, you might say something like, "The word starts like *rice* and rhymes with *bug*. It is something you walk on. What is it?" Now show children how to substitute the beginning letter-sound (the onset) in the first word (the *r* in *rice*) for the beginning letter sound to the second word (the *ug* in *bug*) to solve the riddle (*rug*). (Look in chapter 2 for more information on the phonemic awareness skill of sound substitution.) Give each child a small white board, a dry-erase marker, and a paper towel for an eraser. Make up easy riddles with onset and rime clue words. Children write their answers on the white boards and then hold up the boards to show their solutions. Everyone in the group responds, thus giving you valuable insight into how children use their knowledge of onsets and rimes, as well as children's ability to substitute initial consonants. Examples of riddles include:

- The word begins like *dip* and rhymes with *hog*. It barks. What is it?
- The word begins like *pink* and rhymes with *rig*. It lives on a farm. What is it?
- The word begins like *candle* and rhymes with *rake*. You eat it. What is it?
- The word begins like *fan* and rhymes with *box*. It is a forest animal. What is it?
- The word begins like *jar* and rhymes with *wet*. It flies. What is it?
- The word begins like *rat* and rhymes with *sing*. It is something you wear. What is it?
- The word begins like *girl* and rhymes with *cold*. It is a color. What is it?
- The word begins like *bat* and rhymes with *fox*. It is something you put things in. What is it?
- The word begins like *tan* and rhymes with *sail*. It's something dogs wag. What is it?
- The word begins like *box* and rhymes with *tell*. It rings. What is it?

If you want to make the riddles more challenging, do not give children the meaning clue, such as "It rings." In only considering the clue words (the word begins like *box* and rhymes with *tell*) children must depend completely on their knowledge of onsets and rimes and on their ability to substitute beginning sounds.

Word Family Muffin Words

This word-building activity is especially good for learning centers, and yields a permanent record of the words children build with onsets and rimes.

Things You'll Need: A muffin tin; small cards with onsets and rimes (or small tiles with onsets and rimes); muffin word guide. Put an assortment of onset-rime cards in each compartment of the muffin tin. Tape a small label above each compartment to tell which onset or rime cards are inside. Make a muffin word guide (Figure 4–7) by drawing several circles on a sheet of blank paper to simulate a row on a muffin tin. Write a word family clue word above the simulated muffins. The clue words on the muffin word guide should be the same clue words that help remind children of word family rimes, consistent with best practice. Underline the rime in each word family clue word.

Figure 4–7 The muffin word guide that children fill in when they combine onset with rime cards placed in a muffin tin is a permanent record of the words that children build.

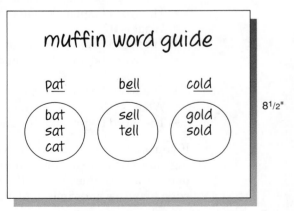

Directions: Children in centers read the word family clue words on the muffin word guide, and use onset and rime cards to build word family words (Figure 4–7). Children write the words in the "muffins." If children build more words than fit in the blank muffins on the muffin word guide, ask them to write the extra words underneath the muffins.

 Fishing for Words

Children fish for words in a bucket "pond." Rather than simply reading words, as is the procedure in the traditional version of the word fishing activity, children substitute one beginning letter-sound for another to read words with familiar rimes. This activity is suitable for small groups of first graders and second graders who need extra help in learning how to read word family words by substituting beginning sounds.

Things You'll Need: A plastic bucket to serve as a pond; a pole (a ruler works well); string; paper clips; a magnet; fish made of laminated construction paper; a marker. To make the fishing pole, tie a string to a ruler and fasten a small magnet to the end of the string. To make the fish, cut colored construction paper into fish shapes. Write a word with a familiar rime on one side of each fish—the word *band* for instance. On the other side, write an onset that creates a word when substituted for the beginning letter in the word on the reverse, such as the letter *s*. Last, fasten a large paper clip to each fish and dump all the fish in the pond (the plastic bucket).

Directions: Children catch a fish, read the word on one side (*band*), substitute the beginning sound written on the reverse side (*s*), and then read the new word (*sand*), as shown in Figure 4–8. Correctly identified words are removed from the pond. If the word is not correctly identified, the fish is thrown back into the pond for another try later in the game.

 Hink Pinks

Hink pinks are two-word rhymes consisting of an adjective and a noun that share a rime.

Things You'll Need: Paper; pencils; crayons or markers.

Directions: Begin by asking children to think of adjectives with the same rimes as the nouns they describe, such as *dairy fairy* or *smelly belly*. Write examples on the chalkboard to serve as illustrations. Children create and illustrate their own hink pinks. Figure 4–9 shows hink pinks and pictures created by a multi-age group of second and third graders. You may want to ask children to write definitions for their hink pinks. For example, "a drippy pet" or "a wet pet" are definitions for the hink pink *soggy doggy*. And you also may want to prop the definitions on the chalk tray, and have children match the definitions with the hink pinks and pictures.

Figure 4–8 Children substitute one beginning sound (onset) for another to discover the words they catch in a "pond" made from a bucket or pail.

foggy doggy

STUPID CUPID

Figure 4–9 Children think about rime and word meaning when they create and illustrate pairs of words that share the same rime.

happy
pappy

Figure 4–9 *(continued)*

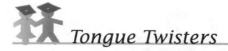

Tongue Twisters

Tongue twisters are sentences in which all (or nearly all) the words begin with the same letter-sound. Use this activity with first, second, and third graders who need practice paying attention to onsets and extra practice in fluently reading short sentences.

Things You'll Need: Tongue twisters remembered from childhood or a good book with lots of twisters, such as *World's Toughest Tongue Twisters* (Rosenbloom, 1986) or Charles Keller's *Tongue Twisters* (1989).

Directions: Write a tongue twister on the board and have children read and reread the twister in chorus for fluency. Ask a volunteer to underline the words with the same beginning letter-sound (onset). Have the whole group join together to write a tongue twister. Children are now ready to write their own tongue twisters. You may designate the onset each child is to use in writing the tongue twister, or children may decide for themselves which beginning sound they would like to use. Share the alliterative tongue twisters children write (Figure 4–10); read

Figure 4–10 Writing and illustrating tongue twisters gives children opportunities to identify the onsets in words and to creatively use this knowledge.

twisters aloud in chorus; put them on wall charts. To develop fluency, have children tape-record tongue twisters. Follow the example of Rosenbloom and fasten together children's alliterative sentences and illustrations to make a book of playful, alliterative language created by the readers and writers in your classroom.

Word Family Egg Words

Children working in centers build words by putting together two halves of colorful plastic eggs—one half with an onset written on it and the other with a rime.

Things You'll Need: A permanent marker; plastic eggs; a basket (optional).

Directions: Write an onset on one half of a plastic egg and a rime on the other half. Put the eggs in a basket, separate them into halves, scramble the halves. Have children fasten together two halves of colored plastic eggs that have a rime and an onset (Figure 4–11). Have children write the words they build.

Word Family Chains

Children make brightly colored paper chains of word family words. Or children may make chains of words that begin with the same letter-sound, depending on which aspect of print (onsets or rimes) you wish to emphasize.

Figure 4–11   Children build words by putting the halves of plastic eggs with onsets on them together with the halves that have rimes written on them.

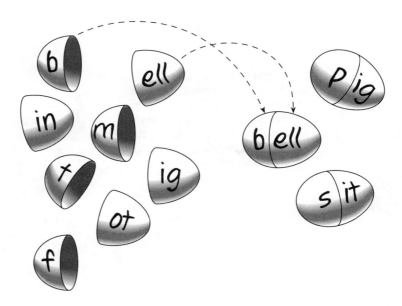

Things You'll Need: Colorful construction paper cut into strips about 1 inch wide.

Directions: Children look for word family words (or words with the same beginning letter-sound) on the word wall, on charts, and on bulletin boards. Children write word family words or words with the same beginning letter-sound on construction paper strips. Tape or staple the ends of strips into a circle, linking the circles with one another to form a giant chain. Before hanging the chain, count the number of words children chained together. Drape chains over bulletin boards; hang them from one corner of the room to the other; tape them to desks, windows, and walls.

Rime Pick-Up

In this gamelike activity, children pick up sticks—either the kind found in popsicles or used as tongue depressors—with word family rimes (or onsets) on them (Figure 4–12). This activity works best when two or three children play together, and fits nicely into centers.

Things You'll Need: Popsicle sticks, craft sticks or tongue depressors with rimes on them (or onsets if beginning letter-sounds are the focus).

Directions: Scatter sticks on a table or floor. Taking turns, children pick up a stick, read the rime or say the beginning letter, and think of a word family word or a word with the same beginning letter-sound. If the child says a real word, the child puts the stick in his or her own personal pile. Each stick is worth one point. The player who gets the most sticks (the most points) wins.

Figure 4–12   Children get lots of practice thinking of the recurring rime in words when they pick up craft sticks with rimes written on them and then think of a beginning sound to make a word.

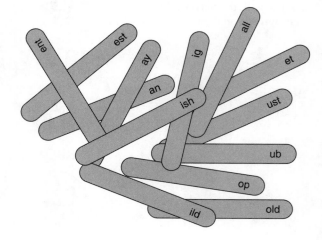

Word Family Tic-Tac-Toe

This old standby fits nicely in learning centers, and is played much like the original version of the game, except word family words are written in tic-tac-toe squares instead of Xs and Os. Or, to focus on onsets, children write words that begin with specified letter-sounds.

Things You'll Need: Oak tag; markers. Make tic-tac-toe cards by drawing the traditional nine-box design and writing two word family clue words with different rimes above the boxes. Underline the rime in each word family clue word (*cat, ran*). If you would rather emphasize onsets, write words with onsets the children are learning and then underline the onsets. Laminate tic-tac-toe cards and have players use erasable markers when they play.

Directions: Two children play; each writes a word with the same rime (or onset) as that at the top of the playing card (Figure 4–13). In this example, one player writes *at* family words, while the other player writes *an* family words. The traditional rules hold—any three words joined in a horizontal, vertical, or diagonal direction win. Note: This game can be used for letter-sound patterns (chapter 5), prefixes (chapter 6), or suffixes (chapter 6) by writing two words with different letter-sound patterns (such as *boat* and *tail* for long o and long a), prefixes (*unhappy* and *replay*), or suffixes (*playing* and *looked*) at the top of the tic-tac-toe cards.

 ## *Word Family Train*

Children make their own train tickets by writing word family words on cards and then putting them inside train cars that have the same word family rime on them. Alternatively, children can write words with beginning letter-sounds that match the letters written on train cars.

Things You'll Need: An engine and train cars made of colorful construction paper; large envelopes. Staple a large envelope with a word family rime (or a beginning

Figure 4–13 Tic-tac-toe challenges children to think of words that share the same rime. This activity can also be adapted for often-used prefixes and suffixes, or for words that have specific letter-sound patterns, such as long vowels or r-controlled vowels.

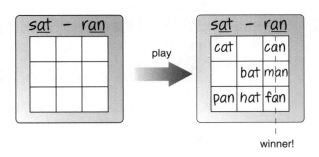

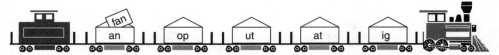

Figure 4–14   Getting on board this train calls for writing word family words (or words with the same beginning letter-sounds) and putting them inside the proper car. When the train leaves the station, all the cards are read and returned to the children, who then take them home for additional practice.

letter-sound), flap side out, to each car. Fasten everything to a bulletin board (Figure 4–14).

Directions: Children make their own "tickets" by writing word family words (or words with beginning letter-sounds) on index cards. Children then put the "tickets" inside the car with the word family clue word on it. When the train is ready to leave the station, take out the tickets, read and discuss the words, and return tickets to their makers so children can take them home to share.

Silly Sentences and Stories

Children write sentences or stories that have many word family words or words that begin alike. Using many words that share the same rime or beginning letter-sound results is silly, often humorous, sentences and stories. This activity is appropriate for children working in small groups and in learning centers.

Things You'll Need: Nothing special.

Directions: Review onsets or rimes, as appropriate for the focus of the activity. Children write silly sentences or stories that predominantly feature either the same rimes or the same onsets. For instance, using the Minnie Moo books (Cazet, 2000) as an inspiration, children might write a silly story that features the *m* onset. Children might write, *One morning Mr. Moo and Mr. Moo's mooing wife (Mrs. Moo) mooed, "Moove over" to their little son Minnie Moo Jr. Minnie Moo Jr. yelled, "Mooomy, I want some m-m-m-ilk and coookie crisps." "I have some cookie crisps, but you will have to make your own m-m-m-ilk," said Mrs. Moo.* Or children might write silly sentences with the same rime, such as *Save brave Dave from the deep, dark cave.* or *The fat cat sat on a hat and squashed it flat.*

Three Kinds of Word Lists

Children make long lists of words that begin with the same onset or end with the same rime. Encourage children to actively participate in list making, to help write the words, and, additionally, have children read and reread the lists to develop word fluency.

Things You'll Need: Nothing special.

A. *Theme-Based Word Family Lists*

Directions: Challenge children to think of words that share rimes with food names, holidays, animals, community places, games, and toys. For example, word family words for an animal, say a *cat*, might include *hat, bat, gnat, fat, sat, rat,* and *mat;* a list of word family words for an outdoor toy, say a *swing,* might be *ring, king, bring, sing,* and *thing.* Fasten lists to walls, bulletin boards, and doors. Compare and contrast words; use words for writing poetry, for studying word spelling, and in games.

B. *Celebrate Onsets*

Directions: Explore onsets with an old-fashioned celebration, an alliterative feast with all sorts of things that begin alike, such as *popcorn, pizza, potatoes, pineapple, pretzels,* and *pie.* Make a list of these words. Write poems and stories about the experience, using lots of words from the alliterative list.

C. *Alliterative Shopping Lists*

Directions: Make a game of creating imaginary shopping lists, saying, "I went to the store and I found a banana to buy." Then ask each child to add something to the list that begins with the same letter and sound as *banana—basket, bread, book, balloon, bean.* Make a list on the chalkboard. Discuss onsets and the sounds they represent, and then invite children to create their own imaginative shopping lists.

 ## *Word Family Slides*

Children pull a strip of oak tag through a device to reveal one word family word at a time, as shown in Figure 4–15. This activity fits nicely into learning centers.

Things You'll Need: While slides can be purchased, they are extremely easy to make from oak tag. To make a slide, write onsets on a strip of oak tag. Then cut a medium-sized shape out of oak tag to serve as the body of the slide. Write a rime on the slide and cut a window (two horizontal slits) beside the rime. Make the window large enough so that the strip with onsets can be threaded through it.

Directions: As children pull the strip through the slide, different words are formed. Ask children to write down the words they make, and then later include these words in the word family word building activity described earlier.

 ## *Word Family Word Binders*

Children save important word family words in binders, and then consult the words either when writing or when participating in other word family activities.

Figure 4–15 Word family slides give children practice identifying word family words that are formed when different onsets are combined with the same rime.

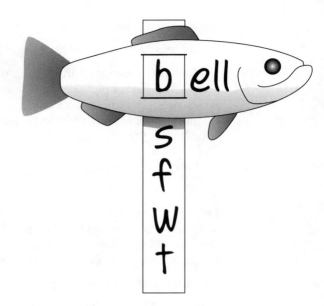

Things You'll Need: One binder for each child; paper for the binders.

Directions: As a group, children make a list of words in the same family, the *at* family, for example. Children then put the *at* family list in their personal word family word binders. Children add to their binders other word family words they meet in reading or need for writing. The words children put in their binders may come from the word family lists in your classroom, from the word wall, from poems, and from writing activities. Put lists in binders alphabetically according to the vowel in the rime, *am, an, at, et, ig, im, ip, it,* and so forth.

Word Family Word Towers

Children build towers of word family words by reading words written on blocks. Or, alternatively, children make towers of blocks with words that have the same beginning letter-sound.

Things You'll Need: Blocks with word family words or words with some of the same beginning letter-sounds. To make blocks, you need square tissue boxes; tape; sticky shelf or drawer liner paper; a permanent marker. Cover the boxes with drawer liner paper, write words on the blocks. It is easier to make towers when blocks have words on only four sides, more difficult when words are on all six sides.

Directions: Children read the words on each block, decide which word belongs to the family (or has the same beginning letter-sound), and then stack the blocks

Figure 4–16 When children make word towers, they have opportunities to read and reread the same words, which helps familiarize children with onsets and rimes and, additionally, helps to develop fluency reading often-used words.

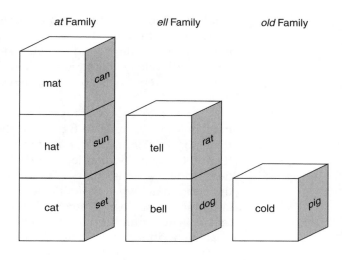

one on top of the other (Figure 4–16). In reading different words on the blocks, children get repeated practice reading the same words, which helps to build word fluency. Count the number of blocks children stack up; ask children to suggest other words that share the same rime or beginning letter-sound; add some of the words to your classroom word wall.

Word Family Hunts

Children search for word family words (or words with the same onsets). In the process, children learn to look for, recognize, and read words with the rimes or onsets you are teaching.

Things You'll Need: Nothing special.

Directions: Children scour the room and familiar books for word family words or words that begin with the same letter-sound. Children write the words they find and share them with the class. If children are keeping their own word family binders, ask them to add the word family words to the binders. Count the words children find. Make a simple bar graph showing how many words belong to the same word family or begin with the same letter-sound.

Looking Beyond the Analogy Strategy:

The number of words children can identify with the analogy strategy depends on three factors: (a) the onsets and rimes readers remember in words, (b) the frequency with which rimes occur in often-read words, and (c) the size of children's fluent reading vocabulary. Using the analogy strategy with onsets and rimes to read new words calls for blending fewer individual groups of sound than decoding letter-sound by letter-sound (/b/ + /ig/ rather than /b/ + /i/ + /g/). Additionally, this strategy gives children a way to read words in which the vowel letter represents an unexpected sound, such as the long *i* in *ight* and the long *o* in *old*.

As a consequence of typical reading and writing experiences, some children may look inside rimes to figure out the sounds that individual letters represent (Peterson & Haines, 1998), but not all readers do this, unless their teachers call attention to the individual letter-sound associations. This may explain why beginning readers who use rimes to make analogies are less proficient at decoding than their classmates who consider letter-sounds (Bruck & Treiman, 1992). Furthermore, although the analogy strategy with onsets and rimes is a helpful and productive tool, it is not entirely suited to unlocking the complete range of words in our alphabetic writing system. Our alphabet is a written map for the sounds in words, not the rimes in syllables.

Anyone who reads and writes a language written in an alphabet must understand how letters represent sounds. Since children develop the analogy strategy and the letter-sound strategy at about the same time, and these two strategies are beneficial for reading new words, teach children to how to use both strategies. Use the activities in this chapter to increase children's strategic use of onsets and rimes, and the activities in chapter 5 to increase their use of letter-sound combinations. After all, word identification is more than one strategy. It is many different strategies; the more strategies readers have at their fingertips, the better.

REFERENCES

Booth, J. R., & Perfetti, C. A. (2002). Onset and rime structure influences naming but not early word identification in children and adults. *Scientific Studies of Reading, 6*, 1–23.

Bruck, M., & Treiman, R. (1992). Learning to pronounce words: The limitations of analogies. *Reading Research Quarterly, 4*, 374–388.

Cazet, D. (2000). *Minni and moo and the musk of Zorro*. New York: Dorling Kindersley.

Ehri, L. C., & Robbins, C. (1992). Beginners need some decoding skill to read words by analogy. *Reading Research Quarterly, 27*, 12–28.

Gaskins, I. W., Ehri, L. C., Cress, C., O'Hara, C., & Donnelly, K. (1996/1997). Procedures for word learning: Making discoveries about words. *The Reading Teacher, 50*, 312–327.

Goswami, U. (1997). Rime-based coding in early reading development in English: Orthographic analogies and rime neighborhoods. In C. Hulme & R. M. Joshi (Eds.), *Reading and spelling: Development and disorders* (pp. 69–86). Mahwah, NJ: Erlbaum.

Goswami, U. (1998). The role of analogies in the development of word recognition. In J. L. Metsala & L. C. Ehri (Eds.), *Word recognition in beginning literacy* (pp. 41–63). Mahwah, NJ: Erlbaum.

Goswami, U. (2001a). Early phonological development and the acquisition of literacy. In S. B. Neuman & D. K. Dickinson (Eds.), *Handbook of early literacy research* (pp. 111–125). New York: Guilford Press.

Goswami, U. (2001b). Rhymes are important: A comment on Savage. *Journal of Research in Reading, 24,* 19–29.

Juel, C., & Minden-Cupp, C. (2000). Learning to read words: Linguistic units and instructional strategies. *Reading Research Quarterly, 35,* 458–492.

Keller, C. (1989). *Tongue twisters.* New York: Simon & Schuster.

Langstaff, J. (1989). *Oh, a-hunting we will go.* Boston: Houghton Mifflin.

Leslie, L., & Calhoon, A. (1995). Factors affecting children's reading of rimes: Reading ability, word frequency and rime neighborhood size. *Journal of Educational Psychology, 87,* 576–586.

Merrill Linguistic Reading Program (4th ed.). (1986). Upper Saddle River, NJ: Merrill/Prentice Hall.

Muter, V., Snowling, M., & Taylor, S. (1994). Orthographic analogies and phonological awareness: Their role and significance in early reading development. *Journal of Child Psychology and Psychiatry, 35,* 293–310.

Nation, K., Allen, R., & Hulme, C. (2001). The limitations of orthographic analogy in early reading development: Performance on the clue-word task depends on phonological priming and elementary decoding skills, not the use of orthographic analogy. *Journal of Experimental Child Psychology, 80,* 75–94.

Peterson, M. E., & Haines, L. P. (1998). Orthographic analogy training with kindergarten children: Effects on analogy use, phonemic segmentation, and letter-sound knowledge. In C. Weaver (Ed.), *Reconsidering a balanced approach to reading* (pp. 159–179). Urbana, IL: National Council of Teachers of English.

Programmed Reading (3rd ed.). (1994). New York: Phoenix Learning Resources.

Rosenbloom, J. (1986). *World's toughest tongue twisters.* New York: Sterling.

Savage, R. (2001). A re-evaluation of the evidence for orthographic analogies: A reply to Goswami (1999). *Journal of Research in Reading, 24,* 1–18.

Stahl, S. A. (2001). Teaching phonics and phonological awareness. In S. B. Neuman & D. K. Dickinson (Eds.), *Handbook of early literacy research* (pp. 333–360). New York: Guilford Press.

Strickland, D. S. (1998). *Teaching phonics today: A primer for educators.* Newark, DE: International Reading Association.

Walton, P. D., Walton, L. M., & Felton, K. (2001). Teaching rime analogy or letter recoding reading strategies to prereaders: Effects on prereading skills and word reading. *Journal of Educational Psychology, 93,* 160–180.

Wylie, R. E., & Durrell, D. D. (1970). Teaching vowels through phonograms. *Elementary English, 47,* 427–451.

CHAPTER
5

The Letter-Sound Strategy

Using Letters and Sounds to Read New Words

This chapter explains how children use the letter-sound strategy to read new words. Here you will learn about the letter-sound relationships of phonics, why the left-to-right sequencing of letters in words is important for word identification, and how using the letter-sound strategy corresponds to movement toward word fluency. In reading this chapter, you also will learn how to sequence phonics instruction, the appropriate place for decodable books in your balanced classroom reading program, 10 research-based best practices for teaching phonics, and 23 activities for teaching letter-sound relationships.

KEY IDEAS

> ➤ Letters that routinely appear next to one another in words, such as the *oy* in *boy* or the *er* in *her,* form patterns of familiar letters that represent sound. Our writing system has many letter-sound patterns.
> ➤ Readers who use the letter-sound strategy associate sounds with letters and then blend sounds together to pronounce words that make sense in reading contexts.
> ➤ Letter-sound patterns are divided into three groups: those that are less challenging to learn and apply, those that are more challenging to learn and apply, and those that are the most challenging to learn and apply when reading new words.
> ➤ Decodable books are helpful when they include the same letter-sound patterns you are teaching in your classroom.

KEY VOCABULARY

Alphabetic stage of movement toward word fluency	Decodable books	Letter-sound pattern
	Digraph	Phonetic spelling
Consonant cluster	Diphthong	Phonetically regular words
	Invented spelling	

Unlike the turtles in Wen Ting's drawing in Figure 5–1, the alphabet is not a jumble of topsy-turvy letter-sound combinations. Readers do not aimlessly tumble as they learn about the alphabetic principle, nor do they stand on their heads when using letter-sound patterns to read unfamiliar words. For readers who do not automatically recognize *topsy, turvy,* and *turtles,* the letter-sound strategy is a quick and sure route to pronunciation. Readers who use this strategy take advantage of the alphabetic principle—the principle that letters of the alphabet represent the sounds in words.

The children in your classroom are likely to be successful readers only when they understand and use the alphabetic principle (Snow, Burns, & Griffin, 1998). Children who learn phonics early and well are better readers and better comprehenders than children who do not learn phonics (Connelly, Johnston, & Thompson, 2001; National Reading Panel, 2000), regardless of children's social or economic background (Armbruster, Lehr, & Osborn, 2001). In addition, because fluent word recognition is related to decoding ability, children are better at automatically reading words when they have already developed decoding skills (Aaron et al., 1999).

Figure 5–1 Unlike the jumbled turtles in Wen Ting's drawing, letters represent sounds in predictable ways and are, therefore, a useful pathway to word identification.

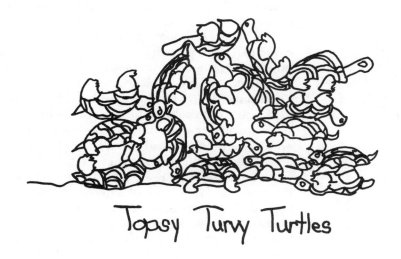

Topsy Turvy Turtles

Using the letter-sound strategy requires a sizable amount of mental attention, phonemic awareness, and letter-sound knowledge. But like so many things in life, the extra time and energy invested in something worthwhile is more than offset by the rewards. One reward is that children can read a large number of new words with a relatively small number of letter-sound patterns. This, in turn, helps children build large fluent reading vocabularies and become independent readers. And finally, as a pathway to the identification of a large number of unfamiliar words, the letter-sound strategy supports the comprehension of increasingly more challenging text.

Letter-Sound Patterns

The 26 letters in our alphabet are a hardworking bunch. This same small group of 26 is systematically arranged, rearranged, and sequenced to build literally tens of thousands of words. With all this arranging and sequencing, it is inevitable that certain letters routinely appear right next to one another in spelling. This creates a type of spelling context—a neighborhood—in which certain letters are frequently and predictably right next to other letters. With many fewer letters (only 26) than sounds (as many as 43), English spelling contains a host of letter neighborhoods. As children become familiar with the letters that are neighbors in spelling, they associate sound with those letters, and hence begin to use the letter and sound patterns of phonics.

Letter-sound patterns may represent one or more sounds in words, such as the *t* in *tap*, the *th* in *this*, and the *thr* in *three*. The left-to-right order of letters in words is immensely important because letter order affects the sounds that the letters represent. Let us use the letter *a* as an illustration. The *a* represents one pronunciation when followed by a consonant and an *e* in the word *made*, a different pronunciation when followed by a consonant letter in *mad,* yet another pronunciation when followed by the *l* in *malt,* and still another when followed by an *r* in *mart.* If we were to look at only the first two beginning letters, *ma,* we might conclude that the *a* in each of these four words—*made, mad, malt,* and *mart*—is pronounced the same. But on closer inspection, we notice that it is the letter following the vowel, the letter to the right of the vowel, that is the cue to sound. In reading English words, we must look to the right of the vowel, in this example the letter *a,* to figure out the sound that *a* represents. That is why is it so important to always encourage the children whom you teach to look all the way through new words, beginning with the first letter and ending with the last letter.

Letter-sound patterns represent sound at the phoneme level, which is the same level used by the alphabet to connect speech with print. Therefore, readers can use their knowledge of letter-sound patterns to pronounce any word that is spelled like it sounds. For instance, though the vowels and consonants in the CVC^1 (consonant-vowel-consonant) pattern may differ from word to word, this pattern generally represents a short vowel sound. Consequently, with a relatively small amount of letter-sound knowledge, in this example the *CVC* short vowel pattern, readers have a good idea as to the vowel sound in many words that include the *CVC* pattern in spelling. We can see this in the short vowel words *jam, back, fled, best, chick, pitch, shop,* and *scrub.*

Because there is almost always more than one way to group the letters in a new word, readers must consider which letters combine to form letter-sound patterns, and which do not. In so doing, readers consider left-to-right letter order. For example, *ba* forms a *CVC* long vowel pattern in *bacon.* This same sequence (*ba*) does not constitute a letter-sound pattern in *bandit* because the *a* belongs to the *CVC* short vowel pattern. Experienced readers know this and, therefore, look for predictable and frequently occurring patterns in words they have never seen before. Table 5–1 summarizes the letter-sound patterns; appendix B gives more detailed explanations of letter-sound patterns and also gives lists of words that include these patterns.

As children have experiences reading and writing, they become sensitive to the letter-sound patterns that recur in many different words. Sensitivity increases as readers move up in the elementary grades (Juel, 1983), and is significantly related to reading ability (National Reading Panel, 2000; Tunmer & Chapman, 2002). So, the more opportunities children have to strategically use letter-sound patterns as they read and write in your classroom, the more children will know about how letters represent sounds.

Reading New Words With the Letter-Sound Strategy

In using the letter-sound strategy, readers associate sounds with the letter patterns in new words, and then blend the sounds to pronounce contextually sensible words. Readers who use this strategy have the full strength and power of the alphabet at

---

1 For brevity, C stands for consonant; V for vowel.

TABLE 5–1 *Summary of Letter-Sound Patterns**	
Consonant Letter-Sound Patterns	**Examples**
Single Consonants Usually represent the sounds associated with the italicizied letters in the key words.	*b*oat, *c*at and *c*ity, *d*og, *f*ish, *g*oat and *g*em, *h*at, *j*eep, *k*ite, *l*ion, *m*oon, *n*ut, *p*ig, *q*ueen, *r*ing, *s*un, *t*urtle, *v*an, *w*agon, fo*x*, *y*o-*y*o, *z*ipper
Qu Qu represents /kw/ as an onset and in the middle of words, and /k/ when it is a final sound.	*qu*een, fre*qu*ent, anti*qu*e
Double Consonants Double consonants usually represent only one sound, and that sound is the same as the single consonant.	ra*bb*it, ri*dd*le, wa*ff*le, wi*gg*le, do*ll*, ha*mm*er, di*nn*er, co*pp*er, carro*t*, gossi*p*, mi*tt*en, da*zz*le
Consonant Clusters Two or three consonant sounds are blended when pronounced. Some teachers' manuals refer to this pattern as a consonant blend. Two-letter clusters consist of *bl, cl, fl, gl, pl, sl, br, cr, dr, fr, gr, pr, tr, sc, sk, sm, sn, sp, st, sw,* and *tw*. The three-letter clusters are *scr, spl, spr, squ,* and *str*. The following three-letter clusters represent only two sounds and consist of a digraph plus one other letter: *chr, sch,* and *thr*.	*bl*ack, *cl*ay, *fl*ag, *gl*ass, *pl*ay, *sl*ip, *br*oom, *cr*ib, *dr*ess, *fr*og, *gr*ass, *pr*etty, *tr*ain, *sc*arf, *sk*ate, *sm*ile, *sn*ail, *sp*ider, *st*ar, *sw*eep, *tw*ig, *scr*een, *spl*ash, *spr*ing, *squ*irrel, *str*eet, *chr*ome, *sch*ool, *thr*ow
Consonant Digraphs The letters in a digraph represent a different sound than the letters represent individually. *Th* represents two sounds: the voiced sound (*that*) and the unvoiced or voiceless sound (*thumb*). The *t* in the *tch* digraph is likely to be more troublesome for spellers than for readers.	*ch*air, *ph*one, *sh*oe, *th*umb, *th*at, *wh*ale, ba*tch*
Three Patterns for the Letter S As an onset *s* represents the /s/ heard in *sack*, never /z/. Only two alternatives, /s/ or /z/, are possible when *s* is the middle or the last letter in a syllable.	Onset /s/ in *s*ack and *s*ave. Middle /s/ in ba*s*ic and ha*ss*le. Middle /z/ in cou*s*in and clo*s*et. Final /s/ in bu*s* and to*ss*. Final /z/ in ro*s*e and hi*s*.
Ca, co, and cu Ca, co, and cu usually represent /k/. Teachers' manuals call the /k/ a hard sound.	*ca*mel, *co*lor, *cu*te
Ce, ci, and cy Ce, ci, and cy generally represent /s/. Teachers' manuals call the /s/ a soft sound.	*ce*nt, *ci*ty, *cy*cle

*Look at Appendix B for more detailed explanations and examples.

(continued)

TABLE 5–1 *Summary of Letter-Sound Patterns (continued)*

Consonant Letter-Sound Patterns	Examples
Ga, go, and gu *Ga, go,* and *gu* usually represent the /g/. Teachers' manuals refer to /g/ as the hard sound.	game, got, gum
Ge, gi, and gy *Ge, gi,* and *gy* generally represent the /j/ as in /jelly/. Teachers' manuals refer to the /j/ as the soft sound. The *ge* and *gi* patterns are not as dependable as the *ga, go,* and *gu* patterns.	gem, giant, gym

Vowel Letter-Sound Patterns	Examples

Short Vowel Patterns

Examples of the Short Vowel Sounds We hear short vowel sounds in the key words.	apple, edge, igloo, octopus, umbrella
CVC** Short Vowel Pattern One vowel in a syllable that ends in a consonant usually represents the short sound. We can represent the vowel and consonants as CVC–consonant-vowel-consonant.	cat, bed, hit, top, bug
VCCe Short Vowel Pattern A vowel followed by two consonants and a final *e* (VCCe) usually represents its short sound.	dance, wedge, hinge, bronze, fudge

Long Vowel Patterns

Examples of Long Vowel Sounds We hear long vowel sounds in the key words.	apron, eraser, ice, overalls, unicorn
VCe Long Vowel Pattern A vowel followed by a consonant and a final *e* usually represents the long sound and the *e* is silent.	bake, gene, bike, bone, cute
CV Long Vowel Pattern The vowel may represent the long sound when a word or syllable ends in a vowel sound.	later, be, tricycle, no, cucumber, cycle
Y in a Short Word or Single Syllable When *y* is the only vowel in a short word or syllable, it generally represent the long *e* sound. At the end of words with no other vowels, *y* typically represents the long *i* sound.	Long *e*: any, baby, body Long *i*: by, sky, why

**2 V = vowel, C = consonant

TABLE 5–1 *Summary of Letter-Sound Patterns (continued)*	
Vowel Letter-Sound Patterns	**Examples**
VV Long Vowel Patterns In the patterns *ai, oa, ay, ee, ey,* and *ea,* the first vowel is generally long and the second is silent.	chain, boat, play, tree, honey, beach
Other Vowel Patterns	
Double oo The *oo* usually represents either the sound heard in *book* or the sound heard in *school*.	book, stood, broom, school
Vowel Diphthongs *Ow* and *ou* often represent the sounds heard in *cow* and *out*, while *oi* and *oy* represent the sounds heard in *oil* and *boy*.	brown, down, cloud, pout coin, soil, boy, toy
Vr Pattern *R* affects pronunciation so that vowels cannot be considered short or long.	farm, her, bird, corn, hurt
Au and aw Patterns *Au* and *aw* usually represent the sound in *fault* and *straw*.	haul, saucer, lawn, jaw
Ew and ue Patterns These patterns generally represent the sound in *blew* and *blue*.	chew, grew, blue, true

their fingertips. And thanks to their constant self-monitoring, self-correcting, and cross-checking, readers identify and pronounce real words that match the reading context. Children who use the letter-sound strategy have good phonemic awareness. They can tell you, their teacher, all the individual sounds in spoken words, and children can blend separate sounds into meaningful words. And of course, children have a solid working knowledge of letter-sound patterns (Adams, 1990; Snow et al., 1998).

As an illustration of this strategy, we will consider how Leslie decodes the new word *shaft* in the sentence *Rosie and Rita crawled down the dark mine shaft to look for the lost puppy.* In using the letter-sound strategy to read *shaft*, Leslie reaps the full benefit of reading a language written in an alphabet, and here is how she does it:

1. Leslie groups the letters in *shaft* into two different letter-sound patterns. She recognizes that *s* and *h* (*sh*) belong in one pattern (the consonant digraph pattern), and that the *a* + *f* + *t* is an example of the *CVC* short vowel pattern. This gives Leslie the clues she needs to figure out the vowel pronunciation.

2. Leslie then associates *sh* with /sh/ and *a, f,* and *t* with the sounds /a/ + /f/ + /t/.

3. Now she blends /sh/ + /a/ + /f/ + /t/ to pronounce /shaft/.

4. Last, Leslie cross-checks to make sure that /shaft/ fits the reading context. She asks herself: Does *shaft* sound and look right? Does *shaft* make sense in the passage? If the answers are yes, Leslie stops decoding and turns her full attention to *meaning,* finishing the page and reading the rest of the chapter. If the answers are no, she returns to decoding.

Interestingly, readers do not have to be a segmenting and blending expert like Leslie to begin to use the letter-sound strategy. All readers need is just enough phonemic awareness to separate and blend the sounds in short words. Likewise, readers need just enough knowledge of letter-sound patterns to associate sounds with the letters in short, uncomplicated words.

Sounding out a short word like *big,* which has only three sounds and a predictable *CVC* short vowel pattern, is far less taxing than sounding out a long word like *hippopotamus,* which has 12 letters, many letter-sound patterns, and a whopping five syllables. For this reason, it is quite possible, and indeed highly likely, that some children who have no difficulty sounding out short words like *big* will have trouble sounding out a long word like *hippopotamus.*

The letter-sound strategy Leslie used (as well as all other strategies explained in earlier chapters) works when, and only when, readers connect the meaning of printed words with the meaning of spoken words. In the example above, *shaft* is among the words Leslie recognizes in conversation. So, as soon as Leslie pronounces /shaft/ when decoding, she knows what this word means. As Leslie connects the written word (*shaft*) with the meaning of a familiar spoken word (/shaft/), she adds a new word to her reading vocabulary. But what would happen if *shaft* were not among the words Leslie recognizes in everyday conversation?

If the words children sound out are not in their speaking vocabularies, sounding out will help with pronunciation, but not with meaning. So when you teach the letter-sound strategy (and previously described strategies), make sure that the words children identify are already in their speaking or listening vocabularies. If you suspect that children do not know the meaning of the words they are to identify while reading, help them build enough background knowledge so as to add these words to their speaking vocabularies before they decode them.

Correcting Misidentifications

Readers who use the letter-sound strategy are experts at correcting their own misidentifications. Given the complexity of our English alphabetic writing system, there is no guarantee that the first try will result in a meaningful word. If the sounds Leslie blends together do not make a sensible word, self-monitoring and cross-checking (explained in chapter 4) bring the misidentification to light. She then draws on her considerable storehouse of letter-sound patterns (and well-developed phonemic awareness) to fix mistakes and correct misidentifications. There are three ways Leslie might self-correct:

1. She might reblend the same sounds, perhaps gliding sounds together more smoothly, and then cross-check for meaning.
2. Leslie might associate different sounds with the same letters and then reblend to pronounce a new word that is then cross-checked for meaning.
3. Leslie could redo the entire process—regroup letters into letter-sound patterns, associate sounds with the letters in patterns, blend, and cross-check all over again.

The children whom you teach are bound to prefer easier, less attention-demanding ways to self-correct over energy-draining alternatives. So you will notice that successful word identifiers often try reblending as their first attempt to correct mistakes. Then, if reblending does not work, they may try different sounds for letters. Only when all else fails do readers typically redo the entire process of re-identifying the letter-sound patterns.

Minor Mistakes

Readers may take minor mistakes in stride. Minor mistakes may not derail decoding because readers actively look for sensible connections between the words they recognize in everyday language and the words in the reading context. Accordingly, as readers self-monitor, self-correct, and cross-check, they find words in their speaking vocabularies that sound similar to minor decoding mispronunciations. When this happens, readers associate minor mispronunciations with real words that make sense in the reading context. Once plausible words are identified, readers automatically adjust mispronunciations so that the sounds in the words they decode match the words in their speaking vocabularies. The net effect is that slight letter-sound mistakes and minor blending miscalculations do not require a lot of extra special effort to repair.

Interestingly, not all misidentifications interfere with comprehension, so not all misidentifications need correcting. Readers have greater tolerance for misidentifications when they read a novel for pleasure than when they read a content subject textbook to learn new information. In this example, Leslie is reading for pleasure, so she is less concerned with absolute accuracy than when she reads a chapter in her science book to complete an assignment. As a consequence, the misidentifications Leslie chooses to ignore as she reads for pleasure may well be, and in some cases absolutely ought to be, corrected if she were reading for technical information in a content subject.

A Sequence for Teaching Letter-Sound Patterns

A good working knowledge of letter-sound patterns contributes to comprehension and vocabulary alike, particularly in the early grades (Rupley & Wilson, 1997). We divide letters into consonants and vowels. Though we know it takes more reading and writing experiences to learn the vowel patterns than to learn the consonant patterns, you may be surprised to learn that research does not support the use of any one particular teaching sequence over another. There is no prescribed order in which the letter-sound patterns must be taught, no immutable learning hierarchy, and no sequence chiseled in stone.

You are free to teach letter-sound patterns in any order whatsoever, as long as children are successful learning and using patterns. If you are using a commercial set of teaching materials that already has created a sequence for learning letter-sound patterns, by all means follow that sequence. However, if you have some flexibility in how you sequence the teaching of letter-sound patterns, you might wish to consider the relative difficulty of learning and applying patterns as a criteria for introducing letter-sound relationships. All things being equal, we find it useful to group letter-sound patterns into those that are less challenging, more challenging, and most challenging for the children whom we teach. We begin with the less challenging patterns and then gradually move toward those that are the most challenging to learn and apply when reading and writing.

Two Less Challenging Patterns

- *Single Consonants* The single consonant at the beginning of a word (the onset) is the easiest for children to learn and use (see appendix B for an explanation). Beginning consonants are especially obvious and can be readily combined with syntactic and semantic cues, which keeps decoding meaning based. It is not surprising, then, that many readers first pay attention to the single consonants at the beginning of words. As children gain more experience reading and writing, they notice this pattern at the end of words.
- *CVC Short Vowel Pattern (Consonant-Vowel-Consonant)* The children whom we teach find the *CVC* short vowel pattern (explained in appendix B) to be the least challenging of all the vowel patterns. The vowels in this pattern usually represent the short sound. The critical feature of the left-to-right letter order in the *CVC* pattern is the consonant following the vowel. Therefore, we may have a short vowel pattern when only one consonant follows the vowel (*at, bat*), two consonants follow the vowel (*bath*), or three consonants follow the vowel (*batch*). Once readers know a few short vowel rimes, we encourage them to look inside the rimes they already know to discover how the *CVC* short vowel pattern represents sound. In looking inside rimes, readers learn to recognize the *CVC* pattern as a signal for a short vowel sound, and then use this knowledge to pronounce many different words.

Seven More Challenging Patterns

- *Consonant Clusters* Letters that form a *consonant cluster* (as the *cl* in *clam* or the *st* in *stop*) are somewhat more challenging to learn. The letters in consonant clusters represent the same sounds as the letters in the single consonant pattern. The only difference is that the sounds of letters in consonant clusters are pronounced by sliding them together rather than saying them separately. The consonants in clusters reliably represent sound, and, as a result, readers have practically no new information to learn to effectively use this letter sequence. However, many of the children whom we teach seem to stumble over blending the sounds in clusters. Some children try to pronounce the *bl* in *block* as two separate sounds, /b/ + /l/, rather than two blended sounds, /bl/, and hence mispronounce consonant clusters. For this reason, we find that consonant clusters take somewhat more time to learn and use than single consonants and the *CVC* short vowel pattern. We first focus on two-letter clusters (*st*) and then move to three-letter clusters (*str*). Clusters that include a digraph (as the *ch* portion of *chr* in <u>*chr*</u>*ome*) are left until after children know how consonant digraphs represent sound. Table 5–1 and appendix B illustrate this concept.

- *Consonant Digraphs* The children whom we teach usually find the consonant *digraphs,* such as the *sh* in <u>*sh*</u>*ade* and the *th* in <u>*th*</u>*umb,* somewhat challenging to learn and apply. Perhaps this is because the letters in digraphs represent a totally different sound than the letters represent separately. Hence, readers cannot generalize, or transfer, what they already know about the sounds represented by single consonants to the consonant digraphs.

- *VCe Long Vowel Pattern (Vowel-Consonant-e)* The *VCe* pattern is, in our teaching experience, usually the easiest of the long vowel patterns (refer to Table 5–1 and appendix B). Though the final *e* is a good visual reminder of the *VCe* long vowel pattern, as in *same* and *dime,* some readers overlook the final *e*, hence treating letters as if they are in a *CVC* short vowel pattern. As a consequence, these readers pronounce *dime* as /dim/ and *same* as /sam/. Additionally, there are some obvious exceptions to the *VCe* pattern (see appendix B for an explanation). Our advice is to tell children to try the long vowel sound first and, if that does not make a sensible word that fits the reading context, to try a short sound.

- *VV Long Vowel Pattern (Vowel-Vowel)* The *VV* pattern is formed when the following two vowels are side by side: *ai* (s<u>*ai*</u>l), *ea* (cr<u>*ea*</u>m), *ee* (s<u>*ee*</u>d), *oa* (b<u>*oa*</u>t), *ay* (st<u>*ay*</u>), and *ey* (hon<u>*ey*</u>). For the most part, children pay attention to the middle of words when associating sounds with *ai* (*train*), *ea* (*treat*), and *oa* (*road*). Children usually look at the end of words when associating sounds with *ey* (hon<u>*ey*</u>) and *ay* (pl<u>*ay*</u>). When associating sound with the *ee* pattern, children look at the end (s<u>*ee*</u>) or the middle of words (s<u>*ee*</u>d). The *VV* pattern usually represents the long vowel sound, with exceptions, of course (see appendix B). Teach readers to try the long vowel sound and then to try the short vowel sound as a back up, if necessary.

- *CV Long Vowel Pattern (Consonant-Vowel)* The *CV* pattern represents a long vowel sound, as in <u>*me*</u> and <u>*sp*</u>*ider* (refer to Table 5–1 and appendix B). When this pattern comes at the beginning of words, it gives readers lots of excellent information to combine with context cues. The *CV* long vowel pattern has some exceptions (particularly in unaccented syllables) and hence takes more experience with print than patterns in the less challenging category (look for a detailed explanation of syllables in chapter 6).

- *Double oo Pattern* The *oo* pattern almost always represents one of two sounds: the sound heard in sch<u>*oo*</u>l or the sound heard in b<u>*oo*</u>k. Advise children to try one sound first and, if that does not make a sensible word, to try the other sound.

Look in appendix B for examples of words with the *oo* pattern and a way to help readers manage the two options for its pronunciation.

- *Diphthongs* The *ow, ou, oi,* and *oy* form *diphthong* patterns. The *ow* represents the sounds heard in *c<u>ow</u>*, *ou* the sounds in *<u>ou</u>t*, *oi* the sounds in *<u>oi</u>l*, and *oy* the sounds in *b<u>oy</u>*. Diphthongs are different from the sounds that these letters represent in other patterns, and, therefore, readers must learn totally new letter-sound associations for them. Added to this, *ow* sometimes represents the long *o* sound, as heard in *cr<u>ow</u>*. For these reasons, diphthongs take more attention and more experience with print than letters in less challenging patterns.

Four Most Challenging Patterns

- *C or G Plus a Vowel* As for the most challenging patterns, we find that letter-sound patterns made up of a *c* or a *g* plus a vowel (*c<u>a</u>ke, c<u>oa</u>t, c<u>u</u>t, c<u>e</u>nt, c<u>i</u>ty, c<u>y</u>cle,* and *g<u>a</u>te, g<u>o</u>, g<u>u</u>m, g<u>e</u>m, g<u>i</u>n, g<u>y</u>m*) are quite challenging for the children whom we teach. Both of the consonants represent two sounds—*c* the /s/ heard in *city* or the /k/ in *candy; g* the /j/ heard in *gem* or the /g/ in *goat*. Not only do readers have to think very carefully about the left-to-right letter order, but also they must consider the exceptions, especially for the letter *g* plus a vowel. We suggest that you help children try more than one sound, should the first fail to produce a real, meaningful word. Look in Table 5–1 and appendix B for more detailed explanations of the *c* and *g* plus a vowel patterns and examples of words with these letters.
- *Vr Vowel Pattern (R-Controlled Vowel)* The r-controlled pattern (*Vr*) is challenging to learn and use because the *r* changes the sound represented by the vowel letter. This is so regardless of which vowel precedes the letter *r*. This combination, *Vr*, may appear at first glance to be a *CVC* short vowel pattern because, after all, *r* is a consonant letter. Readers must learn to pay special attention to the *r* and to anticipate its affect on the vowels it follows, as in *c<u>ar</u>, h<u>er</u>, s<u>ir</u>, f<u>or</u>,* and *f<u>ur</u>*. Do not be surprised if some end-of-year second graders still need practice and targeted instruction to efficiently and effectively use the *Vr* pattern.
- *VCCe Short Vowel Pattern (Vowel-Consonant-Consonant-e)* We also find it takes the readers whom we teach a while to develop competence reading and spelling words with the *VCCe* pattern, as in *ch<u>ance</u>, f<u>ence</u>, br<u>idge</u>, br<u>onze</u>,* and *pl<u>unge</u>*. Perhaps this is so because the *VCCe* short vowel pattern somewhat resembles the *VCe* long vowel pattern and is large, consisting of four or more letters. Unlike the *VCe* long vowel pattern, however, the first vowel in the *VCCe* pattern represents a short vowel sound. This, of course, means that readers have to be especially careful to differentiate long vowel *VCe* words (*lane*) from short vowel *VCCe* words (*lance*).
- *Au, aw, ue,* and *ew Patterns* These four patterns, as in the words *haul, draw, due,* and *blew,* are quite challenging. They take a good bit of practice and, not surprisingly, emerge later in both reading and writing. Give readers lots of practice reading and writing words with these letter-sound patterns.

Figure 5–2 Venn diagrams illustrate how some of the more challenging letter-sound patterns represent more than one sound in words.

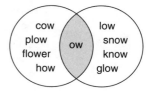

Demonstrating How Some Patterns Represent More Than One Sound

We like to use Venn diagrams to illustrate how some of the challenging patterns represent more than one sound. Venn diagrams are overlapping circles with shared characteristics inside the overlapping portion and unique characteristics inside each separate circle, as illustrated by Figure 5–2. We begin by drawing on the board two overlapping circles and write a letter pattern that represents more than one sound (*ow*, for instance) in the overlapping portion. Then we write a word that represents one pronunciation (*cow*, perhaps) in one circle; a word that represents another pronunciation (*snow*, for example) in the other circle. We challenge children to think of words in which *ow* represents the sounds heard in *cow* and in *snow*, and write those words in the appropriate circles. This gives children opportunities to think of words that fit the pattern and helps them become more sensitive to the two sounds that *ow* typically represent.

In the final analysis, the most challenging patterns typically require that children have much more practice reading all sorts of books, poems, articles, and stories, and many more opportunities to spell and write. So, if the children whom you teach take longer to figure out how to strategically use the most challenging letter-sound patterns, this is perfectly natural. Take opportunities during guided reading to point out and explore letter-sound patterns, help children become sensitive to these patterns through spelling, and use the activities described later in this chapter to support children as they use their letter-sound knowledge to read new words.

Do Phonics Rules Belong in Your Balanced Classroom Reading Program?

Researchers have put tremendous energy into finding out which letter-sound patterns are dependable and which are not. In their quest, researchers investigated 45 phonics rules (Bailey, 1967; Clymer, 1963; Emans, 1967). Take the rule that says, "A vowel in the middle of a one-syllable word represents the short sound." Let us think about this middle vowel "rule," which is a way of explaining the *CVC* short vowel pattern. We would agree that words like *man* and *red* are examples of the *CVC* short vowel pattern and, coincidentally, follow the rule. Surprisingly, researchers find this rule to be relatively unreliable. In a sample of primary grade reading material, both Clymer and Emans report that the middle vowel rule applies only 62% and 73% of the time, respectively. Examining materials for Grades 1 through 6, Bailey reports that this rule is useful a mere 71% of the time.

Some of the examples these authors cite as exceptions to the middle vowel rule reflect a narrow interpretation of this "rule." Narrow interpretations make our alphabetic system seem more complicated than it really is. In this example, a narrow interpretation overlooks the fact that some vowels in the middle of one-syllable words are not in a *CVC* short vowel pattern. Emans (1967) cites the word *hew* and Bailey (1967) the word *her* as examples of exceptions to the middle vowel rule. It is not reasonable to consider either word—*hew* or *her*—as an exception because the vowels in these words represent two different patterns: The *e* in *hew* is part of the *ew* pattern found in words like *jewel, chew,* and *threw* (as explained in Table 5–1 and appendix B). The *e* in *her* is perfectly regular, too, for the *e* in this word is part of an *r-controlled* pattern (*Vr*), and so the sound it represents is characteristic of this pattern, as in *germ* and *clerk,* as described in Table 5–1 and appendix B.

While most readers cannot recite the "rules" of phonics word for word, they do have mental representations—mental images—of the way that phonics patterns represent sound. Their in-depth knowledge of letter-sound patterns gives them a powerful resource which, when combined with cross-checking, self-monitoring, and self-correcting, enables them to pronounce any word that is spelled like it sounds.

Perhaps you are wondering whether you should teach children the "rules" in a balanced classroom reading program. Just because children recite rules does not mean that they know when and how to apply them. Children who memorize rules without connecting them to reading and writing may not be able to use them to support word identification or spelling. In fact, some children are quite skilled at reciting phonics rules yet do not have the foggiest notion of how to use the rules they put so much effort into memorizing. These children learn to "parrot" rules—they recite the wording of rules but do not relate the rules to the words they read and write.

Rather than focus on teaching the rules themselves, a more beneficial and balanced approach is to sensitize children to the way letter-sound patterns affect pronunciation and to ground patterns in the spelling of words children encounter as they read and write. Does this mean that you should never ever say a rule? Of course not. Sometimes it is quite helpful to tell children about a rule, especially when children need some clarification. In fact, explaining a rule from time to time can speed learning along, provided that the rule is solidly related to the words children read and spell. Encourage children to analyze left-to-right letter order and to learn how letter order affects the sounds letters represent. As a result, children will learn how letter-sound patterns look and sound in real words, and create mental pictures of words in which the letter-sound patterns appear. This, in turn, contributes to automatic word recognition and supports the development of a large fluent reading vocabulary.

The Alphabetic Stage of Movement Toward Word Fluency and the Phonetic Stage of Spelling

Children who use the letter-sound strategy are in the *alphabetic stage of movement toward word fluency* (Ehri, 2000). Whereas children in the partial alphabetic stage mainly look at beginning and ending letters, children in the alphabetic stage analyze all the letter-sound relationships in words. As a consequence, these readers can identify any word that is spelled the way it sounds.

Children enter into the alphabetic stage toward the end of kindergarten or, more typically, at the beginning of first grade. The children in your classroom who have reached the alphabetic stage have good phonemic awareness. They can tell you the number of sounds in spoken words and can blend sounds together. They are learning (or have learned) letter-sound patterns and use this knowledge to sound out words that are not already in their fluent reading vocabularies. It's not surprising, then, that these children learn words faster than children with low phonemic awareness and a poor understanding of letter-sound patterns (Stuart, 1995). Children in the alphabetic stage are becoming independent readers whose fluent vocabularies are growing by leaps and bounds. Because they can read new words on their own, their reading ability increases even when they are out of school on summer vacation, provided, of course, that they read over the summer break. These children learn many, many words, and they learn most of them on their own.

Awareness of the single consonant letter-sound pattern emerges early, as we see in Figure 5–3 in the note Roger taped to the gerbil cage in his first-grade classroom. Roger, who is just beginning to make the transition into the alphabetic stage, wrote this note to tell his classmates about the feisty habits of the resident pet, Biscuit. Roger's warning reads: *Biscuit bites. Don't bother Biscuit because he bites.* Roger spells words the way he hears them rather than the way letters are conventionally sequenced. He begins words with single consonants and ends words with consonant letters, too. Roger even includes consonants in the middle of words, as in *Biscuit* (spelled *Bekst*) and *bother* (spelled *brtr*). When we look closely at Roger's

Figure 5–3 The invented spelling in Roger's note shows that he thinks carefully about the relationship between the letters in written words and the sounds in spoken words.

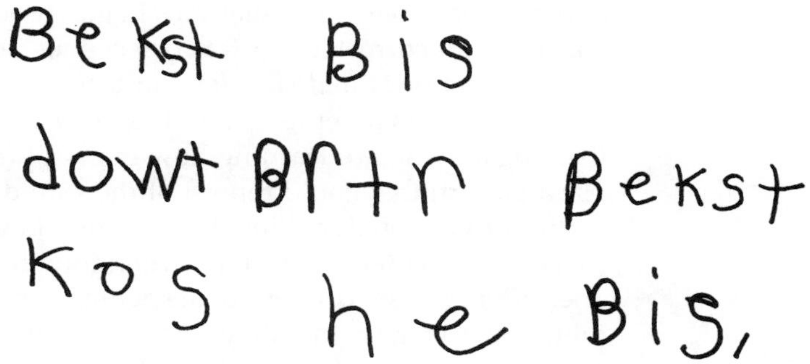

note, we can infer that he is beginning to discover the way that vowel letters represent sound. It is, in fact, this emerging use of vowels that tells us that Roger is moving out of the partial alphabetic stage and into the alphabetic stage.

Although Roger seems to know that vowels are important, he is far from understanding all the vowel letter patterns. This is quite natural because there are several different vowel patterns, and hence many choices for pronunciation. It stands to reason, then, that children need more time and more reading experience to use vowel letter-sound patterns than the consonant patterns (Fowler, Shankweiler, & Liberman, 1979; Zinna, Liberman, & Shankweiler, 1986). Of the 45 phonics rules researchers use to explain letter-sound correspondences, fully two-thirds pertain to vowels (Bailey, 1967; Clymer, 1963; Emans, 1967). Perhaps this explains why children misidentify the sounds represented by vowels far more frequently than the sounds represented by the consonants.

As children move further into the alphabetic stage, they become increasingly adept at learning words on their own and at spelling words in ways that others can read. Logan's story in Figure 5–4 shows that he knows more about letter-sound patterns than does Roger. We can infer from Logan's spelling that he understands how many different patterns represent sound, including vowel letter-sound patterns. While Roger is just moving into the alphabetic stage, Logan is solidly in this stage of word fluency (Ehri, 2000). He has enough phonemic awareness and letter-sound knowledge to completely pronounce many new words; his vocabulary is rapidly expanding; he enjoys reading; and he can read easy books by himself without help.

Logan conventionally spells words in his fluent reading vocabulary. And when he spells unconventionally, you and I can read what he writes. When Logan figures out the spelling of new words on his own, he represents all essential sounds in words, even though there may not be a correct match between letters and sounds (*drest* for *dressed,* for example). This type of spelling is called *phonetic spelling* (Gentry, 1987). *Phonetic spelling, invented spelling,* and temporary spelling all refer to an early problem-solving stance to spelling in which children write a letter for each sound heard in a word (*lisend* for *listened*).

Logan thinks carefully about the sounds in words, and has enough phonemic awareness to associate letters with the sounds he wants to spell, as shown by *drest* for *dressed.* Logan's writing illustrates many characteristics of alphabetic readers and phonetic spellers: Sometimes Logan uses letter names to spell (the *e* in *storey*), substitutes incorrect letters for correct ones (*scholle* for *school*), adds incorrect letters after correct ones (*dide* for *did* and *worke* for *work*), and matches letters with the sounds he hears to represent past tense (*drest* for *dressed*). Also interesting, children like Logan, who are learning how many different patterns represent sound, often use a pattern that could represent the sounds in words, but is not the pattern we use in conventional spelling. For instance, Logan used the *VCe* pattern to spell *shoes* (*shuse*). This pattern, in fact, is a very good representation of sound even though it does not represent conventional spelling. Another interesting characteristic of children in this stage is that they sometimes overgeneralize. For example, Logan adds an extra *e* to *did* (*dide*), *school* (*scholle*), and *work* (*worke*). From this we can assume that he is sensitive to the final *e*, but he is unsure of exactly when to use it in spelling and precisely what its function is in signaling sound.

Figure 5–4 Logan thinks carefully about letter-sound patterns when writing. As he considers which letters represent sound, he sometimes substitutes incorrect letters for correct ones, adds incorrect letters after correct ones, and uses the letter-sounds he hears to represent past tense.

I woke up and got drest and ate.
I put my shuse on then
I went to scholle I dide
all my worke. I ate a toca.
We lisend to a storey. Then we
went out side. Then it was
time for me to go to the doctor.
I didinte have strep. Then we
went home and went to bed.

Phonetic spelling, or invented spelling, has come under fire because some people fear that children will cling to inventions and, as a consequence, will not learn to spell conventionally. Phonetic spelling is a part of the natural course of learning to read and spell; it is helpful for writers who wish to express their thoughts and have only a small number of words they can spell from memory. In concentrating on the sounds in words, phonetic spellers have opportunities to increase their phonemic awareness. In thinking about how letters represent sound, phonetic spellers also have opportunities to develop greater sensitivity to letter-sound patterns. When children edit their own writing, they correct the unconventional spellings. This gives you, the teacher, opportunities to help children learn to conventionally spell often-used words. As children add words to their fluent reading vocabularies, learn letter-sound patterns, and get practice spelling often-used words, they leave behind the unconventional phonetic spellings in preference for correct spelling.

Logan's teacher observes that sometimes he seems to move slowly through text as he focuses on the words. Slow, almost plodding, reading is frequently observed in children like Logan who are just beginning to develop some measure of competence using the letter-sound strategy. Children like Logan try to figure out many more words in text than children who are not learning phonics (Connelly et al., 2001). For Logan and others like him, relatively slow reading is probably a consequence of dedicating a good bit of attention to identifying unfamiliar words, as well as trying to read exactly what the author wrote. As Logan's fluent reading vocabulary grows and as his ability to use the letter-sound strategy improves, his reading will become quite fluent.

Ten Best Practices for Teaching Letter-Sound Patterns

Good readers use their in-depth knowledge of letter-sound patterns with planful flexibility and resourcefulness. They *think* while using the letter-sound strategy; they apply their knowledge of letter-sound patterns to read new words and to build a large fluent reading vocabulary; and they always focus on meaning. You will be a more effective teacher when you follow these 10 best practices:

   1. **Teach letter-sound patterns early, in kindergarten or first grade** (Armbruster et al., 2001; National Reading Panel, 2000). Effective phonics instruction begins early and uses learning activities that are appropriate for a child's age and development. Introducing the letter-sound patterns of phonics early in the elementary school—kindergarten or first grade—is more effective than introducing instruction later in the elementary grades, say second grade and above.

   2. **Teach the same letter-sound patterns in reading as you teach in spelling** (Ehri, 2000). Children use their understandings of letter-sound patterns when they read, and their understandings of sound-letter patterns when they spell. For example, in reading, children know that the *ck* in *back* represents /k/, and in spelling children know that the /k/ sound in /back/ is spelled *ck*. When spelling known words, children recall the letter order in words, write those sequences, and then read words to make sure that they look right (Neuman, Copple, & Bredekamp, 2000). Therefore, teaching the same letter-sound patterns in reading and spelling ensures that instruction in reading and spelling support and reinforce each other.

   3. **Teach letter-sound patterns systematically and in a logical, planful sequence** (Armbruster et al., 2001; National Reading Panel, 2000). Teaching should be sequenced so that kindergartners, first graders, and second graders learn the phonics patterns in Table 5–1 and appendix B well enough to use them when reading and spelling new words.

4.   **Give children plenty of opportunities to use letter-sound patterns in reading and writing**   (Armbruster et al., 2001). Teach letter-sound patterns thoroughly and in conjunction with reading a variety of meaningful text and writing for a variety of purposes. When you teach phonics letter-sound patterns, you anchor knowledge in the real words that children read and spell everyday in your classroom.

5.   **Teach phonemic awareness, when needed**   (Armbruster et al., 2001; National Reading Panel, 2000). If some of the children whom you teach are not yet skilled at separating words into sounds and blending sounds together, combine some of the activities in chapter 2 with the activities in this chapter.

6.   **Teach to small groups, large groups or individuals, depending on children's needs**   (Armbruster et al., 2001; National Reading Panel, 2000). It is not so much the number of children whom you teach—large groups, small groups, or individuals—as what you teach that is important. You will be an effective teacher when you teach the letter-sound patterns in a logical sequence and then create opportunities for children to practice using these patterns when reading and writing.

7.   **Pace instruction to the needs of each child**   (Armbruster et al., 2001). Some children quickly grasp letter-sound patterns and how to use them, while others take more time, more instruction, and more reading and spelling practice. Move children along at a pace that is comfortable for them—fast enough to cover the letter-sound patterns children need to learn and slow enough to assure that children are competent users of the letter-sound strategy.

8.   **Spend only about two years teaching phonics**   (Armbruster et al., 2001). Generally speaking, phonics instruction should be complete by the end of the second grade; sooner for adept learners.

9.   **Use decodable text to give children practice reading words with the letter-sound patterns they are learning in your classroom**   (Armbruster et al., 2001; National Reading Panel, 2000). *Decodable books* have many words that are spelled like they sound and hence the words can be sounded out using letter-sound patterns. Reading these books gives children practice applying letter-sound patterns when reading text, as you will learn later in this chapter.

10.   **Integrate letter-sound instruction into your classroom reading program**   (National Reading Panel, 2000). Phonics is a means to an end, not the end in and of itself. The goal of phonics instruction is to develop independent readers who are skilled at learning new words, and who are fully capable of using reading as a learning tool. If we overteach phonics by emphasizing letter-sound patterns at the expense of comprehension and reading for pleasure, we miss the mark. Make phonics part of your overall classroom reading program, but not the predominant component or the most important component. Balance phonics teaching within your classroom program and measure success in many ways and by many barometers, such as the strategies readers use to read and spell new words, comprehension, the ability to use reading as a learning tool, love of reading, and interest in books.

How Decodable Books Fit Into Your Balanced Classroom Reading Program

Books with unusually high numbers of words that sound like they are spelled are called *decodable* books. These books support word identification by using *phonetically regular* words; that is, words that can be pronounced by associating sounds with letters. For example, *pig* and *sweet* are phonetically regular words because readers can use their knowledge of letter-sound patterns to figure out pronunciation. *Have* and *cafe*, on the other hand, are not phonetically regular because readers cannot completely pronounce them by associating sounds with letters. Many decodable books emphasize one or two patterns by clustering together words that have the same letter-sound patterns, such as the long *e* spellings in *str*ee*t*, *sl*ee*ve*, *tr*ee*, *b*ee*, *cr*ea*m*, *l*ea*ve*, and *r*ea*l*.

Decodable books support word identification by directing readers' attention to the letter-sound patterns they are learning in your classroom, and by allowing readers to actually use their letter-sound knowledge when reading (Mesmer, 2001). These books are beneficial for three types of children: (a) partial alphabetic readers moving into the alphabetic stage, (b) alphabetic readers who lack fluency using particular letter-sound patterns, and (c) alphabetic readers who know letter-sound patterns but do not use them. The high number of phonetically regular words not only gives readers practice applying phonics knowledge, but also encourages them to use this knowledge to read new words (Juel & Roper-Schneider, 1985).

The assumption is that in reading many decodable words children will become convinced that the letter-sound strategy is worth trying and use this strategy to read new words in text. It stands to reason, then, that the letter-sound patterns in decodable books should match the letter-sound patterns children are learning in your classroom (Mesmer, 2001). For example, if you are teaching the *VCe* pattern, a book that predominantly has *CVC* short vowel words is not a good choice, because this book does not match ongoing instruction. In this example, you would want to find decodable books that feature lots of *VCe* long vowel words, and make these books available to readers.

Decodable books serve a specific purpose at a specific time in children's development as readers. These books should never replace good quality literature in your classroom, and their presence in your classroom should not limit children's choices of the books they read. Decodable books are beneficial when they reinforce the letter-sound patterns children are learning, when they are used selectively, and when they are read by children who are transitioning into the alphabetic stage, lack fluency using letter-sound patterns, or know patterns but do not use them.

Twenty-three Easy and Effective Activities for Teaching Letter-Sound Patterns

The following 23 activities help children develop knowledge of letter-sound patterns. You may adapt the activities to focus on the letter-sound patterns children are learning in your classroom, to meet the specific needs of the children whom you teach, and to your own individual teaching style. As you use these activities, ask children to explain in their own words how letter patterns represent sound, when to use the letter-sound strategy to read new words, and how knowing letter-sounds helps in spelling. As children reflect on the letter-sound patterns in the words they read and spell, children become more metacognitively (consciously) aware of how, when, and why to use the letter-sound strategy, as explained in chapter 1. As a consequence, children will learn to use this strategy to read new words and add words to their fluent reading vocabularies.

 ## Two Ways to Build Words With Letter-Sound Patterns

Word building has definitely withstood the test of time, for it has been around for decades in one form or another (Reed & Klopp, 1957). This activity is appropriate for children working in large, small, and flexible groups and for children in any grade. It also can be used with any letter-sound pattern.

Things You'll Need: As many letter cards (or letter tiles, see Figure 5–5) as there are children in a small group.

A. *Learning a New Pattern: Comparing and Contrasting a Known Pattern with a Pattern Children Are Learning*   Focusing on only two letter-sound patterns at once (the *CVC* and *VCe* patterns, for instance) is appropriate for teaching letter-sound patterns. The goal is to help children gain insight into how a known pattern and a new pattern represent different sounds in words.

Directions: If children are not familiar with word building, demonstrate how to build words by writing letters on the board and then using the letters to build different words. Alternatively, you may want to demonstrate word building with magnetic letters. When children are familiar with word building, give each child cards with letters that combine to make words with two different patterns. One pattern should be one that children already know and the other should be a pattern that children are learning. For example, if children already know the *CVC* pattern and are learning the *VCe* pattern, you might give children cards with *t, r, c, n, p, a,* and *e,* and ask them to build *cap - cape; can - cane; pan - pane; nap - nape; rat - rate; tap - tape.* Compare and contrast the patterns. Use this activity to demonstrate how adding an *e* (*cap + e = cape*) turns a short vowel word into a long vowel word. Table 5–2 is a list of *CVC* words that, when the final e is added, make the *VCe* pattern words.

B. *Practicing Known Patterns: Word Building With Several Letter-Sound Patterns*
Building words with several patterns is appropriate for practicing the patterns children have already been taught. Use this version of word building with the letter-sound patterns that require a little extra practice before children effectively use them when reading and spelling new words.

Figure 5–5 In building words with letter cards, children think about the way the letters in a word's spelling form letter-sound patterns that represent pronunciation.

TABLE 5–2 CVC *and* VCe *Words for Word Building and Other Activities*

CVC	VCe	CVC	VCe	CVC	VCe	CVC	VCe
bid	bide	fin	fine	man	mane	shad	shade
bit	bite	gal	gale	mat	mate	sham	shame
can	cane	gap	gape	mop	mope	slat	slate
cap	cape	glad	glade	nap	nape	slid	slide
cod	code	glob	globe	not	note	slim	slime
con	cone	grad	grade	pan	pane	slop	slope
cop	cope	grim	grime	pet	Pete	snip	snipe
crud	crude	grip	gripe	pin	pine	tap	tape
cub	cube	hat	hate	plan	plane	Tim	time
cut	cute	hid	hide	plum	plume	ton	tone
dam	dame	hop	hope	prim	prime	tot	tote
dim	dime	hug	huge	rat	rate	trip	tripe
din	dine	Jan	Jane	rid	ride	tub	tube
dot	dote	kit	kite	rip	ripe	twin	twine
dud	dude	lob	lobe	rob	robe	van	vane
fad	fade	lop	lope	rod	rode	wad	wade
fat	fate	mad	made	Sam	same	win	wine

Directions: Give children a small group of letter cards that combine to make words with the patterns children need to practice. For instance, you might give children cards with *r, t, b, s, a, e,* and *m,* and ask them to use these cards to build *me,* and change *me* into *meat,* and then build *team, seam, sea, sat, same, tame, tar, star,* and so forth. Ask children to write the words they build. Then have children explain why they spelled the words the way they did and how the patterns represent sound. Also ask children to tell how knowing the letter-sound patterns helps them read new words.

 Two Ways to Hunt for Words

This activity focuses on the letter-sound patterns in the familiar words that are on your classroom word wall, on charts, and on the board in your classroom. It is suitable for large, small, or flexible skill groups of first and second graders.

A. *Single Letter-Sound Pattern Word Wall Hunt*   Children look on the word wall (or in other places in your room where words are displayed) for words with the same letter-sound pattern.

Things You'll Need: Nothing special.

Directions: Write a few words with the same letter-sound pattern on the board. Then ask readers to find word wall words with this pattern. Make a list of the words that share the same letter-sound pattern.

B. *Multipattern Board Hunt*   In this hunt, children identify different letter-sound patterns that represent the same sound in words. In so doing, children learn how one sound is represented by more than one letter-sound pattern and also learn to find the patterns in words.

Things You'll Need: Colored chalk (or colored dry erase markers if your classroom has a white board).

Directions: Ask children to think of words that have a certain sound, such as the long *e,* and write those words on the board. Alternatively, you may want to write a variety of words on the board that are spelled with patterns children are learning. Discuss the different patterns, and ask children to find words with the same letter-sound pattern. For example, in focusing on letter-sound patterns that represent the long *e* sound, children might hunt for words on the board that are spelled with a *VV* patterns (the *ee* in *beet* and the *ea* in *heat*), and the *CV* pattern (*be*). Children use a different color of chalk (or dry erase marker) to draw lacy clouds around each different letter-sound pattern. For example, all the *ee VV* words might be circled in blue; the *ea VV* in yellow; and the *CV* words in red.

Personal Word Boxes

Children make their own personal boxes that contain (a) words the children are learning to fluently recognize and (b) words that consist of the letter-sound patterns you are teaching.

Things You'll Need: A recipe-size box for each child; index cards that fit nicely into the boxes; ABC tabs for filing words alphabetically.

Directions: Put ABC tabs on the top of index cards and use the tabs for filing words in alphabetical order. Begin by having children make word cards for a moderate list of often-used words. Children write one word on each card and file cards alphabetically in the box. The benefit of beginning with a common group of words is that you, the teacher, know which basic words readers have at their fingertips. Children then add to their boxes words that contain the letter-sound patterns they are learning, words they need for writing, and words they are learning to recognize fluently. The word cards in boxes are excellent references for writing and letter-sound activities.

People Pattern Words

This is a whole body analog of the word building activity described earlier. Only here, children wearing letter-sound patterns line up one pattern after another to build words with the letter-sound patterns they are learning.

Things You'll Need: Large cards with letter-sound patterns on them; yarn if children are to wear the cards. If children are to wear cards rather than hold them, punch a hole in each corner of the cards, thread yarn through them, and tie it in a bow behind children's necks.

Directions: Distribute one card to each child. For example, if building words with intact letter-sound patterns, one child may hold a card with a *tr,* another a card with *ai,* still another a card with an *n.* Children with letter-sound patterns line up to spell the words you pronounce (see the illustration in Figure 5–6). In this example, children would make the word *train.* Talk about the letter-sound patterns in words; read words in chorus; have the children add the words to their personal word boxes. An alternative is to give each child a card with only one letter: *t, r, a, i, n.* Children then construct letter-sound patterns as they build words.

Letter-Sound Compare and Contrast Charts

Children working in small groups make large charts that show how several patterns represent the same sounds.

Things You'll Need: As many large sheets of paper as there are cooperative groups in your classroom; colored markers.

Figure 5–6   People Pattern Words. Children line up to build words that are spelled with the letter-sound patterns they are learning, read the words in chorus, and then add the words to their personal word boxes.

Directions: Ask children to think of words that have a certain sound, the long *o* sound, for instance. Make a list of these words on the board. Call children's attention to the different letter-sound patterns that represent the long *o*. Have children find words on the board that are spelled with this pattern. Distribute chart paper and have the children divide it into as many sections as there are different spelling patterns for the same sound. In our example, children would divide the chart into four sections, each for a different long *o* pattern. In each section, children write a word with one of the letter-sound patterns and draw a picture of that word, as shown in Figure 5–7. Children then write more words in each section that are spelled with the same letter-sound pattern. Children may select words from the board, from the word wall, or from other print in your classroom. Share finished charts with the class; ask children to compare and contrast the letter-sound patterns in words.

 Paper Sack Letter-Sound Sort

Children working with a learning partner, individually or in learning centers sort words into paper lunch sacks according to the sounds letter patterns represent.

Things You'll Need: As many sets of word cards as there are cooperative groups or individual children in your class; lunch-size paper sacks with a letter-sound pattern on them, as shown in Figure 5–8.

Directions: Give children several small paper sacks and a group of word cards or leave the sacks and cards in a learning center. Children sort by putting words that have the same letter-sound pattern in the sack with that letter pattern on the

Figure 5–7 In making charts, children compare and contrast different letter-sound patterns that represent the same sounds in words.

Figure 5–8 Sorting helps readers become sensitive to the letter-sound patterns that occur in many different words.

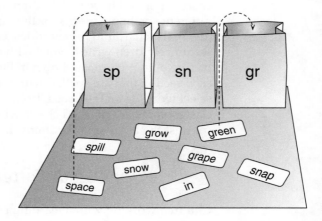

front. When finished sorting, children empty each sack, cross-check to make sure that all the words inside are sorted correctly, and then write each word on the sack in which it belongs. This gives you a record of how children sorted and, additionally, gives children practice writing words that include the letter-sound patterns they are learning.

Fly Away Words

In this gamelike activity, children read words on make-believe flies, bees, or mosquitoes and, as quickly as possible, smack the insects with a swatter. When children quickly read the words you dictate, they get practice recognizing words with targeted letter-sound patterns and have opportunities to develop fluent (quick, accurate, effortless) word recognition. Books like *The Giant Jam Sandwich* (Lord, 1972) and *Why Mosquitoes Buzz in People's Ears* (Aardema, 1975) are examples of stories that feature insects.

Things You'll Need: Two fly swatters; tape; construction paper cut into flies, bees, or mosquitoes with words on them, as illustrated in Figure 5–9.

Directions: Tape the fly away words to the board, spacing them fairly far apart, as shown in Figure 5–9. Divide players into two teams. Call one player from each team up to the board; give each a swatter. Say a word that is spelled with one of the letter-sound patterns children are learning in your classroom. Each player finds and swats the word as fast as possible. Once swatted, the player reads the word and explains or points to the letter-sound pattern you designate. If the player is correct, the swatted word is taken off the board—it "flies away"—and the team gets a point. The team with the most fly away words wins. At game's end, hold up fly away words and ask children to read them in chorus.

Word Puzzles

Children working with a partner, individually, or in a learning center solve puzzles with a clue word (like *steam*) and a set of instructions (− *ea* + *or* =) that transform the clue into a solution word (*storm*), as shown in Figure 5–10.

Things You'll Need: Colored chalk; puzzles with the letter-sound patterns children are learning in your classroom.

Directions: To demonstrate how to solve word puzzles, write a puzzle on the board that includes a letter-sound pattern children are learning in your classroom. Use colored chalk to highlight the transformations children are to perform. For example, you might write: *steam* − *ea* + *or* = _____. Show children that in subtracting the *ea* (*VV*) long vowel pattern and in adding the *or* (*Vr*) pattern in its place, children transform *steam* into *storm*. Puzzle solvers delete letter-sound patterns, add letter-sound patterns, and cross-check to verify

Figure 5–9 An example of fly-away words. In swatting words that the teacher pronounces, children get practice rapidly reading words that contain the letter-sound patterns they are learning.

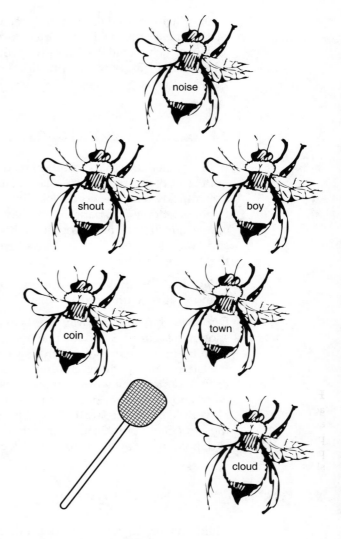

coin	–	oi	+	or	=	_____		steam	–	ea	+	or	=	_____
sheet	–	ee	+	ir	=	_____		house	–	ou	+	or	=	_____
coat	–	oa	+	ar	=	_____		dealing	–	ea	+	ar	=	_____

Figure 5–10 As children solve word puzzles, they think analytically about the sounds that the letters in patterns represent in words.

solutions by sharing them with a classmate. The examples in Figure 5–10 ask children to solve word puzzles with the *Vr* letter-sound pattern.

Mailbox Word Sort

In this center activity, children sort words according to letter-sound patterns, and then mail the words by slipping them into shoeboxes that look like mailboxes.

Things You'll Need: Two or more shoeboxes with tightly fitting lids for mailboxes; mock postcards with words that are spelled with the letter-sound patterns children are learning in your classroom. Cut a slit in the lid of the shoeboxes; cover each lid with construction paper or shelf paper. Above each slit, glue a picture of a word to represent a certain sound, such as a *boat* to represent a long *o* sound, or write a description of the letter-sound patterns children are learning, such as long vowel and short vowel, as shown in Figure 5–11. Stand shoeboxes on end to simulate mailboxes.

Directions: Place mailboxes and postcards in a center. Children sort the postcard words according to their letter-sound patterns by slipping each postcard word through the proper shoebox slot.

Figure 5–11   In this center activity, children sort "postcards" according to the letter-sound patterns in spelling, and mail the postcards by slipping them into shoebox mailboxes.

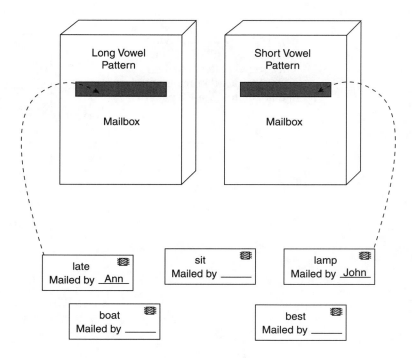

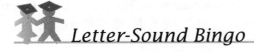

Letter-Sound Bingo

An oldie but goodie for children of any age, bingo is a favorite activity that can be used with any letter-sound pattern children are learning.

Things You'll Need: Bingo cards; pencils. Begin by designing a bingo card that has five rows with five boxes each. Duplicate the model and write incomplete words by omitting letter-sound patterns as needed for the focus of instruction, as shown in Figure 5–12. Words in this example feature the *VV* long vowel patterns of *oa* (*t___st* to make *toast*), *ee* (*tr___* to make *tree*), and *ai* (*tr___n* to make *train*).

Directions: Pass out bingo cards. Say a word and ask children to listen for the sound that a pattern represents. Children then locate the incomplete word and write in the missing pattern. A completed word "covers" the square. Traditional rules hold: any five consecutively covered squares lined up diagonally, horizontally, or vertically wins. Four corners or postage stamps (four squares in any corner) are fun to play, too. Coveralls are always challenging, but they take more time, so save them for days when there is plenty of flexibility in the schedule.

Figure 5–12 In playing bingo, readers fill in missing letter-sound patterns in the words their teacher reads aloud, in this example the *VV* pattern.

str__t	ch __n	fl__t	sl__p	tr__
sn __l	qu__n	t__st	ch__k	s __m
sh__t	p__n	Free	r__st	p__d
tr__l	g__t	br__n	thr__t	c__ch
sp __ch	s__p	l__f	cl__m	p__nt

Use *ee*, *ai*, and *oa* to make the words on this card.

Letter-Sound Scrapbook

Children working in a learning center make scrapbooks of words that are spelled with the same letter-sound patterns.

Things You'll Need: Magazines; markers; large pieces of light colored construction paper with a letter-sound pattern or a word with an underlined pattern at the top; a stapler.

Directions: Place construction paper pages with a letter-sound pattern (*th*) or a word with an underlined pattern at the top (*thumb*), scissors, glue, magazines, and other consumable print in a learning center. When children visit the center, they look for words in magazines and other print that have the letter-sound pattern, cut the words out, and paste them onto a large page that has the targeted letter pattern written at the top. As children learn new letter-sound patterns, have them make a scrapbook page for each one. Fasten pages together to make a large scrapbook. Use the words in scrapbooks when reviewing the letter-sound patterns and as resources for letter-sound activities.

Letter-Sound Wheels

Wheels are two circles, each with one or more letter-sound patterns. To make and read words, children align the letters on the outer wheel with letters on the inner wheel, as shown in Figure 5–13.

Things You'll Need: Two oak tag circles, one larger than the other; a brad; a marker. Make one circle about 9 inches in diameter, the other about 6 inches. On the outermost portion of the large circle, write letter-sound patterns that come at the beginning of words. On the outermost portion of the small circle, write vowel

Figure 5–13   Children think about the sounds the letters in patterns represent and then turn the wheels to form real words.

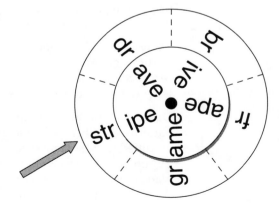

patterns that come at the end of words. Poke a hole in the center of each and fasten them together with a brad.

Directions: Children turn the circles to align letter-sound patterns. Children cross-check to decide which combinations form real words, and then write down all the real words they make.

Word Race

Children working in groups race to write as many words with specific letter-sound patterns as possible within a relative short time. This timed word writing activity draws children's attention to the letter-sound patterns in words, and gives children practice writing words with important letter-sound patterns.

Things You'll Need: One large piece of chart paper for each collaborative group; markers.

Directions: Give each group a large piece of paper with a different letter pattern—such as *oa, sh, oo,* or *tr*— a marker, and a large piece of chart paper. Challenge the groups to write as many words as they can that contain this letter pattern. Set the timer for a specific amount of time. When the timer goes off, children put down their markers. Groups share their words with the class, read the words in chorus, and count the words each group made. Write that number at the top of the chart. Invite children to look for other words with the same letter-sound patterns and to add them to the charts.

Modified Cloze Sentences

A few of the words in modified cloze sentences are partially deleted, as in *str___t* (*street*). The deleted portion consists of a letter-sound pattern children are learning or need to practice. Children use syntactic, semantic, and letter-sound cues to figure out the identity of words and to write in the missing letters.

Things You'll Need: Modified cloze sentences, which consist of sentences that have portions of words deleted and replaced by blanks. To make modified cloze sentences, delete portions of words so as to focus readers' attention on certain letter-sound patterns.

Directions: Children read the sentences; consider syntax, meaning, and letter-sound patterns; and then write the missing letter patterns in the blanks. For example, modified cloze sentences for practice using syntactic, semantic, and the *oy* and *oi* diphthong patterns would look like this: John got a t__y car for his birthday. (toy) Nancy planted the seeds deep down in the wet s___l. (soil) Glenda wanted to j___n the club. (join) The b___s like to play marbles during recess. (boys)

Clothesline Letter-Sound Pattern Words

Children working in small groups create a clothesline of words that share the same letter-sound pattern.

Things You'll Need: A rope for a clothesline; an assortment of clothespins; word cards (or construction paper in the shape of clothes with words written on each clothing article); blank cards (or pieces of construction paper in the shape of clothes); markers.

A. *Hanging Clothesline*

Directions: String a clothesline (rope) across a corner of the room and give each child several cards (or pieces of construction paper cut in the shape of clothes). After discussing the letter-sound pattern; children read the words, then pin the cards to the clothesline, as shown in Figure 5–14. Children also may add their own words to the clothesline by writing words on blank cards. When finished, everyone reads the words in chorus.

B. *Bulletin Board Clothesline*

Directions: As an alternative, you may wish to make a bulletin board by zigzagging a clothesline (rope) from top to bottom, pinning a word on the top of the clothesline (*home*, for example), and underlining the letter-sound pattern (in this example the *VCe* long vowel pattern). In this example, children find words with the *VCe* pattern, read the words to make sure that the pattern represents the long vowel sound, and pin the word cards to the clothesline with a clothespin or thumbtack. Pin any exception words, like *have* and *plaid*, in a bottom corner. Then

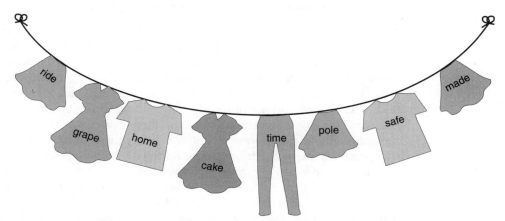

Figure 5–14 Pinning words that are spelled with the same letter-sound pattern to a clothesline gives readers opportunities to analyze the letter-sound patterns inside words and to draw conclusions about how the letter-sound patterns represent sound.

when the bulletin board is finished, read the words that sound like they are spelled, and read, too, the exception words. Discuss how readers need to be ready to try another sound (in this example, a short vowel sound) if the first try does not make a real word.

Letter-Sound Pattern Board Sort

In this activity, children sort words on cards according to the letter-sound patterns they are learning, and then tape words to a chalkboard or white board, thereby making long chalkboard lists.

Things You'll Need: Word cards with masking tape loops on the back.

Directions: Write several letter-sound patterns on the board—preferably patterns that have a letter in common, such as the long *a* in *stay* (*VV*), *made* (*VCe*), and in *train* (*VV*). Give children word cards with masking tape loops on the back. Children sort the words by putting them under the words on the board (*stay, made,* and *train,* in this example) that share the same letter-sound pattern. When finished, read the words in chorus; point out the patterns; ask children to explain why they pronounce each word as they do. If, on reading the lists, children find a few mistakes, simply move the words to the proper columns.

Movie Words

Children produce "homemade" movies and, in the process, get experience writing and reading words with the letter-sound patterns they are learning.

Things You'll Need: A cardboard box; two dowels; a knife; tape; butcher paper. To make a movie projector, cut a rectangle in the bottom of a cardboard box to serve as a viewing screen. Cut two sets of holes on either side of the box: Cut one set toward the top of the box (one above the "screen"), the other toward the bottom (one below the "screen"). Make the holes large enough for a dowel to fit through. Slide each dowel through one set of holes. Now, working through the back of the box, tape the movie (which is written on the butcher paper) to the dowels. Wind the entire movie around one dowel; wind only the lead (the blank butcher paper that precedes the movie frames) around the other dowel. Turn the dowels to simulate a movie as the paper film moves from one dowel to another as illustrated in Figure 5–15. Adjust the tension by turning either the top or bottom dowel. Advise children to make the pictures and text a little smaller than the actual frame. This way there is some leeway in case the frames drawn on butcher paper are not positioned quite right on the movie screen.

Directions: Discuss and review the letter-sound patterns you are teaching. Then ask children to write and illustrate their own movies, and to underline the words

Figure 5–15 Children produce homemade movies and, in the process, get experience writing and reading words with the letter-sound patterns they are learning.

John's cake had six candles.

in their stories that are spelled with the letter-sound patterns they are learning. Or you might ask children to write scripts with as many words as possible with a targeted letter-sound pattern. After editing their stories, children divide the stories into brief episodes consistent with the story line. Partition a long piece of butcher paper into movie frames by drawing horizontal lines at equal distances. Make two extra frames, one at the beginning and one at the end of the movie. These extra frames are later wound around and fastened to the dowels. Working from their edited stories, children write one episode in each frame, draw an appropriate picture, and underline words with the special letter-sound patterns they are learning. Fasten the butcher paper to dowels and insert it in the homemade movie projector. As the dowels are turned, different frames appear on the screen and children read their stories frame by frame. Have children talk about the movies, the story structure, and some of the words with the letter-sound patterns they are learning. Reread the movies for fluency. Have children read in chorus; ask them to put their thumbs up for every word they see with a specified letter-sound pattern; share the movies with other classrooms.

 ## Vowel Pattern Grid

This small group activity is beneficial for any age reader who needs more practice identifying and comparing and contrasting long, short, and r-controlled vowel patterns.

Things You'll Need: A grid showing spaces for long, short, and r-controlled vowel pattern words, as shown in Figure 5–16; pencils; cards with a variety of long, short, and r-controlled vowel pattern words.

Directions: Ask children to work with a partner. Give each set of partners a piece of paper with a grid that has different letter-sound patterns, and a stack of word cards. Partners sort the words according to the vowel letter patterns—long vowel, short vowel, or r-controlled—and then fill out the grid by writing each word in the appropriate square. Use the completed sort to compare and contrast

Figure 5–16 Sorting words
by their vowel letter-sound pattern
gives children opportunities to
compare and contrast the sounds
the letters in patterns represent.

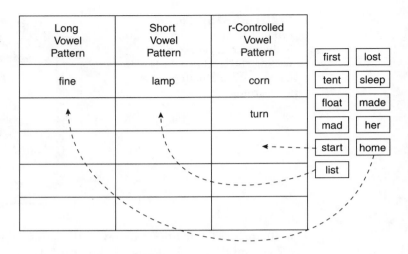

Long Vowel Pattern	Short Vowel Pattern	r-Controlled Vowel Pattern
fine	lamp	corn
		turn

first   lost
tent   sleep
float   made
mad   her
start   home
list

the different vowel patterns and how they represent sound. Ask children to find
or think of other examples of familiar words that include the vowel patterns.
Make this activity easier by asking children to sort for only two letter-sound
patterns.

Crossing Out Silent Consonants

This activity calls attention to the "silent" double consonants in words, such as
rabbit and *mitten*.

Things You'll Need: Nothing special.

Directions: Write several words with silent consonants on the chalkboard. Ask a
child to pronounce a word and then to come to the chalkboard and draw a line
through the "silent" consonant. For example, the second *b* in *rabbit* and the
second *t* in *mitten* would be crossed off.

Bag Books

Children use their knowledge of letter-sound patterns when writing stories, which
are then edited and slipped inside plastic bags to make durable books.

Things You'll Need: Gallon-size plastic bags that lock at the top; a hole punch;
ribbon; paper and pencils; colored highlighters.

Directions: Children write, revise, and edit stories. In so doing, children use their
knowledge of letter-sound patterns to spell the words they wish to write. You

Figure 5–17 Writing stories that are then made into bag books gives children opportunities to use their knowledge of letter-sound patterns when writing.

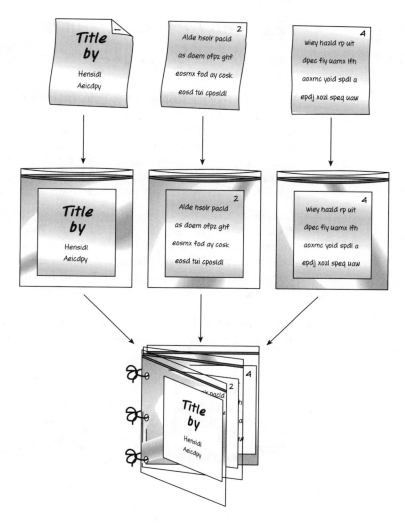

may wish to have children use a highlighter to draw attention to words with a letter-sound pattern they are learning. Put two pages back-to-back. Slip them into a gallon-size plastic bag and seal the bag. When all the pages are inside bags, use a paper punch to make three holes on the far left of the bags as shown in Figure 5–17. Thread colorful ribbon through holes and tie the ribbon in a bow. This fastens the pages of the book together and adds a cheerful splash of color, too. Share bag books with the class, and, when you do this, talk about story sequence, meaning, and the letter-sound patterns in words.

Interactive Bulletin Board

Children in a small group sort words according to shared letter-sound patterns and then put the words on a bulletin board.

Things You'll Need: Construction paper; markers; word cards. Before introducing this activity, think of everyday objects (nouns are best) that are spelled with the letter-sound patterns children are learning. Cut construction paper into the shapes of the objects. For instance, if you are going to focus on consonant clusters and digraphs, you might make a *shoe* for *sh*, a *cloud* for *cl*, and a *truck* for *tr*. Make a word card for each cutout—*shoe, cloud,* and *truck.* Fasten the construction paper cutouts and accompanying words to the bulletin board.

Directions: Read the words on the bulletin board, drawing attention to the phonics letter-sound patterns children are learning. Give children word cards. You may wish to give children some cards with words that have the letter patterns on the bulletin board and some cards with words that do not include the targeted letter-sound patterns. If a word has the same letter-sound pattern as one of the bulletin board words (*shoe, cloud,* or *truck* in this example) children add it to the bulletin board, illustrated in Figure 5–18. You may wish to leave a few blank cards for children to add their own words and words they find on the word wall, on charts, and in the books they are reading in your classroom.

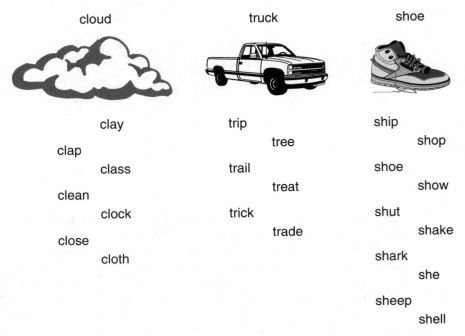

Figure 5–18   An interactive bulletin board. Children make colorful bulletin boards by sorting words according to their letter-sound patterns.

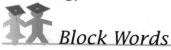

Block Words

Children working in small groups or in centers build words with blocks that have letter-sound patterns on them.

Things You'll Need: Blocks with a letter-sound pattern on each side; markers. Purchase blocks at a craft store or make your own out of square tissue boxes covered with shelf paper. Each block has six sides, so you will want to think of three letter-sound patterns for each block and write each pattern twice per block. For instance, to build words with the *Vr* pattern, children would use three blocks, each with the same pattern written twice: one block might have *p, d,* and *sh;* the second *ar, or,* and *ir;* the third *t, k,* and *e.* Block-building is more challenging when blocks have six different letter patterns, one pattern on each of the six sides.

Directions: Place blocks in a learning center or distribute them to children in a small group. Using the blocks you provide, children build as many words as possible and then write the words they build as shown in Figure 5–19.

Figure 5–19 An example of block words. Children apply their knowledge of letter-sound patterns when building words with blocks that have letter-sound patterns on them and then writing the words they build.

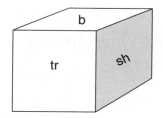
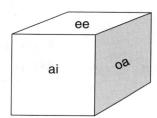

ee	oa	ai
tree green	boat	train

How Many Words Can You Make?

This is a variation of the party game where players make as many words as they can from one large word, usually the name of a famous person, place, thing, or event. It is easy to integrate with social studies, science, math, and health by using words from these content subjects, and helps build fluency writing and reading words. This activity is best used with second graders and up, and lends itself to working with children in large or small groups.

Things You'll Need: Other than paper and pencils, you do not need anything special.

Directions: Challenge children to use the letters in the long word to spell as many short words as they can and to write words on a sheet of paper. Set the timer and, when the timer goes off, word writing stops. Writing words in a short period of time helps children bring their word knowledge to fluency and, additionally, gives children practice thinking of and writing words with many different letter-sound patterns. Have children share the words they make; count the words; read the words in chorus.

Moving Toward Word Identification With Multiletter Chunks

In using the letter-sound strategy, readers associate sounds with letters to read new words. Remembering how the letters in written words represent sounds in spoken words helps children learn words, even when words are visually similar (Adams, 1990). The letter-sound strategy takes advantage of the basic principle of alphabetic writing—the use of letters to represent sounds. Children who are skilled at using the letter-sound strategy have good phonemic awareness, know many different letter-sound patterns, and can read any new word that is spelled like it sounds. Added to this, the letter-sound strategy paves the way for developing sensitivity to the large multiletter groups, or chunks, in the structure of long words, such as the *–ment* in *excitement*. The use of large multiletter chunks to identify words typically matures only after children have had lots of experience using letter-sound patterns to read and spell words. Not only does the use of large multiletter chunks make word identification quicker, but knowing the meaning of one or more of the large multiletter chunks in a word often gives readers insight into that word's definition, as you will learn in chapter 6.

References

Aardema, V. (1975). *Why mosquitoes buzz in people's ears*. New York: Dial Books for Young Readers.

Aaron, P. G., Joshi, R. M., Ayotollah, M., Ellsberry, A., Henderson, J., & Lindsey, K. (1999). Decoding and sight-word naming: Are they independent components of word recognition skill? *Reading and Writing: An Interdisciplinary Journal, 11,* 89–127.

Adams, M. J. (1990). *Beginning to read: Thinking and learning about print.* Cambridge, MA: MIT Press.

Armbruster, B. B., Lehr, F., & Osborn, J. (2001). *Put reading first: The research building blocks for teaching children to read.* Washington, DC: National Institute for Literacy.

Bailey, M. H. (1967). The utility of phonic generalizations in grades one through six. *The Reading Teacher, 20,* 413–418.

Clymer, T. (1963). The utility of phonic generalizations in the primary grades. *The Reading Teacher, 16,* 252–258.

Connelly, V., Johnston, R., & Thompson, G. B. (2001). The effect of phonics instruction on the reading comprehension of beginning readers. *Reading and Writing: An Interdisciplinary Journal, 14,* 423–457.

Ehri, L. C. (2000). Learning to read and learning to spell: Two sides of a coin. *Topics in Language Disorders, 20,* 19–36.

Emans, R. (1967). The usefulness of phonic generalizations above the primary grades. *The Reading Teacher, 20,* 419–425.

Fowler, C. A., Shankweiler, D., & Liberman, I. Y. (1979). Apprehending spelling patterns for vowels: A developmental study. *Language and Speech, 22,* 243–252.

Gentry, J. R. (1987). *Spel . . . is a four-letter word.* New York: Scholastic.

Juel, C. (1983). The development and use of mediated word identification. *Reading Research Quarterly, 18,* 306–327.

Juel, C., & Roper-Schneider, D. (1985). The influence of basal readers on first grade reading. *Reading Research Quarterly, 20,* 134–152.

Lord, J. V. (1972). *The giant jam sandwich.* Boston: Houghton Mifflin.

Mesmer, H. A. E. (2001). Decodable text: A review of what we know. *Reading Research and Instruction, 40,* 121–142.

National Reading Panel. (2000). *Teaching children to read: An evidence-based assessment of the scientific research literature on reading and its implications for reading instruction: Reports of the subgroups* (NIH Publication No. 00-4754). Washington, DC: U.S. Government Printing Office.

Neuman, S. B., Copple, C., & Bredekamp, S. (2000). *Learning to read and write: Developmentally appropriate practices for young children.* Washington, DC: National Association for the Education of Young Children.

Reed, L. C., & Klopp, D. S. (1957). *Phonics for thought.* New York: Comet Press Books.

Rupley, W. H., & Wilson, V. L. (1997). Relationship between comprehension and components of word recognition: Support for developmental shifts. *Journal of Research and Development in Education, 30,* 255–260.

Snow, C. E., Burns, M. S., & Griffin, P. (Eds.). (1998). *Preventing reading difficulties in young children.* Washington, DC: National Academy Press.

Stuart, M. (1995). Through printed words to meaning: Issues of transparency. *Journal of Research in Reading, 18,* 126–131.

Tunmer, W. E., & Chapman, J. E. (2002). The relation of beginning readers' reported word identification strategies to reading achievement, reading-related skills, and academic self-perceptions. *Reading and Writing: An Interdisciplinary Journal, 15,* 341–358.

Zinna, D. R., Liberman, I. Y., & Shankweiler, D. (1986). Children's sensitivity to factors influencing vowel reading. *Reading Research Quarterly, 21,* 465–479.

CHAPTER 6

The Multiletter Chunk Strategy

Using the Multiletter Groups in Word Structure
to Read New Long Words

This chapter describes how readers use the multiletter groups in

word structure to read long and complex new words. You will learn

about the multiletter groups that indicate meaning and sound, and

about syllables that indicate pronunciation. In reading this chapter

you will find out about 5 research-based best practices for teaching

prefixes and suffixes, 3 best practices for teaching syllables, ways to

support readers as they use the multiletter chunk strategy, and

22 activities for teaching the multiletter chunks in word structure.

KEY IDEAS

➤ Chunks consist of the large, intact letter groups that readers automatically recognize and pronounce in words.
➤ Many multiletter chunks indicate meaning—for example, the prefix *un-* in *unhappy,* the suffix *-ly* in *friendly,* and the root word *sign* in *signal* and *signature.*
➤ Syllables indicate pronunciation, such as the syllables *dis, trib,* and *ute* in *distribute.*
➤ The multiletter chunk strategy is more efficient than other word identification strategies and, by extension, takes less time away from comprehension.
➤ The multiletter chunk strategy is the last strategy to develop before readers reach the stage where they automatically recognize all the words in the text they read every day.

KEY VOCABULARY

Prefixes	Base words	Transitional stage of spelling
Suffixes	Greek and Latin roots	Automatic recognition stage of movement toward word fluency
Affixes	Compound words	
Inflectional suffixes	Contractions	
Derivational suffixes	Consolidated stage of movement toward word fluency	
Syllable		
Accent		

At a mere glance, you know how to pronounce *astroport* as used in Figure 6–1, recognize that it is most likely an interstellar station for the space traveling public, know it is a noun, and, if asked, could use *astroport* in a sentence. All this is quite interesting since *astroport* is not a real word, at least not yet.

The way to unlock this word's pronunciation and at the same time to get insight into its meaning is to divide *astroport* into the two large, meaningful multiletter chunks—*astro* and *port.* Each multiletter chunk is spelled the way it sounds and contributes to the word's definition, provided you know that *astro* means *star* and *port* means *to carry.* With this knowledge, you might logically infer that an *astroport* is a site to which space travelers are transported, just as an *airport* is a site to which airline passengers are transported.

Figure 6–1 Meaningful chunks
give insight into pronunciation and
word meaning. The student who
drew this picture used knowledge of
astro and port to show what they
might mean if put together.

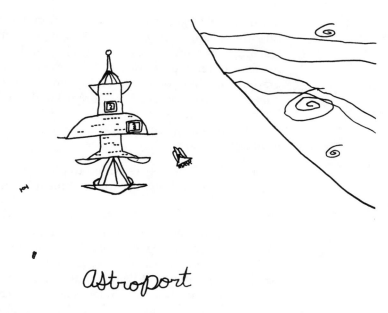

After reading and writing the same letter sequences time and time again, readers perceive these groups as large, intact units (Stuart & Coltheart, 1988). In so doing, readers chunk, or join together, groups of letters in their minds. Multiletter chunks significantly reduce the energy readers put into word identification and, when readers know the meaning of letter groups, they have some insight into the definition of words as well. Readers who use multiletter chunks do not recall analogous onsets and rimes in known words to identify unknown words as do users of the analogy strategy, nor do they sound out and blend letter-sound patterns as do users of the letter-sound strategy. Instead, readers recognize and pronounce all at once entire groups of letters in words (*complete = com + plete; unworkable = un + work + able*).

When you, the teacher, help readers use multiletter chunks to read new words, you are teaching structural analysis[1]. Rather than focus on the sound level, which is the scope of phonics instruction, structural analysis focuses on

---

1 Analysis of meaningful units in words is part of morphology, a specialized study in linguistics which concentrates on word forms and their connections to meaning. Prefixes, suffixes, contractions, compound words, base words and root words are more accurately described as morphemic analysis because each deals with meaning. Syllables, accents, and other pronunciation units, such as rimes, represent sound and therefore are associated with phonic analysis. Combining meaningful and nonmeaningful chunks under the umbrella of structural analysis makes sense for the purpose of teaching inasmuch as readers recognize these letter groups as single, intact units.

teaching the large structural units that make up words. When you demonstrate how the meaning of *effort* changes when we add *-less* to make *effortless*, you are teaching structural analysis. You also teach structural analysis when you help readers understand how *isn't* consists of *is* and *not*. And when you help a fifth grader use a hyphen to divide the word *government* into syllables so as to write part of the word on one line (*govern-*) and part on another (*ment*), you are teaching structural analysis.

In analyzing word structure, readers pay attention to the following seven multiletter chunks:

1. *Prefixes*   Prefixes are added to the beginning of words to change meaning (the *un-* in *unhappy*) or to make meaning more specific (the *mid-* in *midweek*).
2. *Suffixes*   Suffixes are added to the end of words to clarify meaning (the *-s* in *cats*) or to change grammatical function (the *-able* in *drinkable*).
3. *Base Words*   Base words are the smallest meaningful units, or words, in English that can stand alone (*play, go, come, here, father, cowboy*).
4. *Greek and Latin Root Words*   Latin and Greek roots are word parts we borrowed from these two languages (*astro* borrowed from Greek and *port* from Latin) that are combined to form English words.
5. *Compound Words*   Compound words are two base words that, when combined, make an entirely new word (*cow + boy = cowboy*).
6. *Contractions*   Constractions are short cuts for writing two words together (*isn't, we're*).
7. *Syllables*   Syllables are the basic units of pronunciation in our English language (the *ta* and *ble* in *table*). All words have one or more syllables, and each syllable has one vowel sound.

Interestingly, the use of large multiletter groups is not unique to reading, because we group—or chunk—together, all sorts of information, and we do this for good reason. Before we explore each of the seven important multiletter chunks, we will consider *why* readers use multiletter chunks in the first place.

Why Readers Chunk Letters

We form multiletter chunks whenever we bundle several small bits of information into one single unit. For example, when you combine the letters $p + r + e$ in *precook* into one whole unit *pre-*, you create a multiletter chunk in your mind. We group information to prevent a bottleneck in short-term memory. All information goes through short-term memory on its way to long-term memory. Our short-term memory holds all the information about whatever we happen to be paying attention to at the moment. Long-term memory, in turn, is the storehouse for all the information, words, ideas, and memories we accumulate throughout our lives.

Consequently, we want to get as much information as possible out of short-term memory and into long-term memory.

While there is a great deal of space to store information in long-term memory, the storage space in short-term memory is extremely limited. In fact, only five to seven thought units are held in short-term memory at once (Miller, 1956), and this information lasts only a few seconds before it is either forgotten or moved into long-term memory. A thought unit can be small (one letter, such as *p*) or large (a group of letters, such as *pre-*). A bottleneck occurs when there are so many separate thought units, or pieces of information, in short-term memory that some are forgotten before the information is sent to long-term memory.

When we combine small units, or bits, of information (a single letter, *p*) into a large chunk (a group of letters, *pre-*), we pack more information into a single thought unit. This prevents overcrowding and makes it easier to keep more information in short-term memory. It also makes it possible to get more information into long-term memory because a number of small bits of information are grouped in each thought unit.

Take *astroport* as an example. If we consider the nine letters separately ($a + s + t + r + o + p + o + r + t$), we are almost certain to overburden short-term memory. However, if we consider multiletter groups, we reduce information to just two thought units: *astro* and *port*. With only two thought units in short-term memory, we are less likely to forget information, and there is room left over to make a little sense of *astroport* before it goes to long-term memory. Added to this, the use of multiletter chunks decreases the number of spoken language segments to be blended. Blending a few large chunks—/astro/ + /port/—makes it less likely that individual sounds will be forgotten or reversed.

Given the advantages of multiletter chunks, it is not surprising that as readers increase the number of chunks they recognize, their efficiency in word identification improves (Invernizzi, 1992). All in all, readers who use multiletter chunks put less mental attention and less mental energy into reading new words than is the case with other forms of word identification. This means that readers who use large multiletter groups return to textual reading more quickly, and the disruption to comprehension created by new words is reduced.

Using the Multiletter Chunks in Word Structure to Read Long Words

Reading new words with the multiletter chunk strategy takes less mental attention than sounding out words with the letter-sound strategy and, by extension, requires less time away from comprehending text. Readers who use the multiletter chunks in word structure know that spoken and written words can be divided into a variety of units, some small and some large. They can separate spoken words into individual sounds and multisound groups, and they can blend individual sounds and multisound groups together to form meaningful words. These readers know that the same chunks are part of many different words, as the *ter* in *butter* and *terrific*. They recognize multiletter chunks that indicate pronunciation only (the *ter* in *butter*), as well as multiletter chunks that indicate meaning and pronunciation (the *ing* in *playing*). The more reading and writing experiences children have in school, the more they learn about the multiletter groups in language, and the more accomplished they become at using the multiletter chunks in word structure.

Use of the multiletter chunk strategy hinges on recognizing the multiletter groups in words, as you will see when Peter comes across the new word *antiseptic* in this sentence from his science book: "Perhaps you recall getting a cut on your knee. Someone may have disinfected the cut with an antiseptic" (Hackett, Moyer, & Adams, 1989, p. 27). Peter's science class has already discussed *antiseptics* and their function, so this word is in his speaking and listening vocabularies. Peter also knows that *anti* means *against* or *preventing* when it is in common words like *anti-smoking* and *antitheft*. All things considered, Peter brings a good deal of prior knowledge to word identification. He knows (a) what the spoken word *antiseptic* means, (b) how *anti* contributes to a word's definition, and (c) how to recognize many different types of multiletter chunks in the words he reads. Here is how Peter goes about using the multiletter chunk strategy:

1. Peter recognizes *anti* and, in so doing, instantly recalls its pronunciation and meaning.
2. He identifies two additional multiletter chunks—*sep* and *tic*. Peter now has divided *antiseptic* into three pronounceable groups: /anti/ + /sep/ + /tic/.
3. Peter blends /anti/ + /sep/ + /tic/ into /antiseptic/.
4. Last, he cross-checks to make sure that he pronounces and understands the word in the context in which it is used in his science book. He asks himself: Does *antiseptic* sound and look right? Does *antiseptic* make sense in the passage? If *antiseptic* makes sense, Peter continues reading.

In the way he separated them, the first group of letters is *anti*, the second *sep* and the third *tic*. But there are other ways Peter might have chosen to group letters. Though the *septic* in *antiseptic* is a meaningful multiletter chunk, it is not in Peter's speaking or listening vocabulary. Had he known the meaning of *septic*, Peter might have divided *antiseptic* into the two meaningful chunks—*anti* + *septic*. Or he could have divided *antiseptic* into *an* + *ti* + *sep* + *tic* or into *an* + *ti* + *septic*. Though the specific multiletter groups individual readers use will vary depending on each reader's background knowledge, all readers who use this strategy are sensitive to which letters form chunks and which do not, and which chunks are meaningful and which are not.

Take *ing* as an example. Readers know that *ing* represents meaning and sound in *playing*, and only signals pronunciation (a rime) in *swing*. They also know that *ing* is not a viable multiletter chunk in *hinge*. When identifying multiletter chunks, readers bring to bear their knowledge of the letter-sound patterns in a word. This explains why Peter did not identify the *ise* as a multiletter chunk in *antiseptic*. Though *ise* is a pronounceable multiletter chunk in *rise, wise,* and *revise,* it is not a viable chunk in *antiseptic* because it is not consistent with the surrounding letter-sound patterns of phonics. Peter and readers like him use their knowledge of letter-sound patterns to determine the letters in new words that are most likely to belong in groups. This kind of in-depth knowledge is not an overnight phenomenon. Rather, it develops gradually as readers strategically use the multiletter chunks in word structure to read and write.

Correcting Misidentifications

Readers who do not successfully identify words on the first try may choose from among the following four alternatives:

1. Rechunk letters (divide words into different multiletter groups and then reblend).
2. Fall back on either the letter-sound or analogy strategy.
3. Look up words in the dictionary.
4. Ask expert readers for help.

Rechunking or falling back on the letter-sound or analogy strategies are, of course, less efficient ways to identify never-seen-before words. With its dependence on an in-depth knowledge of word structure cues, the multiletter chunk strategy does not come into its own until after readers have had experience using the analogy and letter-sound strategies.

Roots of the Multiletter Chunk Strategy

The multiletter chunk strategy is rooted in both the analogy and the letter-sound strategies. In fact, there is reason to believe that the very origin of multiletter chunks in readers' minds comes from using rimes and letter-sound patterns to identify words (Ehri, 1991). When readers use the analogy strategy, they learn how to capitalize on large, predictable letter groups in spelling. This helps them develop a predisposition to look for and to use rime groups (the *ig* in *pig,* for example). So, the use of analogous rimes presents early opportunities for readers to strategically use multiletter chunks and, in this sense, constitutes a step toward the more sophisticated chunk strategy.

When readers use the letter-sound strategy, they think analytically about the letter-sound patterns in words. In so doing, they have opportunities to form hypotheses about the recurring letter sequences in word structure. As a consequence of reading and writing the same letter sequences, readers eventually fuse letters together to recognize common chunks (Stuart & Coltheart, 1988). Children then refine their knowledge of multiletter chunks through even more reading and writing experiences and, as reading maturity increases, so too does the ability to take advantage of multiletter chunks (Santa, 1976–1977).

Once the multiletter chunk strategy develops, it coexists with the analogy and letter-sound strategies. As readers become sensitive to more and more multiletter chunks in word structure, they become much better at word learning (Ehri, 1998).

Readers who use the multiletter chunk strategy are in the *consolidated stage of movement toward word fluency* and the *transitional stage of spelling*, as you will learn in the next section.

The Consolidated Stage of Movement Toward Word Fluency and the Transitional Stage of Spelling

Readers who use the multiletter chunks in word structure are at the *consolidated stage of movement toward word fluency*. These readers are not neophytes just cutting their teeth on our alphabetic writing system. They have insight into the letter-sound patterns of phonics and have consolidated, or grouped, letter sequences in memory (Ehri, 1998). Readers at the consolidated stage recognize meaningful letter chunks, such as the *un-* and *-ed* in *unfinished*, as well as nonmeaningful syllables, such as the *cir* and *cle* in *circle*. While the transition into the consolidated stage comes toward the end of second grade for most readers, some will move into this stage during the third grade.

Readers at the consolidated stage use the reading context to help them identify words and use cross-checking to determine whether words make sense in the passages that they read. These readers know when to self-correct and, because their focus is on meaning, know when it is necessary to fix a word identification miscue and when it is not profitable to do so. They do not sound out words letter-sound by letter-sound, nor do they think about analogous portions of known words to identify unknown words. Instead, these readers automatically recognize large intact letter groups in words. They recognize syllables, such as the *tion* in *nation*, and they also automatically recognize prefixes (the *pre-* in *preheat*); suffixes (the *-er* in *smaller*); base words (the *clean* in *cleaning*), compound words (*snowman*), and contractions (*she'd*). Using the large multiletter chunks in word structure is the last word identification strategy to mature before readers reach the stage where they automatically recognize all words they see in text.

Readers at the consolidated stage are at the *transitional stage of spelling*. Transitional spellers have insight into the structure of words, and use this understanding when spelling (Gentry, 1987). When you look at the writing of transitional spellers, you will notice that they (a) conventionally spell common word endings (such as *-s*, *-ed*, *-ing*, and *-ly*), (b) include a vowel in every syllable, (c) put a vowel before the letter *r* (though not necessarily the correct vowel, *buttur* instead of *butter*), and (d) use the *VCe* long vowel pattern and the *VV* long vowel pattern (though not always correctly, *trale* instead of *trail*). You also will notice that the transitional spellers in your classroom sometimes substitute alternative spellings for the same sound; *naym* or *naim* for *name* is an example.

By late spring of second grade, Shania, a transitional speller, is sensitive to some of the meaningful multiletter chunks that make up word structure. She correctly spells common word endings (*lives*, *fishing*, and *lunches*, for instance), uses the *VV* long vowel pattern (*street* and *each*), and puts a vowel in every syllable as

Figure 6–2 Shania recognizes the multiletter chunks in word structure, and uses this knowledge when she reads and spells.

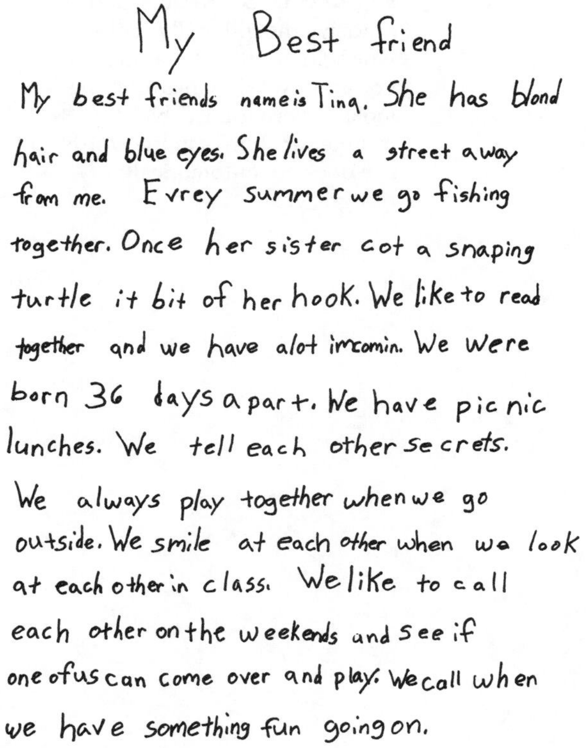

My Best friend

My best friends name is Tina. She has blond hair and blue eyes. She lives a street away from me. Evrey summer we go fishing together. Once her sister cot a snaping turtle it bit of her hook. We like to read together and we have alot in comin. We were born 36 days apart. We have picnic lunches. We tell each other secrets.

We always play together when we go outside. We smile at each other when we look at each other in class. We like to call each other on the weekends and see if one of us can come over and play. We call when we have something fun going on.

you can see in Figure 6–2. She writes a vowel before the letter *r* (*togeth_er_* and *ov_er_*), though she sometimes writes letters in the wrong sequence (*evrey*). And, of course, she conventionally spells most of the words in her fluent reading vocabulary. When Shania misspells, she writes words the way she believes they sound (*comin* for *common*). From her misspelling of *snaping* for *snapping*, we can infer that Shania is still learning how to add endings to words that require doubling the last consonant. The more literacy experiences she has the more sensitive she will become to the multiletter chunks in words and the more effectively she will use this knowledge when she reads and spells.

Fifth grader Kristen spells all words conventionally, with the exception of *restaurant*, which she spells *restarant* (see Figure 6–3). She has a large fluent reading vocabulary and, therefore, automatically identifies many words. When she does not automatically recognize a word, she is most likely to look for pronounceable multiletter chunks in its structure. Kristen's knowledge of multiletter chunks will continue to grow in middle and high school. This is important because she will rely on this strategy when she is challenged to learn the long, complex technical terms in high school textbooks.

In due time, children's reading vocabulary becomes so enormous that it includes all the words they typically see in text. Children who automatically recognize

Figure 6–3 Kristen, a fifth grader, conventionally spells the words in her fluent reading vocabulary. When reading, she looks for pronounceable multiletter chunks in the words she does not automatically recognize.

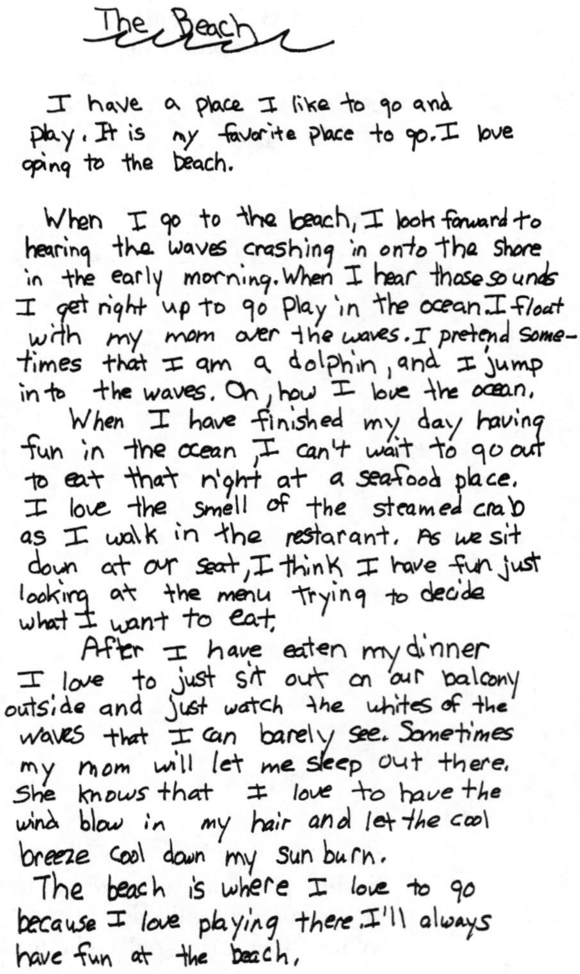

The Beach

I have a place I like to go and play. It is my favorite place to go. I love going to the beach.

When I go to the beach, I look forward to hearing the waves crashing in onto the shore in the early morning. When I hear those sounds I get right up to go play in the ocean. I float with my mom over the waves. I pretend sometimes that I am a dolphin, and I jump into the waves. Oh, how I love the ocean.

When I have finished my day having fun in the ocean I can't wait to go out to eat that night at a seafood place. I love the smell of the steamed crab as I walk in the restarant. As we sit down at our seat, I think I have fun just looking at the menu trying to decide what I want to eat.

After I have eaten my dinner I love to just sit out on our balcony outside and just watch the whites of the waves that I can barely see. Sometimes my mom will let me sleep out there. She knows that I love to have the wind blow in my hair and let the cool breeze cool down my sun burn.

The beach is where I love to go because I love playing there. I'll always have fun at the beach.

all the words they read are at the fifth and final stage—the *automatic recognition stage of movement toward word fluency.* Now word recognition is completely automatic, with the exception, of course, of unusual words and some content subject words (Ehri, 1998). These children spell known words conventionally, including irregular words; they know when words are not spelled right and fix their own misspellings (Gentry, 1987). Accomplished high school readers use many effective comprehension strategies and, because they automatically recognize words, they concentrate on comprehending and learning from their textbooks. When these readers encounter new words, they use the multiletter chunk strategy, calling on their extensive knowledge of multiletter groups to learn words in subjects like geometry, physics, geography, and American literature.

Prefixes, Suffixes, and Base Words

Prefixes are added to the beginning of words, and *suffixes* are added to the end of words. We will use *affixes* when referring to both prefixes and suffixes. Prefixes and suffixes cannot stand alone; they must be attached to words. For example, the word *like* can stand alone, but the prefix *un-* and the suffix *-ly* cannot. When *un-* and *-ly* are added to *like*, we create a word with a different meaning and grammatical function, *unlikely*. Prefixes and suffixes make words longer, as we see in *unlikely*, *reworked*, and *returnable*.

Prefixes

Prefixes either change word meaning completely, as in *non* + *fat* = *nonfat* (which results in an opposite), or make meaning more specific, as in *re* + *write* = *rewrite* (which means to write again). A mere smattering of prefixes, four to be exact, account for 58% of the words with prefixes that third through ninth graders are likely to read (White, Sowell, & Yanagihara, 1989). The four most frequently occurring prefixes are: *un-* (*unhappy*), *re-* (*rewrite*), *in-* (meaning *not* as in *inaccurate*), and *dis-* (*dislike*). *Un-* accounts for the lion's share: A full 26% of words with prefixes begin with *un-* (White, Sowell, & Yanagihara, 1989). While *un-*, *re-*, *in-*, and *dis-* are certainly useful, older readers benefit from knowing more difficult prefixes, because these prefixes offer considerable insight into word meaning (Harris & Sipay, 1990). The 20 prefixes in Table 6–1 are the most important prefixes to teach children in grades 3 through 9. When the prefixes in Table 6–1 have more than one meaning, the meaning listed is that given by White, Sowell, and Yanagihara.

Suffixes

Suffixes either clarify word meaning or change grammatical function. There are two types of suffixes: *inflectional suffixes* and *derivational suffixes*. Inflectional endings make word meaning more specific or change the verb tense. The *–s(es)*, *-ed*, *-ing*, *-er*, *-est*, and *-ly* are inflectional suffixes. These suffixes are the most frequently occurring of all the suffixes (White, Sowell, & Yanagihara, 1989). Look in appendix C for generalizations about adding these six suffixes to words.

Derivational suffixes change the part of speech, such as changing *dirt* (noun) to *dirty* (adjective), *history* (noun) to *historic* (adjective), and *agree* (verb) to *agreeable* (adjective). Children's knowledge of derivational suffixes increases from the third to the sixth grade (Mahony, Singson, & Mann, 2000; Singson, Mahony, & Mann, 2000). So you can expect older readers to more readily recognize and understand suffixes like *–ment*, *-able*, and *–ic* than younger, less experienced readers. Table 6–2 is a list of the 20 most common suffixes (White, Sowell, & Yanagihara, 1989).

Ross's story in Figure 6–4 (see p. 166) illustrates how a precocious first grader uses common suffixes. Ross conventionally spells words with *-ed*, *-ing*, and *-s/es*, and correctly forms contractions. Ross has learned these multiletter groups so well

TABLE 6–1	*The 20 Most Common Prefixes*	
Prefix	**Meaning**	**Examples**
anti	against	antitrust, antiknock, anticrime, antiglare, antitheft
de	from, away	debug, defog, decaf, defrost, deplane, derail
dis	apart from, not	disarm, disbar, disown, disuse, disable, dislike
en, em	in	enact, enclose, enable, embark, embody, embattle
fore	in front of, before	foresee, forego, forewarn, foreground, foretell
in, im, ir, il	not	invisible, improbable, irresponsible, illogical
in, im	in or into	inborn, inflow, inward, immigrant, immoral
inter	between, among	interact, intermix, interlace, interlock, interplay
mid	middle	midair, midday, midway, midweek, midnight
mis	wrong, bad, not	misfit, misplace, mislay, misuse, misdeed
non	not	nonfat, nonskid, nonprofit, nonstick, nonstop
over	too much	overage, overdue, overeat, overlap, overlook
pre	in front of, before	precut, premix, prepay, predate, precook
re	back, again	rearm, retell, redo, renew, repay, rerun
semi	half, partly	semicircle, semisoft, semifinal, semisweet
sub	under, inferior	subplot, subzero, subset, submarine, substandard
super	above, in addition	superman, superfine, superhero, superheat, superstar
trans	across, through	transact, transport, transplant, transform, transpolar
un	not	uncut, unfit, unlit, untie, unzip, unhappy, unsure
under	too little	underage, underfed, underpay, underdone, underfed

that they are second nature when he reads and writes. For example, he drops the final *y* in *try* and writes an *i* before adding -*ed* to spell *tried*. Notice the word *cutted*, which does not need an -*ed* to signal past tense. Ross writes the way he talks, and he sometimes says *cutted* when he means *cut*. Though Ross does not use *cut* conventionally, he shows us that he understands the convention of doubling the last consonant, the letter *t*, before adding the -*ed*. Ross's teacher thinks he will benefit from learning more about writing in complete sentences, and using periods and capitals, so she has formed a small, flexible skill group to give Ross and a handful of his classmates extra help with punctuation. Ross reminds us that streamlined word identification and a large fluent reading vocabulary are not tied to readers' grade in school but instead are a consequence of in-depth knowledge of our alphabetic writing system coupled with a plethora of reading and writing experiences.

The number of words with affixes doubles from fourth to fifth grade, and doubles again by the seventh grade (White, Power, & White, 1989). It is estimated that fifth graders may meet an average of 1,325 words a year that include the pre-

TABLE 6–2	*The 20 Most Common Suffixes*	
Suffix	**Meaning**	**Examples**
al, ial	relating to	bridal, global, rental, burial, memorial, personal
ed	past tense	played, jumped, painted, hopped, kicked
en	relating to	liken, ripen, olden, frozen, waken, wooden
er, or	one who	painter, player, reader, worker, visitor, actor, sailor
er	comparative	quicker, higher, fatter, uglier, faster, slower
est	most (comparative)	biggest, slowest, highest, largest, fastest, nicest
ful	quality of	artful, joyful, beautiful, plentiful, careful, fearful
ible, able	able to, quality of	readable, eatable, fixable, defensible, divisible
ic	like, pertaining to	historic, scenic, acidic, atomic, poetic
ing	ongoing	reading, listening, running, jumping, helping
ion, ation, ition, tion	act or state of	action, addition, adoption, construction, donation
ity, ty	state or quality of	dirty, dusty, nutty, salty, fruity, oddity, activity
ive, ative, itive	tending to, relating to	creative, active, massive, formative, additive
less	without	joyless, aimless, fearless, endless, jobless, useless
ly	every, in the manner of	friendly, badly, kindly, dimly, boldly, calmly
ment	result or state of	payment, argument, judgment, excitement, shipment
ness	quality of	fitness, illness, happiness, madness, goodness
ous, eous, ious	full of, state of	studious, joyous, envious, furious, gaseous
s, es	plural	dogs, houses, boys, girls, ashes, boxes, teachers
y	quality, full of	ability, muddy, baggy, bossy, bumpy, chewy, jumpy

fixes *in-, im-, ir-, il-* (meaning "not"), *un-, re-,* and *dis-*. Seventh graders may identify 3,000 words, and perhaps as many as 9,000 words, with these prefixes and with a variety of suffixes. As readers move into higher grades, their knowledge of suffixes also increases (Nagy, Diakidoy, & Anderson, 1993), quite possibly as a consequence of increased grammatical awareness (Nunes, Bryant, & Bindman, 1997). So, it is not surprising that fourth, sixth, and eighth graders use their knowledge of suffixes to read new words in context, and that sixth and eighth graders are better at this than fourth graders (Wysocki & Jenkins, 1987).

Base Words

Base words are the smallest real English words to which we might add prefixes and suffixes. Unlike prefixes and suffixes, base words stand alone; they are what is left

Figure 6–4 Through his writing, Ross demonstrates that he knows how to correctly use and conventionally spell common suffixes, and how to form contractions.

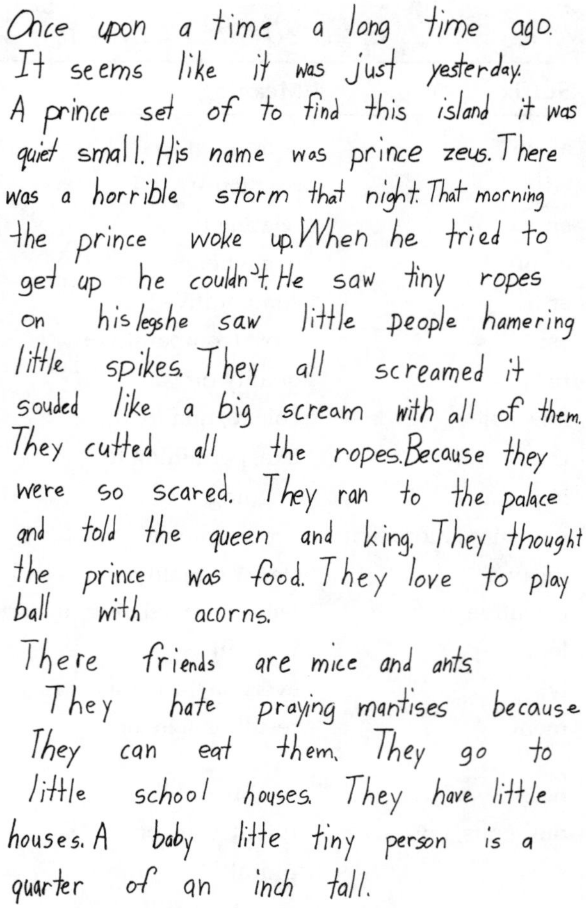

Once upon a time a long time ago. It seems like it was just yesterday. A prince set of to find this island it was quiet small. His name was prince zeus. There was a horrible storm that night. That morning the prince woke up. When he tried to get up he couldn't. He saw tiny ropes on his legs he saw little people hamering little spikes. They all screamed it souded like a big scream with all of them. They cutted all the ropes. Because they were so scared. They ran to the palace and told the queen and king. They thought the prince was food. They love to play ball with acorns.

There friends are mice and ants. They hate praying mantises because They can eat them. They go to little school houses. They have little houses. A baby litte tiny person is a quarter of an inch tall.

when we take away the prefixes and suffixes (*drinkable* − *able* = *drink*; *unhappy* − *un* = *happy*). For example, *unlikely* consists of the base word *like*, one prefix (*un-*), and one suffix (*-ly*). *Jump* is the base word in *jumps*, *jumped*, and *jumping*; *stop* in *nonstop*, *stopping*, and *stopper*; *sick* in *sickest*, *sickly*, and *sickening*.

Butterfly is a base word because we cannot divide it into *butter* and *fly* and still maintain the meaning of *butterfly*. We can, however, add a suffix to *butterfly*. We might refer to several *butterflies*. In this example, the *-es* ending is not part of the base word. The purpose of *-es* is to indicate that there is more than one *butterfly*. Likewise, we cannot take letters away from base words and still preserve their meaning. For example, if we find a "little word," such as *wag*, in a "big word," such as *wagon*, we cannot say that *wag* is the base word for *wagon*. *Wagon* is the base word, as it conveys the meaning. *Wag* is an English word, to be sure, but it conveys a totally different meaning from that of *wagon*.

Five Best Practices for Teaching Prefixes and Suffixes

Third through fifth graders who understand how prefixes and suffixes affect word meaning are better comprehenders than children who do not understand affixes (Carlisle, 2000). In using the following five best practices, you will effectively teach children how to recognize, read, and write words with prefixes and suffixes.

1.   Teach readers how to peel away affixes to reveal familiar base words. Sometimes readers are confused by words with prefixes or suffixes. Analyzing words into prefixes, suffixes, and base words gives readers a way to read new long words (Alverman & Phelps, 1998). Peeling prefixes and suffixes away from long words is helpful because this may reveal base words that are already part of readers' fluent reading vocabulary. We will use the word *unfriendly* as an illustration. Show readers how to:

1. **Look for a prefix.**   Ask, "Do I see a prefix I know?" If so, peel it off: Peeling *un-* away from *unfriendly* (*unfriendly – un = friendly*) reveals *friendly*.
2. **Look for a suffix.**   Ask, "Do I see a suffix I know?" If so, peel it off, too. Peeling *-ly* away from *friendly* (*friendly - ly = friend*) reveals the base word *friend*.
3. **Look at the base word.**   Ask, "Do I see a word I can read?" If so, "What does it mean?"

2.   Teach inflectional suffixes (-s/es, -ed, -ing, -er, -est, -ly) in the first and second grades.   Though words with affixes do not make up the major portion of text in the storybooks for younger children (Ives, Bursuk, & Ives, 1979), it is wise to begin to explore meaningful multiletter chunks early, and suffixes are a better investment in learning than are prefixes (Durkin, 1993). Authors who write for young readers frequently use words that end with *-s/es, -ing,* and *-ed,* which makes these suffixes extremely important (Templeton, 1991). The comparative suffixes *-er* and *-est* are useful because they are important for understanding comparisons such as *quick, quicker,* and *quickest* or *large, larger,* and *largest.*

3.   Teach derivational suffixes in the third grade and above.   By the third and fourth grades children have enough reading and writing experience to begin to understand and use suffixes like *-able* and *-ous* (Henderson, 1990; Richek, Caldwell, Jennings, & Lerner, 2001). Generally speaking, derivational suffixes present greater challenges than more frequent endings that do not change the grammatical function of words. For this reason, endings like the *-ous* in *furious,* and the *-ment* in *judgment* are more easily learned when readers are in the upper grades.

4.   Give children practice reading and writing many different words with the same prefixes and suffixes.   As children's reading ability increases, you can expect their knowledge of multiletter chunks to expand as well (Gibson & Guinet, 1971; Invernizzi, 1992; Santa, 1976–1977). In reading and writing words with the same prefixes and suffixes, such as the *re-* and *-ing* in *replaying, reloading, retelling,* and *rerunning*, children learn how these affixes contribute to word meaning. Prefixes and suffixes are significant features of syntax, and therefore contribute to the strength of syntactic cues. This is especially true for the inflectional endings (Heilman, Blair, & Rupley, 2002). When children read and write in your classroom, take naturally occurring opportunities to ask them to find base words with affixes and to explain in their own words how the affixes affect word meaning.

   5.   If children *do not* know the meaning of base words or cannot already read base words, teach the base words first and then teach the prefixes and suffixes.   Children need to know the meaning of the base words and need to be able to read the base words to which the affixes are added. Once children understand base word meaning and recognize base words in text, then it is appropriate to teach them how affixes affect base word meaning.

Greek and Latin Roots

Greek and Latin roots are word parts we borrowed from these two languages. When the scholars, philosophers, and authors of the Renaissance became interested in writing in their own language, English, they borrowed liberally from ancient Greek and Latin (Ayers, 1980). Just as the great thinkers and writers of the Renaissance used Greek and Latin words to coin lots of new words, so too do we continue this tradition today. When we ventured into space in the middle of the 20th century, a new word was needed for space explorers. Rather than devising a whole new word from scratch, the term *astronaut* was coined by combining the Greek root *astro*, meaning *star*, with *naut*, meaning *sailor*. Considering the Greek origin, modern-day *astronauts* are *star sailors*, a term that suggests all sorts of engaging images.

   Words that share the same Greek or Latin roots, such as the *aud* (meaning to hear) in *auditory*, *audible*, and *audience*, form meaning families (Henderson, 1990; Templeton, 1991). By organizing words into meaning families, readers have a platform for figuring out the meaning of unfamiliar words with the same Greek or Latin root. For example, *aqua* (of Latin origin) means *water*, and therefore words with *aqua* also have something to do with *water*, as in *aquarium*, *aquatic*, *aqueduct*, and *aquaplane*. Likewise, *magni* (from Latin) means *great* or *large*. Consequently, *magnify*, *magnificent*, *magnanimous*, and *magnitude* all pertain to conditions in which an object or action is great or large. From a practical standpoint, you can expect readers who recognize and appreciate Greek and Latin roots to learn a great many technical terms with relative ease, and to do so with less guidance from you than their classmates who do not understand the contribution Greek and Latin roots make to English words.

   By and large, readers in middle school and above learn how Greek and Latin roots affect English word construction and meaning. However, when social studies, science, and mathematics terms contain Greek and Latin roots, or when some of the words in children's reading material are built of frequently occurring Greek and Latin roots, pointing out these roots may help fourth and fifth graders gain more in-depth understandings of, and appreciation for, word meaning. The point, then, is to include in your balanced reading program often-used Greek and Latin roots that will expand children's fluent reading vocabulary. Look in appendix D for common Greek and Latin roots, their meanings, and examples of words that contain the roots.

Readers are not likely to figure out the meaning of borrowed word parts from normal reading experiences. In part, this is because Greek and Latin roots are semi-hidden in words, and in part each English word that includes them has a slightly different meaning. *Magni-*, for example, in buried in *magnify*. Readers must look for *magni-* to find it in *magnify* and *magnificent*. *Aquarium* and *aquaplane* both pertain to *water*, but the meaning of the individual words is quite different. Consequently, to develop the ability to strategically use Greek and Latin roots, readers need explicit explanations of them and modeling of how to use them to unlock word meaning, as well as many opportunities to read and write words with them.

Compound Words

Compound words are formed when two words—for example, *finger* and *print*—are glued together to create a third word—in this case, *fingerprint*. Compounds differ depending on how far afield meaning wanders from the definitions of the individual words that are put together (Miller & McKenna, 1989). In the case of *fingerprint*, the general definition of each word is unchanged. A second sort of compound is made of words whose meanings are somewhat different than that of the combined form, such as *basketball, driveway, skyscraper,* and *spotlight.* In a third category, the meaning of the compound has practically nothing to do with the meaning of the individual words. Examples include *butterfly, fireworks, dragonfly, hardware, turtleneck,* and *peppermint.* Knowing the words that make up this sort of compound provides precious little insight into the meaning of the compound words themselves.

The readers whom we teach find compound words to be relatively easy to learn. Perhaps this is because compounds are made of two whole words, and hence are not overly challenging to identify. When the words that make up compounds are already in children's fluent reading vocabularies, pronunciation is merely a question of saying the words together. As for the meaning of compounds, we find that readers are intrigued by the changes in meaning that occur when words are glued together. First graders enjoy finding words that are glued together in compounds. Older readers, on the other hand, have had so many rich experiences with print that the compounds they see in everyday reading usually pose no challenge whatsoever.

Contractions

Contractions are formed when one or more letters (and sounds) are deleted from words. Missing letters are replaced by an apostrophe, which is a visual clue telling readers that a word is abbreviated, as in *hasn't, he's, she'll,* and *let's.* Words mean exactly the same thing whether they are written as a contraction or individually. First graders meet contractions in everyday reading material, so it is important that these readers learn to recognize the contractions they see in storybooks.

All children encounter contractions in reading and use them in writing, so teaching contractions is a good large group activity. We use a set of magnetic letters and a magnetic apostrophe to illustrate how contractions are formed. We ask first and second graders to use magnetic letters to change words like *she* and *will* into *she'll*, as well as to reverse the process by changing contractions (*she'll*) into two words (*she* and *will*). We also write pairs of sentences on the board. In the first sentence, we underline two words that can be combined to form a contraction. In the second sentence, we leave a blank where the contraction should be:

1. The dog <u>did not</u> find the bone.
2. The dog _____ find the bone.

Children then read the first sentence, form a contraction from the two underlined words (*did* and *not*), and write the contraction (*didn't*) in the blank in the second sentence. Everyone then reads both sentences together in chorus while we sweep our hands under the words as they are read.

Syllables

The *syllable* is the basic unit of pronunciation. Each syllable has one vowel sound, so the number of syllables in a word equals the number of vowels heard. Try saying *lilac*. How many vowels do you hear? /Li/ – /lac/ has two vowel sounds and hence two syllables. Now try *table*. When you pronounce the last syllable, *ble*, you do not notice a distinct vowel. You hear instead a vowel-like sound—/bul/. So when we divide words into syllables, we listen for vowel and vowel-like sounds. One vowel or vowel-like sound equals one syllable.

Readers can identify the syllables in unfamiliar written words by counting the vowel letter-sound patterns. Just as a spoken word has as many syllables as vowel sounds, so too is a written word divided into as many syllables as vowel letter-sound patterns. Words with one vowel pattern have one syllable—the *CVC* short vowel pattern in *got*; *CV* in *go*; *VV* in *goat*; *VCe* in *gave*. Words with two vowel patterns have two syllables—*ba - con* and *be - gin* each with a *CV* and *CVC* pattern, for example. Those with three vowel patterns have three syllables (*in - ter - nal*), four patterns have four syllables (*in - ter - nal - ize*) and so on.

Five Syllable Patterns

When we say words aloud, it is sometimes hard to decide where one syllable ends and another begins. And when consulting the dictionary, we find occasionally that syllable division does not reflect pronunciation. Our goal is to help children read new long words by dividing them into pronounceable syllables, not to have readers memorize dictionary-style syllabication. Syllable patterns are guidelines for dividing words into pronounceable multiletter chunks, although with exceptions, of course. The following five syllable patterns and clues to syllable division are intended to help you, the teacher, organize and focus instruction.

1. Open syllable (*CV*).   An open syllable ends in a vowel that generally represents a long sound. You can easily recognize the open syllable because it is the *CV* long vowel pattern. For example, the one-syllable word *go* is an example of the *CV* long vowel pattern. *Table,* a two-syllable word, begins with a *CV* long vowel pattern (*ta - ble*), as does *motor* (*mo - tor*), *major* (*ma - jor*), and *bugle* (*bu - gle*).

Clue to syllable division: When there is a single consonant between two vowels, as in *favor,* divide the word right after the first vowel. The second consonant frequently begins the second syllable, as in *fa - vor, be - gan,* and *si - lent.* Other examples of a single consonant between two vowels are *lo - cal, fe - ver,* and *si - lo.* The *Vr* vowel pattern is a logical exception to this syllable division pattern because the vowel is not separated from the *r* in the *Vr* pattern (*car - ol,* not *ca - rol; mer - it,* not *me - rit;* and *chor - us,* not *cho - rus*). There are other exceptions, so advise readers to first try the long vowel sound and, if that does not work, to next try the short sound.

2. Closed syllable (*CVC*).   A closed syllable ends in a consonant, and the vowel typically represents a short sound. The closed syllable includes the *CVC* short vowel pattern, as in the one-syllable words *cat* and *chin.* Examples of words with closed syllables include *button* (*but - ton*), *pencil* (*pen - cil*), and *cactus* (*cac - tus*).

Clue to syllable division: If there are two consonants between two vowels, as in the words *rabbit* and *napkin,* the syllable usually divides between the consonants (*rab - bit* and *nap - kin*). When words have double consonants, divide the syllable between the two like consonants (*pup - pet* and *rab - bit*). Generally speaking, advise readers to avoid dividing between the letters of a digraph (*fash - ion*) and a consonant cluster (*se - cret*).

3. Prefix and suffix syllables.   In general, prefixes and suffixes are separate syllables, with the exception of *-s,* which does not have a vowel sound and hence cannot be a syllable, and *- ed* when pronounced as /t/, as in *jumped.* In examining the prefixes in Table 6–1 you will notice that a few have more than one vowel sound, and hence more than one syllable, as the *semi -* in *semisweet* (*sem - i*). Readers who already recognize these multisyllable prefixes will automatically know how to pronounce them, so the fact that a few prefixes represent two syllables should not deter readers from figuring out the pronunciation of these prefixes in long words.

Clue to syllable division: Divide the syllable after the prefix and before the suffix as in *non - stop - able, un - help - ful,* and *re - fill - able.*

4. Consonant-le (*Cle*) syllable.   When a word ends in a *consonant + le* (*Cle*), the *Cle* usually forms a syllable, as in *table* (*ta - ble*), *title* (*ti - tle*), and *sprinkle* (*sprin - kle*).

Clue to syllable division: In words that end in *le* preceded by a consonant—*ble, cle, dle, fle, gle, kle, ple, sle,* and *zle*—the consonant usually begins the syllable. Examples include *fum - ble, cy - cle, can - dle, ri - fle, bea - gle, wrin - kle, dim - ple, has - sle, ti - tle,* and *driz - zle. Ble* is pronounced as /bul/, *cle* as /cul/, *dle* as /dul/, *fle* as /ful/, *gle* as /gul/, *kle* as /kul/, *ple* as /pul/, *sle* as /sul/, *tle* as /tul/, and *zle* as /zul/.

5. Compound word syllables.   Compounds are divided between the two words, for instance *pop - corn, snow - man,* and *cow - boy.*

Clue to syllable division: Divide compounds between the two words.

Looking at the five syllable patterns, we see that the closed syllable explains why we double the last consonant when adding suffixes to words ending with a *CVC* short vowel pattern like *hop* and *sit*. By doubling the last consonant in a *CVC* short vowel pattern, we spell *hopped* and *pinned*, thereby keeping the vowel in its proper pattern. When the final consonant is not doubled, this indicates a long vowel letter-sound pattern, as in *hoped* and *pined*. It takes a lot of reading and writing experience for children to learn when to double (or not to double) the last consonant. Anticipate spending extra time helping children edit their writing and, perhaps, form a flexible skill group to give special practice to those who need it.

Accent Patterns

The syllables in long words are given different stress. *Accent,* the stress given to syllables, is very important, for it affects vowel pronunciation. There are three levels of stress: primary, secondary, and reduced (or unaccented). For simplicity, we will call the syllable with the most stress the primary accent. The vowels in accented syllables tend to follow the pronunciation we would expect from their placement in letter-sound patterns. Most vowels in unaccented syllables have a soft, or short, sound. We will therefore focus on the accented syllable and will put a (') after the syllable to indicate primary stress.

When we shift the primary accent, we also shift pronunciation. Try saying these words by placing the primary accent on the first or second syllable, as indicated: *con'- tent* and *con - tent'; ob'- ject* and *ob - ject'; con'- vict* and *con - vict'*. In these examples, shifting the primary accent from the first to the last syllable changes word meaning. Reread *con'- tent, ob'- ject,* and *con'- vict*. What do you notice about these words? If you conclude that they are nouns, you are right. The primary accent tends to fall on the first syllable of a noun. Here are five guidelines to indicate where to place the primary accent:

1. All one-syllable words are accented syllables.
2. The primary accent most often falls on the first syllable of a two-syllable word (*ma'- ple* and *sal'- ad*), unless the last syllable includes two vowels (*con - ceal'* and *ap - proach'*) and then that syllable is stressed.
3. Prefixes and suffixes are ordinarily not accented. The base word receives the primary accent, as in *name'- less* and *ex - chang'- ing*.
4. The primary accent usually falls on the first word of compounds, such as *snow'- man* and *base'- ball*.
5. When a word has two like consonants, the primary accent generally falls on the syllable that closes with the first letter, as in *rab'- bit* and *ham'- mer*.

Two additional tips help with certain spellings: First, *Cle* (consonant-le) syllables are generally not accented, as in *tram'- ple* and *tur'- tle*. And second, syllables ending in *ck* are often accented, such as *buck'- et* and *nick'- el*. And when teaching readers about the manner in which dictionaries represent syllables and pronunciation, point out that the way we divide words in writing does not always correspond to the way we group sounds together when speaking. The boldface type indicates how we divide a word when writing; the type in parentheses shows how we pronounce words when speaking. It is the type in parentheses that shows where to place the accent.

Three Best Practices for Teaching Syllables

1. Use clue words to illustrate syllable patterns. Clue words illustrate syllable patterns and help readers remember how to pronounce the five syllables types. Examples of clue words include:

1. Open syllable clue words (*CV*): *go*; *he*.
2. Closed syllable clue words (*CVC*): napkin (*nap* - *kin*); rabbit (*rab* - *bit*).
3. Prefix and suffix syllable clue words: replayed (*re* - play - *ed*); unlikely (*un* - like - *ly*).
4. Consonant-le (*Cle*) syllable clue words: table (*ta* - *ble*); maple (*ma* - *ple*).
5. Compound word syllable clue words: cowboy (*cow* - *boy*); popcorn (*pop* - *corn*).

2. Teach the syllables and accent patterns only after readers have a good understanding of phonics letter-sound patterns. Because syllables are multiletter chunks that include letter-sound patterns, readers first need to know how letter-sound patterns, particularly vowel patterns, represent sound (Burns, Roe, & Ross, 1999). Combining a knowledge of letter-sound patterns with an understanding of syllable patterns helps readers decide which letters form syllables and which do not.

3. Give readers opportunities to apply their syllable knowledge when reading and writing. Asking children to engage in activities that are far removed from real reading and writing, such as memorizing lists of affixes (Lapp & Flood, 1992), syllable patterns, or accent patterns is pointless because readers are unlikely to use the memorized lists.

After children have had a great deal of practice reading and writing long words, they automatically apply syllable and accent patterns. In fact, as an expert reader you can read, with the proper accent, nonsense words that conform to English spelling, even though you may not be able to "say" the rules. To prove this, read and divide into syllables these two nonsense words: *quimlar* and *plygus.* Did you divide them into the syllables of *quim - lar* and *ply - gus*? And did you pronounce them with the accent on the first syllable—*quim'- lar* and *ply'- gus*? If so, you are doing what other good readers do, using your in-depth knowledge of our writing system, including syllable and accent patterns, to read and pronounce new words.

Twenty-two Easy and Effective Activities for Teaching the Multiletter Chunks in Word Structure

The following 22 activities help readers learn and use the multiletter chunks in word structure. The more readers know about the multiletter chunks in word structure, the more effective and efficient they will be at reading and spelling new words, and the closer they will move toward the last stage of word fluency—automatic recognition of all the words they read in everyday text. Select the activities that will be most beneficial for the children whom you teach, and adapt activities to suit your own special classroom environment and teaching style.

Fold-Over Contractions

This easy activity graphically demonstrates how we form contractions. It is manipulative and appropriate for working with children in large or small groups. Fold-over contractions look like accordions with deleted letters simply folded out of sight and replaced by a piece of masking tape with an apostrophe on it. The tape holds the fold-over contraction in place, as shown in Figure 6–5.

Things You'll Need: Construction paper strips about 2 inches wide and 6 inches long; markers; masking tape.

Directions: Distribute a paper strip and a small piece of masking tape to each child. Children decide on the contraction that they wish to make or follow your lead in making the contraction you designate. Children count the letters in the two separate words and fold their paper strips accordion style to make as many boxes as there are letters in the two words. For example, in turning *are not* into a fold-over contraction, children would make six boxes on the paper strip. Children write the two words one after the other, putting one letter in each box. In this example, children write six letters: *a, r, e, n, o, t.* Children write an apostrophe on the small piece of masking tape. Turn the accordion into a contraction by folding the square with the letter to be deleted (*o*) under the square with the preceding letter on it (*n*), and putting the masking tape apostrophe at the top to hold the contraction together, thus forming *aren't.* Encourage children to describe in their own words the idea behind missing letters, as well as the purpose and placement of the apostrophe.

Figure 6–5 Fold-over contractions is a hands-on activity in which children fold deleted letters in contractions out of sight and replace them with an apostrophe.

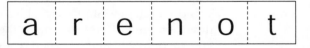

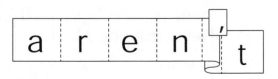

Create Your Own Compounds

In this small or large group activity, first through third graders put everyday words together to create their own unique compounds.

Things You'll Need: Pencils; crayons or colored markers.

Directions: Readers think of two words they use every day, and then put those words together to make a brand-new compound word. Have children illustrate their own compound words, as in Figure 6–6.

Prefix Binders

Children collect words with the prefixes they are learning, put the words in binders, and then use the words as references when writing and participating in other classroom activities.

Things You'll Need: Each child needs a binder with tabs that have prefixes on them; notebook paper for the binder.

Directions: Children write one prefix on each tab, and put the tabs in the binder to separate pages with different prefixes. Children then write one prefix at the top of each page of notebook paper followed by words to which the prefix is added. For instance, one page may have the prefix *un-* at the top, and words like *unhappy*, *unkind*, and *unplugged* underneath. Ask readers to be on the look out for words with prefixes in everyday reading, and to add these words to their prefix binder. Use the prefixes and base words as a ready resource for other word study activities.

Affix Graffiti

Here's a quick and easy opportunity for children to spontaneously express themselves while using prefixes and suffixes. This activity is appropriate for end-of-year second graders and above.

Things You'll Need: A large piece of newsprint; colorful markers.

Directions: Fasten a large piece of newsprint to a bulletin board or put it on the floor. Write one or two affixes at the top of the paper. Over the course of several days, children write words on the newsprint that contain one or more of the affixes. Children may write in any color marker, and may write words in any script, so long as the words are legible. At the end of several days, ask the whole class to read the words in chorus and to find graffiti words with certain affixes. Add some of the words to the word wall, or, if children are keeping personal binders for words with prefixes, add some of the words to the binders.

TooThCoat

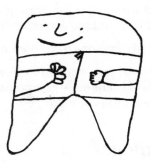

A tooth coat is a coat for your teeth

Figure 6–6 Coining new compounds gives children opportunities to creatively use their knowledge of word meaning and to write definitions for the unusual compounds they create.

Prefix-Base Word Chalkboard Sort

This activity, which allows children to move around as they compare base words with prefixes, is appropriate for second through fifth graders.

Things You'll Need: Two, three, or four cards with prefixes; cards with base words only; masking tape loops.

Directions: Tape on the board two, three, or four cards with prefixes the children are learning (such as *un-*, *re-*, and *dis-*). Discuss how the prefixes contribute to word meaning. Give each child one or more base word cards, each with a masking tape loop on the back. Children read the base words, find prefixes on the board to which their word might be added, and then tape the base words underneath the prefixes, thereby creating columns of words, as shown in Figure 6–7. Children then analyze the chalkboard lists to answer the questions: Does every combination make a real word? Are there base words that might be combined with more than one prefix? Rearrange cards, when appropriate. Give children blank cards; ask

Figure 6–7 In this sorting activity, readers pay attention to prefixes and base words, talk about how prefixes affect word meaning, and cross-check for accuracy and meaning.

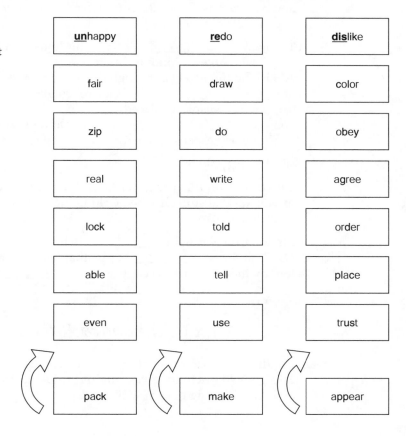

them to write their own base words on the cards and to add them to the
chalkboard lists.

Modified Cloze Sentences (Use for Prefixes or Suffixes)

In this activity, readers use context and their knowledge of word structure to fill in
the missing words in sentences. This activity is appropriate for all grades, and suitable for readers working in small groups or in centers.

Things You'll Need: Modified cloze sentences in one of two formats: (a) sentences
in which deleted words are replaced by a blank with three base word-affix
choices underneath, or (b) sentences in which the affix is deleted from base
words and replaced by a blank.

A. *Base Word-Affix Choices*

Directions: In completing these cloze sentences, readers consider sentence context
and base words with different prefixes or suffixes when selecting the right word
to complete the sentence.

The man _____ his house bright red.
        (painted, painting, painter)
After John threw a ball through the window, Mrs. Jones had to
_____ the broken glass.
    (replace, displace, placed)
Tom _____ the door and peeked into the room.
    (opening, opens, opened)

B. *Missing Affixes*

Directions: Children use syntactic and semantic cues along with their knowledge
of prefixes and suffixes when writing the affix before or after the incomplete
word in the blank.

Mr. Johnson was work _____ in his garden.
Ms. Smith was _____ happy that his favorite team lost.
Johnny thought the blue car was fast _____ than the red car.

Affix Chalkboard Race

Children write as many affixed words as possible within a relatively short time.
This gamelike activity gives children valuable practice thinking of affixed words
and remembering how to spell them.

Things You'll Need: Nothing special.

Directions: Have children line up in two teams. As the children on each team look on, write on the board a base word that is already in children's fluent reading vocabulary. Alternating teams, ask a child to go to the board and add as many affixes as possible to the base word within a specified amount of time, say 30 seconds or so. Depending on children's needs, you may want to ask them to add only prefixes or only suffixes. Every correct answer earns one point. Writing must be legible for the team to earn a point. The team with the most points wins.

 Affix Hunts

Readers scour magazines and newspapers in search of words with the prefixes and suffixes they are learning in your classroom. Hunting for affixes is a good small group or center activity that is appropriate for children from late second through fifth grade.

Things You'll Need: Print that is appropriate for children's reading level, including a variety of magazines, coupons, and newspapers; a highlighter for each child.

Directions: Give children a variety of age-appropriate print, such as old magazines, coupons, and newspapers. Children use a highlighter to flag words with the prefixes or suffixes you specify. Write the words on the board; use them when making affix wall charts.

 Wall Charts (Use for Prefixes, Suffixes, and Words With Greek and Latin Roots)

In making large wall charts, readers think about words that include the multi-letter chunks they are learning in your classroom, read the words, and then refer to them when participating in many different classroom reading and writing activities.

Things You'll Need: A large piece of newsprint for each wall chart. Or if you make a word wall, lots of cards with words spelled with affixes or words that include Greek and Latin roots.

Directions: Invite readers to find words with affixes in the books they read every day, and on signs and posters in the hallways of your school. Make large wall charts that consist of lists of words with prefixes, suffixes, or Greek and Latin roots. Count the number of words in which the same affix or Greek or Latin root occurs. Make a bar graph showing the frequency of occurrence, and talk about how affixes or Greek or Latin roots contribute to word meaning.

Complimenting Classmates (Use for Suffixes)

Children use their knowledge of suffixes to write compliments for their classmates.

Things You'll Need: One piece of oak tag cut in the shape of a shield for every child in your class; a list of everyone in the class (one list per child) with a line beside each name; several thesauruses.

Directions: Talk about how adjectives describe nouns, like the compliments *cheerful* and *artistic*. Discuss also how suffixes change a noun (*friend*) or a verb (*imagine*) into an adjective (*friendly* or *imaginative*), and how *-er* and *-est* show comparative relationships, such as *kind, kinder,* and *kindest*. Give a class list to each child, and ask the children to think of one compliment—a positive character trait—for each of their classmates. Ask the children to write the compliment on the line beside each child's name. When writing, children cannot (a) use worn-out adjectives or (b) use the same compliment twice. For example, if a child uses *imaginative* to describe one classmate, the child cannot use that same word to compliment another classmate. Have children use the thesaurus to find synonyms. After each child has written one compliment next to the name of each of their classmates on the class list you provided, give each child an oak tag shield. Each child then writes his/her name on the shield. Using the list of classmates and compliments the children already have filled out, the children refer to their list and write a compliment *in pencil* on each individual child's shield. When finished, a shield will have as many compliments as there are children in your class. When everyone has contributed, have the person to whom the shield belongs trace over the penciled compliments in ink. Any mistakes children accidentally make when writing the original compliments are easily erased and so the finished shields are smudge-free and error-free. Laminate shields and put them on the bulletin board. Fourth graders made the shield in Figure 6–8.

Base Word-Suffix Chart

Children working together in groups combine base words with suffixes to create a chart that shows the same base words with many different suffixes.

Things You'll Need: Each cooperative group needs the following: a large piece of oak tag; a ruler; a dictionary; a pencil; a set of directions; a large piece of plain paper; colorful markers.

Directions: Make a base word-suffix chart ahead of time. Show it to the children and leave it on display as a model. Distribute to each group a set of directions, a large piece of oak tag, a ruler, a colored marker, and a dictionary. Directions consist of two pages: One page is a list of 20 words and 8 suffixes, as shown in

Figure 6–8 Making shields to compliment classmates gives readers opportunities to better understand adjectives and to consider how suffixes affect word meaning.

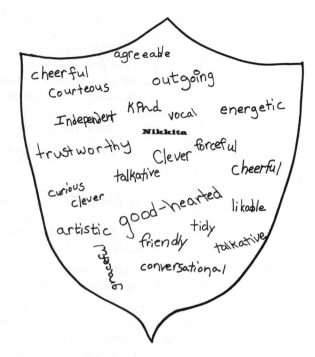

TABLE 6–3	*Sample Base Words and Suffixes for the Base Word-Suffix Chart*

Base Words				Suffixes	
act	calm	drive	last	-ed	-ing
blame	cheer	elect	like	-er	-ive
bold	color	happy	play	-est	-ly
bubble	cool	help	pass	-ful	-s/es
burn	create	jump	sick		

Table 6–3. The second page explains the following steps for developing a chart showing the same base words with many different suffixes:

1. Use a ruler to make a chart with 21 rows and 9 columns.
2. Color in the first box. Begin next to the colored box. Write one suffix in each box at the top of each column. When finished you should have written: *-ed, -er, -est, -ful, -ing, -ive, -ly,* and *-s/es.*
3. Write one of the words in the first box in every row. Write the 20 words in alphabetical order. Begin writing words in the row under the colored box.

4. Write base word-suffix combination in the rows. BEFORE writing the base word-suffix combinations, check in the *dictionary* to be sure that you are writing REAL words.
5. Leave spaces empty when you cannot make a real word with the base word-suffix combination. Use a colored marker to color in each empty space.
6. Sign the names of everyone in your group on the back of the chart when it is finished.
7. Share your chart with the class.

Table 6–4 shows a base word-suffix chart grid completed by a group of fourth graders.

Prefix and Suffix Cartoons

Children create their own cartoons using dramatic illustrations, dialogue balloons, and words with the prefixes and suffixes they are learning in your classroom.

Things You'll Need: Large pieces of construction paper or oak tag; colored markers for decorating the final drafts.

Directions: Have children divide a large piece of oak tag into boxes. Each box will be used for one scene in the cartoons children are to write. After deciding on a story line, children divide the story into four scenes, create fictional characters, write dialogue that uses a smattering of designated prefixes and suffixes, and illustrate their work, as shown in the cartoon in Figure 6–9. Give writers opportunities to share their cartoons with their classmates. And when children share their cartoons, have them point out base words with affixes. Talk about how the affixes affect word meaning and, if your classroom curriculum is currently focusing on derivational suffixes, discuss how these suffixes sometimes change a word's grammatical function.

Suffix Shoebox Words

In this gamelike activity, two teams draw suffix cards out of a shoebox, select a base word from a chalkboard list, and then write the base word-suffix combination. In so doing, children get practice reading and writing affixed words and you, the teacher, have an opportunity to target nettlesome base word-suffix combinations, such as correctly spelling *CVC* and *VCe* words when adding suffixes.

Things You'll Need: Cards with suffixes the children are learning; a shoebox.

Directions: Put several suffix cards a shoebox, such as *-ed, -ing, -ly, -s/es, -er, -est,* and *-ly.* Write several base words on the board, like *talk, hop, slow, hope, try, jump, please, short, fast, large, drive, simple, happy,* and so forth. Divide the class (or group) into two teams. Alternating from team to team, a child draws a suffix card from the shoebox, goes to the board, selects one of the base words (*hop,* for

TABLE 6–4 Completed Base Word-Suffix Chart

	-ed	-er	-est	-ful	-ing	-ive	-ly	-s/es
act	acted				acting	active		acts
blame	blamed				blaming			blames
bold	bolded	bolder	boldest				boldly	
bubble	bubbled	bubbler			bubbling		bubbly	bubbles
burn	burned	burner			burning			burns
calm	calmed	calmer	calmest		calming		calmly	calms
cheer	cheered			cheerful	cheering			cheers
color	colored			colorful	coloring			colors
cool	cooled	cooler	coolest		cooling			cools
create	created				creating	creative		creates
drive		driver			driving			drives
elect	elected				electing	elective		elects
happy		happier	happiest				happily	
help	helped	helper		helpful	helping			helps
jump	jumped	jumper			jumping			jumps
last	lasted				lasting			lasts
like	liked				liking			likes
pass	passed				passing	passive		passes
play	played	player		playful	playing			plays
sick		sicker	sickest				sickly	

Figure 6–9 Writing cartoons is a natural opportunity to use suffixes and to explore the contribution that suffixes make to word and passage meaning.

example), writes the word, and adds the suffix (*hopping*). If the base word-suffix combination is a meaningful, correctly spelled word, the team gets a point, and that base word is erased. Continue playing until all the words are erased. Take the opportunity to discuss examples of base word-suffix combinations that the children are learning, such as when and when not to double the final consonant or change the *y* to *i* before adding a suffix to a base word.

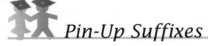

Pin-Up Suffixes

This activity can be used for practice with a suffix children are learning, and is appropriate for large and small groups of first graders and beginning-of-the-year second graders.

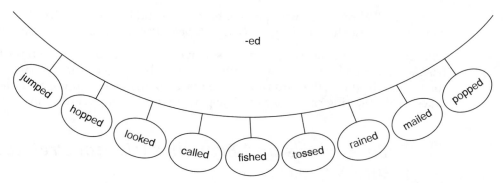

Figure 6–10 In this example, children pin up words to which the suffix *-ed* can be added. Later, words are taken down and children write them on the board with the suffix.

Things You'll Need: One lightweight rope several yards long; construction paper cut into either rectangles or objects that are consistent with the theme of a book children are reading; clothespins; a sack or a shoebox; 3-inch-by-5-inch cards with base words. Put the 3-inch-by-5-inch word cards in the sack or shoebox.

Directions: Write a suffix on the board, such as *-ed,* and a few base words, perhaps *jump, hop, help,* and *hope.* Demonstrate how to add *-ed* to the base words to make *jumped, hopped, helped,* and *hoped.* Explain that there are lots of words in the sack (or the shoebox), but that *-ed* (or any other suffix the children are learning) cannot be added to every one of them. Children pick a word from the shoebox or sack, and then decide if *-ed* can be added to it. If so, children write the word with the *-ed* suffix on a piece of construction paper (or a shape consistent with a theme in a book children are reading), and use a clothespin to put the word on the line, as shown in Figure 6–10. Words that cannot have an *-ed* added to the end stay in the shoebox or sack. After all the words with *-ed* are pinned up, read them in chorus and have children practice writing them on the board. Reinforce the concept of adding suffixes to base words. In this example, you would want to reinforce the idea of doubling the final consonant when adding *-ed* to *CVC* words by asking children to write words like *hopped* and *hoped* on the board. And then you would want to talk about why the consonant (*p*) in *hop* is doubled when adding *-ed* and why the *p* is not doubled when adding *-ed* to *hope.* End by asking children to find words with doubled consonants on the pin-up clothesline.

 Flip-Up Affixes

This is another version of the memory game in which players remember which two facedown cards of 20 (or less) match. Because children must not only remember which cards make a pair, but also remember which base word and base word-affix combinations match (*tall - taller* or *happy - unhappy*), children get lots of practice looking for affixes and remember how words look when an affix is attached to the end.

Things You'll Need: Cards with pairs of base word and base word affix combinations, such as *joy - joyous, happy - happier, happy - unhappy,* and *like - dislike.*

Directions: Put cards face down in rows. Players flip up cards one at a time. If the base word card and the base word affix card match (*joy - joyous*), the player keeps the two cards. If not, the cards are flipped face down again, and the next player takes a turn flipping cards face up. The player with the most cards wins.

Base Words and Branches (Use for Prefixes and Suffixes)

This activity uses a tree to illustrate how many different words are built by adding prefixes and suffixes to the same base words. It is appropriate for third graders and above, and suitable for children working individually, in centers, or with a learning partner.

Things You'll Need: Pencils; dictionaries; copies of base words and branches; paper with several drawings of different trees as shown in Figure 6–11.

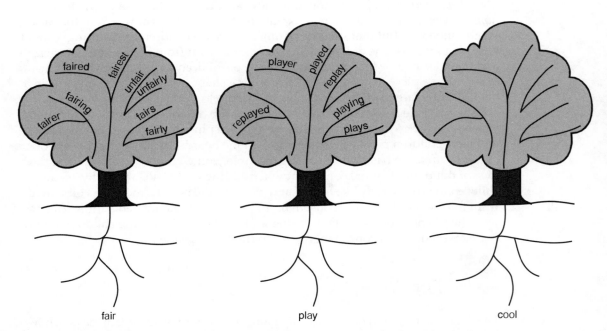

Figure 6–11   Writing words on branches that grow from the same base word helps readers develop more in-depth knowledge of the relationship among prefixes, suffixes, and base words.

Directions: Review base words, prefixes, and suffixes. Give children the base words and branches paper (see Figure 6–11). Explain that each tree shows the many different "branches" that may be created by adding affixes to a single base word. Children think about the word at the base of each tree, decide which prefixes and suffixes can be added to that base word, and then write those words on the branches. Children may consult dictionaries. Children share the base words with affixes that grew from the base word tree.

Tactile Syllables

Children actually feel syllables as they pronounce words. Tactile syllables is quick and easy, and suitable for working with children working in small groups, large groups, or individually.

Things You'll Need: Nothing special.

Directions: Children lightly touch their chins with the back of their hands. You say a word and the children repeat it. In saying a word, children will notice that their chins drop as they pronounce the vowel sounds. Each chin movement represents one syllable. Count the syllables in a word. Write the word on the board and repeat the process, noting how many syllables the children feel. Divide the written word into syllables; discuss how syllable cues help us read new long words.

Building Words With Syllables

Children combine syllables into words and cross-check to make sure that the combined syllables make real words. This activity is appropriate for children working individually, with a learning partner, or in a center.

Things You'll Need: Cards with syllables on them.

Directions: After discussing syllable patterns, ask the children to fold a sheet of paper vertically to form two columns, and to write "Real Words" at the top of one column, and "Nonsense Words" at the top of the other. Give each child or set of learning partners a few syllable cards. Children put the syllable cards together to build words, cross-check for meaning, then write the real words in the "Real Words" column and the nonsense words in the "Nonsense Words" column. When finished, discuss the words the children built. Talk about how syllables help us read new words. Discuss, too, the importance of cross-checking to be sure that the words are real, not nonsense. Table 6–5 shows an example of separate syllables, and real and nonsense words that might be built from the syllables.

TABLE 6–5 *Building Words With Syllables*	

Syllables

car	par
ty	pet
son	per
ter	bat

Real Words	Nonsense Words
party	perter
carpet	carty
person	sonter
parson	parpet
petty	perty
carpenter	batson
Carter	terson
batty	
batter	
car	
pet	
son	
Bart	

Using syllables to build words gives readers experience working with syllables and also gives readers opportunities to cross-check to identify syllable combinations that make real words.

 ## Word Roundup (Use With Prefixes, Suffixes, or Greek and Latin Roots)

Teams compete for three days to find words with the prefixes, suffixes, or Greek and Latin roots they are learning in your classroom.

Things You'll Need: Nothing special.

Directions: Create groups of four to six readers. Ask the groups to find as many words as possible in three days that include the prefixes, suffixes, or Greek and Latin roots they are learning in your classroom. Teams write the words on a sheet of paper and indicate where the words were found. Teams earn one point for each different word (or word variation) they find. At the end of the third day, teams share the words and, if appropriate, teams get a prize for finding different types of words, such as (a) the most words, (b) the most unusual word, (c) the longest word, or (d) the word with the most syllables.

 ## Coin-a-Word (Use With Common Greek or Latin Roots)

Children use common Greek and Latin roots to coin their own words. (*Astroport,* the word at the beginning of this chapter, is the invention of a fifth grader.)

Things You'll Need: Nothing special.

Directions: Children work individually or in pairs to coin words by combining Greek and Latin roots, write a definition for the coined words, and illustrate their new words. Put the coined words and illustrations on bulletin boards, along the chalk tray, or anywhere else where they are in plain view. Discuss the coined words. Children then decide in which meaning family the coined words belong. For instance, *biology, biohazard, biodegradable, biography,* and *bioenergy* all belong to the *bio-* meaning family.

 ## Creating Words (Use With Common Greek and Latin Roots)

This activity illustrates how common Greek and Latin roots are found in many English words. It is suitable for end-of-year fifth graders who are reading words with Greek and Latin roots in content area textbooks.

Things You'll Need: Oak tag sentence strips cut in half; markers; masking-tape loops; dictionaries.

Directions: Select two or three common Greek or Latin roots that usually come at the beginning of words. Write on the board several long words that begin with the Greek or Latin roots, such a *geography, biology,* and *microscope.* Talk about how common Greek and Latin roots contribute to word meaning. Discuss how *bio* means *life, geo* means *earth,* and *micro* means *small.* Explain further that children are going to "create" each word by finding other English words that include its Greek or Latin root. Write the Greek or Latin roots on sentence strips. Tape the strips fairly far apart on the board. Distribute dictionaries, blank oak tag strips, markers, and tape to small groups. Assign (or ask groups to choose) one of the Greek or Latin roots on the oak tag strips. Each group then finds words in dictionaries and context area textbooks that include the roots. Groups write the words they find on an oak tag strips, and tape the strips under the designated roots on the board, as shown in Figure 6–12. Talk about meaning families that include the same Greek or Latin roots. Conclude by inviting a volunteer from

Figure 6–12 Creating Words. In writing words with often-used Greek and Latin roots, children learn how these roots contribute to the meaning of many different words.

Words found in *Merriam-Webster's Elementary Dictionary: The Student's Source for Discovering Language,* (2000), Springfield, MA: Merriam-Webster, Inc.

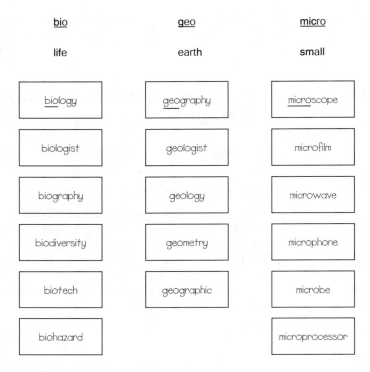

<u>bio</u>	<u>geo</u>	<u>micro</u>
life	earth	small
<u>biology</u>	<u>geography</u>	<u>microscope</u>
biologist	geologist	microfilm
biography	geology	microwave
biodiversity	geometry	microphone
biotech	geographic	microbe
biohazard		microprocessor

each group to explain how their Greek or Latin root contributes to word meaning.

 Word Webs (Use With Prefixes, Suffixes, or Common Greek and Latin Roots)

Word webs begin with a single, often-used prefix, suffix, or Greek or Latin root, and then spin off into many different miniwebs, as shown in Figure 6–13. Webs with prefixes and suffixes are appropriate for third through fifth graders, while webs with common Greek and Latin roots are best suited for fifth graders. This activity is most successful when readers work cooperatively in groups.

Things You'll Need: Dictionaries; a large piece of chart paper for each cooperative group; colored construction paper; colorful markers.

Directions: Write an often-used prefix, suffix, or Greek or Latin root in the center of the board and draw a bubble around it. Write a word with the prefix, suffix, or Greek or Latin root to the upper right; draw a bubble around it; and draw a straight line from this word to the prefix, suffix, or Greek or Latin root, as shown

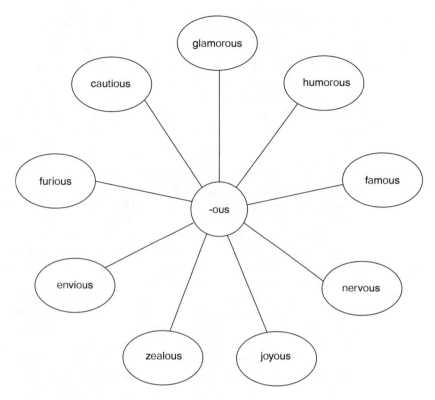

Figure 6–13   Word Web for the Suffix -ous. Creating word webs helps readers draw the conclusion that many words share the same prefix, suffix, or Greek or Latin root.

in Figure 6–13. Challenge readers to think of another word that includes the same prefix, suffix, or Greek or Latin root. Add suggested words to the web, drawing bubbles around them, and drawing a line from each word (called a web strand) to the prefix, suffix, or Greek or Latin root in the center. If children are making webs with common Greek or Latin roots, have them create miniwebs around each word by adding prefixes or suffixes. Children now are ready to work together in small groups to make their own word webs, using words found in materials they study throughout the day, as well as words they find in dictionaries, wall charts, signs, and posters. After webs are perfected to the satisfaction of group members, invite the groups to share their webs with the entire class, and to explain the connections among words, telling why and how each word is a member of the meaning family. Figure 6–13 shows a word web for the suffix *-ous.*

Insight Into Word Meaning and Pronunciation

Many English words have affixes attached to them; others are built from borrowed Greek and Latin roots; still others are short cuts—contractions—for writing words separately. The multiletter chunks in word structure give readers insight into word meaning, which explains why these multiletter groups are so important for word recognition (Nagy, Anderson, Schommer, Scott, & Stallman, 1989). On the other hand, syllables, while seldom providing readers with insight into meaning, do help readers figure out the pronunciation of long words that may be daunting to readers because of their length.

Insight into the meaning and pronunciation of long words becomes increasingly important as children move up in the elementary grades. As children move from third to fourth grade and then on to the fifth grade, they come into contact with more and more long words in content subject and leisure reading material. Many of these words are not in readers' speaking and listening vocabularies. However, when readers combine their understanding of the multiletter chunks in word structure with syntactic and semantic context cues, growth in reading vocabulary extends and expands the number of words in children's speaking and listening vocabularies. Now, at last, vocabulary learning by reading surpasses learning by speaking and listening. By the time children leave the elementary school and move on to middle school, they are learning more new words through reading and writing than through talking and listening. The power of literacy transforms children; it opens to them new ideas, new information, new intellectual horizons and new English words. It also gives them tools for lifelong learning and lifelong reading pleasure.

Though most children develop word identification strategies as they advance in school, some have difficulty strategically using our alphabetic writing system. These children have limited fluent reading vocabularies and, consequently, are often frustrated when reading and writing. Younger children who lack reading fluency cannot read age-appropriate library books on their own; the ideas and concepts in content area textbooks vex older children because the technical vocabulary is out of their reach. Children who have had a great many reading and writing opportunities and who still cannot use word identification strategies to read new words need extra help to do so. This is the topic of the chapter that follows.

REFERENCES

Alverman, D. E., & Phelps, S. F. (1998). *Content reading and literacy* (2nd ed.). Boston: Allyn & Bacon.

Ayers, D. M. (1980). *English words from Greek and Latin elements.* Tucson: University of Arizona Press.

Burns, P. C., Roe, B. D., & Ross, E. P. (1999). *Teaching Reading in Today's Elementary Schools* (7th ed.). Boston: Houghton Mifflin.

Carlisle, J. F. (2000). Awareness of the structure and meaning of morphologically complex words: Impact on reading. *Reading and Writing: An Interdisciplinary Journal, 12,* 169–190.

Durkin, D. (1993). *Teaching them to read* (6th ed.). Boston: Allyn & Bacon.

Ehri, L. C. (1991). Development of the ability to read words. In R. Barr, M. L. Kamil, P. Mosenthal, & P. D. Pearson (Eds.), *Handbook of reading research* (Vol. II, pp. 383–417). New York: Longman.

Ehri, L. C. (1998). Grapheme-phoneme knowledge is essential for learning to read words in English. In J. L. Metsala & L. C. Ehri (Eds.), *Word recognition in beginning literacy* (pp. 3–40). Mahwah, NJ: Lawrence Erlbaum.

Gentry, J. R. (1987). *Spel . . . is a four-letter word.* New York: Scholastic.

Gibson, E. J., & Guinet, L. (1971). Perception of inflections in brief visual presentations of words. *Journal of Verbal Learning and Verbal Behavior, 10,* 182–189.

Hackett, J. K., Moyer, R. H., & Adams, D. K. (1989). *Merrill Science.* Upper Saddle River, NJ: Merrill/Prentice Hall.

Harris, A. J., & Sipay, E. R. (1990). *How to increase reading ability* (9th ed.). New York: Longman.

Heilman, A. W., Blair, T. R., & Rupley, W. H. (2002). *Principles and practices of teaching reading* (10th ed.). Upper Saddle River, NJ: Merrill/Prentice Hall.

Henderson, E. H. (1990). *Teaching spelling* (2nd ed.). Boston: Houghton Mifflin.

Invernizzi, M. A. (1992). The vowel and what follows: A phonological frame of orthographic analysis. In S. Templeton & D. R. Bear (Eds.), *Development of orthographic knowledge and the foundations of literacy* (pp. 105–136). Hillsdale, NJ: Erlbaum.

Ives, J. P., Bursuk, L. Z., & Ives, S. A. (1979). *Word identification techniques.* Chicago: Rand McNally.

Lapp, D., & Flood, J. (1992). *Teaching reading to every child* (3rd ed.). New York: Macmillan.

Mahoney, D., Singson, M., & Mann, V. (2000). Reading ability and sensitivity to morphological relations. *Reading and Writing: An Interdisciplinary Journal, 12,* 191–218.

Merriam-Webster. (2000). *Merriam-Webster's Elementary Dictionary: The Student's Source for Discovering Language,* Springfield, MA: Author.

Miller, G. A. (1956). The magical number seven, plus or minus two: Some limits on our capacity for processing information. *Psychological Review, 63,* 81–97.

Miller, J. W., & McKenna, M. (1989). *Teaching reading in the elementary grades.* Scottsdale, AZ: Gorsuch Scarisbrick.

Nagy, W. E., Anderson, R. C., Schommer, M., Scott, J. A., & Stallman, A. C. (1989). Morphological families and word recognition. *Reading Research Quarterly, 24,* 262–282.

Nagy, W. E., Diakidoy, I. N., & Anderson, R. C. (1993). The acquisition of morphology: Learning the contribution of suffixes to the meaning of derivatives. *Journal of Reading Behavior, 25,* 155–170.

Nunes, T., Bryant, P., & Bindman, M. (1997). Morphological spelling strategies: Developmental stages and processes. *Developmental Psychology, 33,* 637–649.

Richek, M. A., Caldwell, J. S., Jennings, J. H., & Lerner, J. W. (2001). *Reading problems: Assessment and teaching strategies* (4th ed.). New York: Allyn & Bacon.

Santa, C. M. (1976–1977). Spelling patterns and the development of flexible word recognition strategies. *Reading Research Quarterly, 12,* 125–144.

Singson, M., Mahony, D., & Mann, V. (2000). The relation between reading ability and morphological skills: Evidence from derivational suffixes. *Reading and Writing: An Interdisciplinary Journal, 12,* 219–252.

Stuart, M., & Coltheart, M. (1988). Does reading develop in a sequence of stages? *Cognition, 30,* 139–181.

Templeton, S. (1991). *Teaching the integrated language arts.* Boston: Houghton Mifflin.

White, T. G., Power, M. A., & White, S. (1989). Morphological analysis: Implications for teaching and understanding vocabulary growth. *Reading Research Quarterly, 24,* 283–304.

White, T. G., Sowell, J., & Yanagihara, A. (1989). Teaching elementary students to use word-part clues. *The Reading Teacher, 42,* 302–308.

Wysocki, K., & Jenkins, J. R. (1987). Deriving word meanings through morphological generalization. *Reading Research Quarterly, 22,* 66–81.

CHAPTER
7

Children Who Need Extra Help

This chapter explains why some children struggle with word identification and what you can do to help them. You will learn how to give extra help to readers who over-rely on picture cues, do not effectively use the analogy and the letter-sound strategies, or who speak languages other than English at home. And you will also learn about best practices for teaching reading to children who speak English as a second language.

KEY IDEAS

➤ Some children need extra help because they do not effectively use word identification strategies to read and learn new words.

➤ Some children whose families speak languages other than English need extra help because the language spoken at home is different from the language of instruction in school and the language in which English-speaking authors write.

➤ When you give children extra help, it is important to strike a balance between (a) the knowledge and abilities children bring to reading and writing, and (b) the challenges of reading interesting and age-appropriate literature and of writing for a variety of purposes.

Perhaps you are wondering why the first illustration in this chapter—Figure 7–1—is a seesaw. As it turns out, a simple playground seesaw demonstrates a fundamental principle of physics that has a great deal of relevance to teaching and learning. Seesaws are simple levers. The purpose of levers is to make it easier to lift heavy loads, in this case the weight of playmates at either end of the seesaw. The seesaw board is the lever and the support on which the board is balanced is called the fulcrum.

The weight of the playmates in Rich's drawing in Figure 7–1 is about equal, so the effort needed to push each playmate into the air is exactly the same. Should a heavier playmate get on one end, the lighter playmate must push harder. If the heavier playmate weighs quite a bit more, the lighter playmate will not have the strength (or force) to lift the heavier one. The way to make the seesaw work is to balance the load at either end, to make the effort needed to lift each playmate equal to the weight of each child. Moving the fulcrum changes the balance point. With a new balance point, it takes less effort (force) to lift the heavier playmate (load).

Figure 7–1 A simple seesaw demonstrates a fundamental principle of physics that is relevant to supporting literacy in today's classrooms.

Just as seesaw playmates differ in weight, so do the children we teach differ in the knowledge, abilities, and strategies they bring to reading. While some children develop a full complement of word identification strategies through the normal reading and writing experiences in your classroom, others do not. Just as the success of a seesaw hinges on finding the right balance point between the force and the load, so does the success of learning and using word identification strategies hinge on finding the right balance point between the force (children's abilities) and the load (reading and writing activities). Sometimes regular classroom activities (the load) are too great for the knowledge and strategies children bring to activities (the force). Under this condition, children are in a similar position to that of a lightweight seesaw playmate who lacks the strength to lift a heavier playmate. When this happens, children need extra help.

Children who need extra help succeed when classroom activities (the load) are roughly in balance with their ability to use word identification strategies (the force). In practical terms, this means finding activities with which children are successful and then using those activities to improve achievement. In this chapter we focus on children who do not understand the alphabetic principle, lack knowledge of letter-sound patterns, are confused when prefixes and suffixes are added to familiar words, or do not effectively use word identification strategies.

Children Who Over-rely on Picture Cues

When children over-rely on picture cues, they take advantage of some, but not nearly enough, of the information available in written language. These children do not strategically use onsets, word family rimes, letter-sound patterns, or multiletter chunks in word structure. Children overlook words, focusing instead on pictures and on creating their own stories that coincide with the picture content, although not necessarily with the meaning of the words on the page.

Shandra

First-grader Shandra, whose story is shown in Figure 7–2, over-relies on picture cues. If you were to listen to Shandra read easy books with which she is familiar, you would hear something akin to fluent reading. Shandra's fluency is misleading, however, because she memorizes the text in familiar books. Shandra thinks about print, but she does not pay attention to the rimes and letter-sound patterns in words. For this reason, Shandra recognizes a mere handful of words. What's more, the words she reads with ease in familiar, memorized stories are seldom recognized when she meets them in other reading materials.

Shandra is aware of spoken words and is developing insight into rhyme. However, Shandra has not developed phonemic awareness and hence cannot segment or blend sounds. From Shandra's writing, we might infer that she understands that written language is made up of letters and that writing goes from top-to-bottom and from left-to-right on the page. Shandra also seems to be developing awareness of

Figure 7–2 Children who are glued to pictures by the end of first grade may be trying to figure out exactly which written symbols—letters, numbers, or shapes—make up words.

punctuation and is working out exactly which written symbols make up words and which do not. Even with these understandings, toward year's end, Shandra has fallen far behind her classmates.

After a year of kindergarten and most of first grade, Shandra is still at the prealphabetic stage of movement toward word fluency and the precommunicative stage of spelling. She knows how to read and write her name; can name some, but not all, of the letters; and recognizes a few words. In these respects, Shandra's print knowledge does not resemble that of a typical prealphabetic kindergartner at the beginning of the school year because she has developed some understandings as a consequence of spending nearly two years in school. However, Shandra does not understand the alphabetic principle, which is a hallmark of children at the prealphabetic stage. To make up for this lack of insight, Shandra has become very good at interpreting pictures. When she reads short books that she has not memorized, she combines picture cues with her background knowledge to construct plausible stories.

What Shandra Needs to Know to Move Toward Word Fluency: For starters, Shandra needs to become more print-focused. She needs to know how the onsets, rimes, letter-sound patterns, and multiletter chunks in word structure represent sound. She must also increase phonemic awareness and learn to cross-check, self-monitor, and self-correct to keep word identification meaning centered. The most immediate aim is to help her strategically use onsets and context cues together, and then to use onsets and the rimes in word family words to decode unfamiliar words in text. Although the ultimate goal is for Shandra to develop the ability to use all the strategies described in this book, the letter-sound and structural analysis strategies will demand (load) more than Shandra is able to successfully handle (force) at this time in her literacy development. In studying beginning sounds and word family rimes, however, Shandra will begin to gain insight into the sounds in words and move toward developing sound awareness and blending.

Teaching Rhyme and Beginning Sound Awareness: Children like Shandra who over-rely on picture cues usually have very low phonemic awareness. These children benefit from activities that first target rhyme and beginning sounds, and then quickly move on to ending sounds and middle sounds. As we learned in chapter 2, this is the typical sequence in which phonemic awareness develops. Since spoken rhymes are easier to detect than individual sounds, the load is lighter when activities help children develop sensitivity to the rhyming sounds in words and heavier when activities focus on the middle and endings sounds in words (Cardoso-Martins, Michalick, & Pollo, 2002).

Beginning sound awareness and rhyme awareness are considered to be a single phonological awareness skill (Armbruster, Lehr, & Osborn, 2001), perhaps because children usually become aware of rhymes and beginning sounds at about the same time. Not only are the beginning sounds relatively easy to identify from a phonemic awareness standpoint, but beginning letter-sounds plus the reading context also give children considerable insight into the identity of unfamiliar words. The eight suggestions for bringing rhyme into your classroom, as well as the rhyme and beginning sound awareness activities that are described in chapter 2, are beneficial for helping Shandra identify rhyme. And as you use these activities, share books with rhyming words, engage children in language play that offers them opportunities to enjoy, use and repeat rhyming language, and teach children the sounds represented by the beginning letters and rimes in words.

Teaching Shandra to Pay Attention to Print: Because of the mutually supportive relationship between awareness of the sounds in language and letter-sound knowledge, you can expect Shandra's awareness of the beginning sounds in words to improve as she learns how to use onsets and context cues together to read new words. Show children like Shandra how to read to the end of the sentence, and then to think of a word that makes sense and begins with the sound that the first letter represents. In this way, children stay focused on the meaning and at the same time have opportunities to become aware of the beginning letters and sounds in words.

Read aloud to children like Shandra. And when you read aloud, draw children's attention to print; that is, to the words, letters, and letter-sound patterns in the text. Focusing on print results in significantly better phonemic awareness and more knowledge of words and letters than focusing only on the storybook pictures (Justice & Ezell, 2002). Also call attention to print by pointing out words in your classroom that begin with the same sounds and letters; make lists of words that begin with the same sound; and ask children to find examples of words with the same beginning letter-sounds in familiar storybooks. Activities in chapter 4 that focus on beginning letter-sounds are tongue twisters, celebrate onsets and alternative shopping lists. Activities that can be modified to emphasize onsets are: word family word hunts, word family binders, word family train, rime pickup, word family chains, and sticky note word family word books. Look, too, in chapter 5 for activities that can be adapted to focus on beginning letter-sounds.

To reinforce the concept that specific written words represent specific spoken words and to encourage children to pay more attention to print, ask children like Shandra to point to each word as it is read. If you are not already sweeping your hand under words as you read them aloud, now is the time to do so. Talk about print; point out individual words in big books, poems, and familiar storybooks; make wall charts of often-used words; and ask children to arrange word cards into sentences. When asking children like Shandra to arrange words into sentences, bear in mind that (a) arranging words into sentences is easier when children match the individual words on cards with the words in a sentence you have written on an oak tag strip, (b) it is more difficult to arrange individual words into sentences that children have already dictated to you, and (c) the most difficult form of this easy activity is to give children word cards and to ask children to arrange the cards into the sentences you dictate.

Predictable books offer immediate success, in part because children easily memorize the repeated text and in part because the pictures typically tell the story. Predictable books are best used when children are just entering into reading, and, therefore, are appropriate for Shandra and children like her. With pictures highly supportive of the text and some text repeated over and over, predictable books will help children develop many critical and preliminary concepts, such as (a) reading is meaningful, (b) print is important, (c) writing goes from left-to-right and from top-to-bottom on pages, (d) white spaces separate words, and (e) there is a one-to-one match between spoken words and written words.

Children like Shandra frequently memorize predictable books, so make sure that children actually look at the words when reading. And as soon as Shandra has mastered basic book-handling skills and understands that reading is meaningful and that spoken words match written words, it is time to move beyond predictable books. Children with book-handling skills and who can match spoken words with written words benefit from lots of opportunities to combine context and beginning letter-sounds to identify and learn new words. Of course, children like Shandra also need opportunities to read and write word family words.

Activities that highlight written rime are important for children like Shandra because rime knowledge paves the way for development of the analogy strategy. To help Shandra and children like her expand their knowledge of rimes, invite them to work collaboratively with other children to make wall charts of word family words. This activity is appropriate for many children, so include children like Shandra who are glued to picture cues, as well as better readers who bring more in-depth letter-sound knowledge to reading. When the charts are complete, tape them to the chalkboard and challenge children to explain in their own words why words are included in lists and to think of other words that might be added. In so doing, children have opportunities to think critically about spelling and everyone has a chance to participate.

As Shandra tunes into the rhyme in spoken language and the rime in written words, the lessons in chapter 4 that become helpful include word family word building, rewriting familiar poems, paper plate word family words, fishing for words, word family egg words, word family chains, word family train, and word family word towers. Since Shandra already may have made sticky note books for beginning letter-sounds, making sticky note books for word family words requires less explanation and, therefore, allows for more time spent on talking about word family words, writing word family words, and reading word family sticky note books. In addition, certainly give children like Shandra ample opportunities to find rimes in the words they read in storybooks and poems, and to learn the sounds that the individual letters in rimes represent.

Children Who Do Not Effectively Use the Analogy and the Letter-Sound Strategies

Children who do not effectively use the analogy or the letter-sound strategy tend to misidentify words, get bogged down in the middle of words, blend sounds into the wrong words, and associate the wrong sounds with rimes or letter-sound patterns. These difficulties impair word identification and, of course, interfere with comprehension. You will notice that, while the fluent reading vocabulary of these children does increase over time, the pace of vocabulary growth is much slower than that of average readers. Because children's fluent reading vocabulary is limited and because children cannot effectively use the analogy and letter-sound strategies to read new words, they may bypass many of the words authors write, opting instead to reconstruct the meaning of stories from their own prior knowledge, picture cues, and perhaps a few letter and sound cues.

Relying predominantly on background knowledge, picture cues, and a few letter and sound cues works well enough when children read stories about familiar events. In fact, material that closely parallels children's life experiences is understood remarkably well, given the fact that children do not read many of the words authors write. These are the children about whom you hear teachers say, "He does not know many words in the story, but his comprehension is good." Or you hear, "Even though her reading vocabulary is weak, her comprehension is okay." Bypassing a large number of words does not work at all well when pictures do not tell the story and the reading materials do not closely parallel children's own lives. This approach fails altogether when the reading material introduces new ideas, concepts, and information. To take a closer look at children who have difficulty using analogous rimes and letter-sound patterns when reading new words, consider the following descriptions of three children who do not effectively use the analogy or the letter-sound strategies. The first child, Raymond, brings less knowledge of letter-sound patterns and less phonemic awareness to reading and writing than Melissa, the second child, and Mike, the third child.

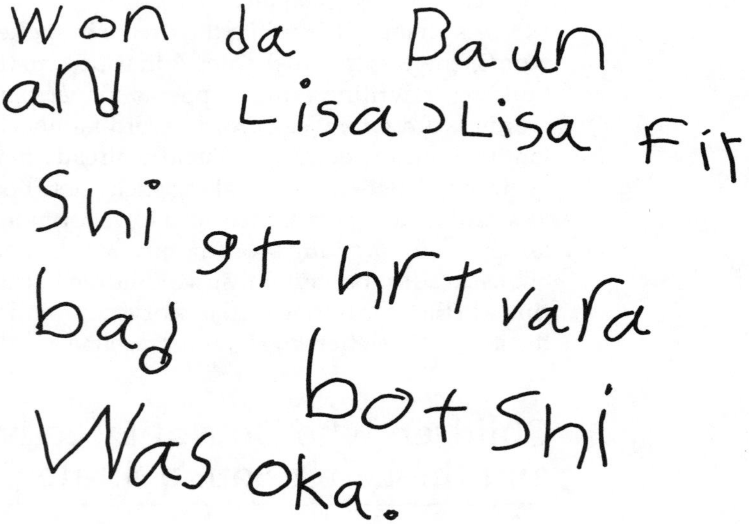

Figure 7–3 The writing of children who have underdeveloped phonemic awareness and who lack full knowledge of letter-sound patterns may include words that are copied, high-frequency words spelled conventionally, words spelled phonetically, and words in which the sounds do not match the letters.

Raymond

By the end of the second grade, Raymond's reading progress has come to a near standstill, as can be seen in Figure 7–3. His fluent reading vocabulary is growing very slowly which, in turn, has a negative affect on comprehension. When he meets an unfamiliar word while reading, Raymond looks for picture cues and/or letter-sound cues from the beginning (and sometimes ending) letters in words. We can infer from his story in Figure 7–3 that Raymond uses some knowledge of onsets and ending letters when he writes, and that he is working out how vowel letter patterns represent sounds in words. He copies words from the print in his classroom, such as *was, Lisa,* and *bad,* and he conventionally spells a few high-frequency words in his fluent vocabulary, such as *and* and *go.* Although letters and sounds are not always completely on target, some of the letters Raymond chooses are similar to the sounds in words.

Raymond's spelling includes a few words that are spelled semiphonetically (spelling that includes some, but not all, of the important sounds in words), as we see in his use of *gt* for *got* and *hrt* for *hurt.* Sometimes Raymond spells phonetically by writing letters that he thinks represent the sounds he hears in words, as in *bot* for *but, won* for *one,* and *vara* for *very.* The way he pronounces the /ot/ in /bot/ is not far from the sounds heard in /but/. This is also true for the word *very,* spelled *vara.*

Although Raymond strategically uses some letter-sound patterns when he spells, he is a long way from spelling conventionally and a long way from reading the kinds of books his second-grade classmates enjoy. Raymond is moving from the partial alphabetic stage into the alphabetic stage, as evidenced by his use of the *CVC* short vowel pattern and his attempts to represent other vowel patterns. From his writing we can infer that he has not yet developed a good working knowledge of letter-sound patterns. Raymond has not made a full transition into the use of letter-sound patterns, as is expected of a an end-of-year second grader. To develop the foundation on which the efficient and effective use of word identification strategies rests, the load and the force must be brought into balance to nurture Raymond's use of word identification strategies and, through effective use of word identification strategies, the expansion of his fluent reading vocabulary.

What Raymond Needs to Know to Move Toward Word Fluency: The most immediate aspects of phonemic awareness that children like Raymond need to develop are the abilities to identify and blend individual phonemes. You will want to develop phonemic awareness through direct instruction (chapter 2) combined with teaching the onsets and word family rimes (chapter 4) and the letter-sound patterns of phonics (chapter 5). If children have difficulty with both the analogy and letter-sound strategies, as is the situation with Raymond, then analogous rimes are the place to begin. Teaching children like Raymond to use analogous rimes helps them become aware of relationships among written and spoken language and helps them overcome their over-reliance on the sounds represented by the first and last letters in words (Greaney, Tunmer, & Chapman, 1997). Hence, the most immediate things that children like Raymond need to know about our writing system are (a) how rimes represent sounds, (b) how to strategically use analogous rimes to identify unfamiliar word family words, and (c) how the letters in phonetically regular rimes in word family words represent (rimes that sound like they are spelled) sound. As children begin to gain insight into the way that the rimes in word family words represent sound, call attention to the individual letter-sound associations within the rimes and call attention to the vowel letter-sound patterns in rimes.

Teaching Phonemic Awareness: Children like Raymond may have difficulty detecting individual sounds in spoken words. Assuming that children already are aware of beginning sounds and rhyme, you will want to focus their attention on ending sounds and, when children are able to identify ending sounds, turn children's attention to sounds in the middle of words.

Look in chapter 2 for activities to develop the ability to detect rhyme and the individual sounds in words. And when you share these activities with children like Raymond, be sure to include arm blending (which is also described in chapter 2). Children like Raymond may find blending quite difficult, and arm blending is a highly successful technique. Arm blending is easy, gives children a visual and kinesthetic platform from which to blend, and transfers to many different reading situations. The description in chapter 2 says to divide words into individual sounds, which places high demands on children who are not completely aware of the middle sounds in words. To lighten the load, divide words

into beginning sounds (onsets) and rimes. Hence, the word /bat/ would be separated into /b/ and /at/, which is well within Raymond's capability. Modify the
directions in chapter 2 by placing your hand in the crook of your elbow when you
say /b/ and then on your wrist when you say /at/. Then, when Raymond has
blended /b/ + /at/, ask him to repeat the whole process, only this time to blend
/b/ + /a/ + /t/. Learning to blend individual phonemes into words increases
the force children like Raymond bring to reading, which means they are then capable of reading materials in which authors use more challenging words. Combine phonemic awareness activities with teaching onset-rimes and letter-sound
patterns, with reading and with plenty of opportunities to write.

Teaching Beginning Letter-Sounds, Word Family Rimes, and Letter-Sound Patterns: If
children like Raymond are to develop greater force, they must bring greater knowledge of the rimes in word family words and a better understanding of letter-sound
patterns to reading. Additionally, children must use word identification strategies
to support comprehension. Once children know a handful of frequently occurring
rimes in word family words, challenge them to look inside the rimes to discover
the manner in which the letters in phonics patterns represent sounds. The idea is
to use what children know, in this case a few high-frequency rimes, as a basis for
teaching something they do not know—the letter-sound patterns of phonics. Teach
children to look inside rimes so as to analyze the vowel patterns. When children do
this, help them understand that one vowel in a short word most likely represents
a short sound (*CVC* pattern). For example, you would teach Raymond how *CVC*
rimes in word family words in the *an* (*man, tan, fan*), *ad* (*mad, had, glad*) and *at* (*mat,
fat, hat*) all represent the short *a* sound. As children look for letter-sound patterns in
rimes, children's knowledge of letter-sound relationships increases and their ability
to use this knowledge while reading also improves. In this way, children use their
knowledge of common rimes to learn how a phonics letter-sound pattern, in this example the *CVC* short vowel pattern, represents the sounds of a whole host of different vowel and consonant combinations.

Next, compare and contrast the *CVC* short vowel pattern in common rimes
with the *VCe* long vowel pattern. An effective way to do this is to challenge children to think of words that include a *CVC* or a *VCe* pattern in their spelling. Analyze the spelling of *CVC* words—*mad, tap, dim*, and *fin*—and *VCe* words—*made,
tape, dime*, and *fine*. Discuss the sounds that vowel letters represent in these two patterns; talk about how and when children might use this information as they read.
Then invite children to work with a partner or in small groups to make charts of
words that are spelled with *CVC* (short vowel) and *VCe* (long vowel) patterns. Ask
children who have less knowledge of letter-sound patterns to work with those who
have more knowledge. Encourage children to find words that include the *CVC* and
VCe letter-sound patterns on the word wall, bulletin boards, and wall charts in
your classroom. Support children as they work with one another to make charts;
share finished charts with the whole class; display charts in your classroom; and
use them as references. (Consult the letter-sound patterns in chapter 5 that are less,

more, and most challenging, and look in appendix B for an explanation of letter-sound patterns.)

The effect of beginning with large segments of spoken and written language (rimes) and then moving to smaller segments (letter-sound patterns) is that activities progress from less demanding to more demanding. Hence, the load (the demands of reading new words) is first brought into line with the force (children's abilities). Then the load can gradually increase as the force children bring to reading grows, that is, as children learn the sounds that the letters in patterns represent and use this knowledge to read new words.

Melissa

At the end of second grade, Melissa is far behind her classmates. Her fluent reading vocabulary is limited, and she can barely read easy first-grade books. When Melissa meets an unfamiliar word, she sometimes considers the beginning letter but not always. When the pictures are highly supportive of the text, Melissa's comprehension is good. When pictures do not help tell the story, Melissa creates in her mind a plausible story, filling in details from her background knowledge. Because Melissa's reading development lags far behind her peers, the load (the type of reading expected of end-of-year second graders) and the force (Melissa's underdeveloped phonemic awareness, rudimentary knowledge of letter-sound patterns, and weak fluent reading vocabulary) are significantly out of balance. It is the load imposed by the reading difficulty of second-grade books, not the ideas in the books, that creates the mismatch.

When someone else reads to her, Melissa easily understands stories written on or above her second-grade level. Melissa dictated her experience of a snake in the rabbit hutch to her teacher, reprinted in Figure 7–4. From her story, we can infer that Melissa is not at a loss for words when talking and that she has a sense of the sequencing of events, and of cause and effect. She has a rich family background and has been read to since she was a very young child. As you might expect, Melissa also uses language effectively when communicating with her friends and adults. Melissa's difficulty, then, is not a lack of prior knowledge, early print experiences, or spoken language.

At this point in her development as a reader, Melissa is hampered by her underdeveloped fluent reading vocabulary, low phonemic awareness, poor knowledge of letter-sound patterns, and ineffective use of the letter-sound strategy. Melissa spells conventionally the words in her fluent reading vocabulary, other words she spells phonetically, as we see in Figure 7–5. She knows enough about letter-sound patterns to be beyond the partial alphabetic stage. She has made the transition into the alphabetic stage of word fluency and the phonetic stage of spelling, yet her progress moving through the alphabetic stage is very slow. While many of her second-grade classmates are entering the consolidated stage of movement toward word fluency, Melissa lingers at an immature state in the alphabetic stage.

Melissa's reading vocabulary is growing very slowly, her reading progress is minimal, and she does not like to write. If Melissa is to succeed, there must be a

One day I was on my mommy's bed watching T.V. Then my mom said, "I am going to go check on the baby rabbits." When she got to the rabbit cage, she opened the back and saw a black snake eating the baby bunnies. The mother rabbit was in the back corner. My mom saw her shivering and she thought she was scared. Then she ran to the house as fast as she could. She called my grandma and grandpa and they sent Matt and my grandma over to kill the snake. Then Matt got a shovel and opened the back door and mommy held the door. Then he tried to hit the snake with the shovel, but he missed the snake. Then the snake crawled out of the back of the pen and went under the barn. They put something on the ground that snakes don't like the smell of to keep the snake from ever coming back. Matt and grandma went home and mommy and I went back in the house.
The End

Figure 7–4 Melissa dictated this story about a snake in the rabbit hutch to her second-grade teacher. Melissa's story shows us that she effectively uses spoken language when telling about the events in her life.

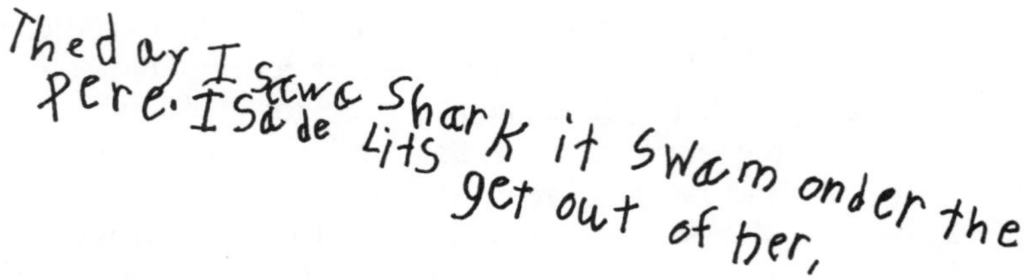

Figure 7–5 By end of second grade, Melissa is far behind her classmates in reading. She spells known words conventionally and others she spells phonetically. Sometimes she looks on the word wall for words she wishes to write but does not know how to spell.

The day I
pere. I sawe de Lits Shark it Swam onder the
get out of her,

better balance between the load (reading demands) and the force (Melissa's abilities and knowledge). Melissa frequently confuses words, cannot remember words, and ignores letters in words—most frequently the vowel letters. If her fluent reading vocabulary and her ability to comprehend grade-level chapter books are to develop, Melissa must consider all the letters in words, including the trick vowels. She must forego overdependence on picture cues and guessing without enough letter-sound information, and she must learn to efficiently and effectively use the analogy and the letter-sound strategies in combination with syntactic and semantic cues, as well as learn to cross-check, self-monitor, and self-correct so as to keep decoding meaning-based.

What Melissa Needs to Know to Move Toward Word Fluency: Melissa readily identifies rhyming words, so you will want to focus instruction on developing her ability to segment and blend the sounds in words. Melissa needs to improve her ability to separate words into sounds, to substitute sounds in words (exchange the /p/ in /pig/ for a /d/ thereby making /dig/), add sounds, delete sounds, and blend sounds (see chapter 2). Melissa already has learned to read word family words, she uses high-frequency rimes when spelling, she knows how to find words on the word wall, and she knows the *CVC* short vowel pattern. At this point in her development as a reader, Melissa needs to learn more about the letter-sound patterns of phonics, and how to use these patterns when reading new words.

Teaching Phonemic Awareness: Melissa easily separates short words (words of two phonemes, such as *me* and *so*) into individual sounds. However, Melissa has to carefully think about sounds before separating three- and four-sound words into phonemes. For example, when asked to separate a three-phoneme word—/mad/, for example—into sounds, Melissa very slowly identifies the sounds. Whereas Melissa's second-grade classmates effortlessly divide /mad/ into sounds, Melissa ponders her answer. As word length increases, Melissa has more and more trouble identifying and manipulating the individual sounds in words. Not surprisingly, Melissa is a very weak blender. Melissa and children like her blend two sounds together quite well, but they frequently have trouble blending three or four sounds together. When blending, Melissa omits, adds, and rearranges sounds, which interferes with use of the letter-sound strategy.

    To further develop Melissa's phonemic awareness, combine the sound awareness and blending activities in chapter 2 with the lessons and activities in chapter 5 that teach letter-sound patterns. As mentioned in chapter 2, there is a mutually supportive relationship between phonemic awareness and letter-sound knowledge. Children like Melissa are in just the right position to take advantage of this two-way (phonemic awareness and letter-sound knowledge) relationship. Of the activities in chapter 2, we find sound squares, interactive spelling and sound boxes with letters to be especially helpful. In using sound squares, write the letters on the squares after Melissa has used them to identify the sounds in words. Writing letters in sound squares and sound boxes reinforces and extends Melissa's letter-sound knowledge, while at the same time developing phonemic awareness. As for blending sounds, Melissa needs lots of direct instruction and practice blending three- and four-sound words. Arm blending is remarkably beneficial for Melissa and children like her. Combine arm blending with sliding sounds together (both explained in chapter 2). When using blending activities, encourage children like Melissa to pay attention to the *middle* sounds in words, to pay special attention to correct blending when using the letter-sound strategy, and to always cross-check for meaning.

Teaching Letter-Sound Patterns: Melissa already knows the sounds represented by the single consonant, consonant cluster, and consonant digraph patterns. Generally speaking, it is the vowel letter-sound patterns that are the most troublesome for children like Melissa. Use the lesson word building with letter-sound patterns (described in chapter 5) to develop vowel letter-sound knowledge. When building words, ask children like Melissa to make changes that affect the vowel patterns, such as changing *CVC* into *VCe* long vowel words (changing *mad* into *made* or *plan* into *plane*), changing *CVC* words into *VV* long vowel words (changing *met* into *meet* or *set* into *seat*), changing *CVC* or *VCe* words into *r-controlled* words (change *cat* into *car; cage* into *care; date* into *dare*). Consult chapter 5 and appendix B for other vowel patterns to highlight when building words. Of course you will want to always have children begin building words with patterns they know and then use this knowledge to help them learn new phonics patterns.

The word puzzles activity in chapter 5 combines phonemic awareness with letter-sound patterns, and thus reinforces and extends the foundations on which the letter-sound strategy rests. The children whom we teach succeed when they first solve puzzles as a whole group activity. Then, when children are confident of their own ability, we ask them to solve puzzles individually. We also find letter-sound pattern board sort, letter-sound compare and contrast charts, and modified cloze sentences (described in chapter 5) to be very beneficial in calling special attention to vowel patterns. After children apply basic vowel letter-sound patterns when reading and spelling, teach other letter-sound patterns and how to use them (these patterns are described in chapter 5 and appendix B).

Children like Melissa benefit from reading decodable books—books with words that are spelled like they sound and therefore can be pronounced using the letter-sound strategy. Decodable books give children practice using the letter-sound strategy while reading (Mesmer, 2001). Using the letter-sound strategy in turn reinforces children's knowledge of the sounds the letters in patterns represent (Juel & Roper-Schneider, 1985). Because so many words can be successfully identified using the letter-sound strategy, decodable books help children like Melissa appreciate the benefits of applying this strategy when reading. Melissa and children like her need many and varied opportunities to use phonemic awareness (particularly blending) along with letter-sound knowledge when reading and spelling new words. The more opportunities to apply knowledge of phonemic awareness and letter-sound patterns the better.

Melissa's reading ability will improve as she develops more phonemic awareness, knowledge of letter-sound patterns, and the ability to strategically use this information to identify and learn new words. As Melissa's fluent reading vocabulary expands, she will be able to read more difficult chapter books and content area books, and hence the load (the requirements of grade-level reading materials) and the force (what Melissa knows and can do) will come into balance.

Figure 7–6 The reading and writing ability of children like Mike, who is midway through the fourth grade, will improve when they increase sound awareness and knowledge of letter-sound patterns.

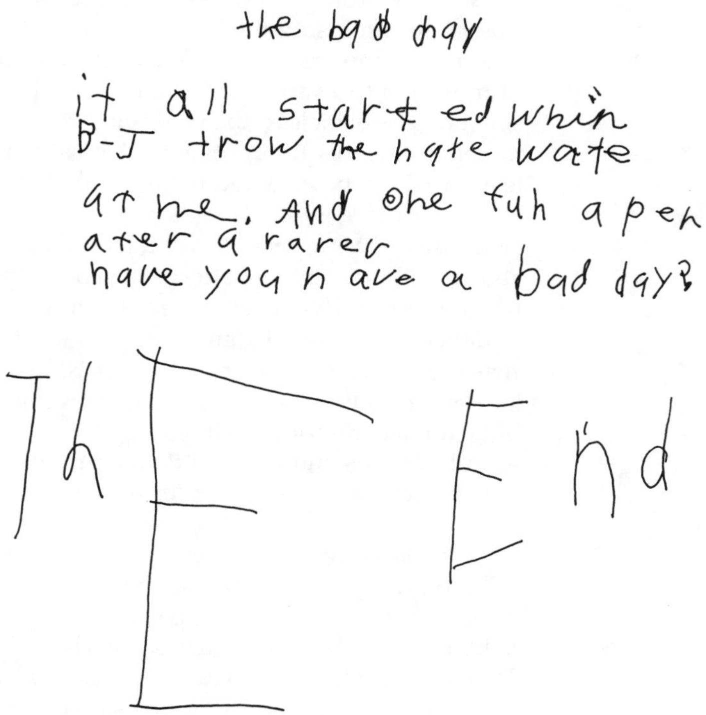

Mike

Mike, whose story is shown in Figure 7–6, has learned to read and spell onsets and common rimes, and he is able to read and spell some letter-sound patterns. Even so, Mike has not learned enough about letter-sound patterns to support reading the material his fourth-grade classmates enjoy. Hence, the force that Mike brings to reading and writing is far less than the load imposed by everyday fourth-grade reading and writing activities.

When Mike writes, he conventionally spells highly frequent words, such as *it, all, you, bad, day,* and *have.* He also spells phonetically, as we see in the word *weight,* written as *wate.* In so doing, Mike uses the *VCe* long vowel pattern (*ate*), which suggests that he has some knowledge of this more challenging vowel letter pattern (chapter 5). Mike still has a good deal to learn about letter-sound patterns in words, for even with the support of story context, we cannot figure out words such as *fuh* (intended to be the word *thing*), *ararer* (meant to be *another*), and *hate* (supposed to be *heavy*). Like Melissa, Mike has moved beyond the semiphonetic stage of word fluency. Also like Melissa, Mike's development as a reader is encumbered by his inability to effectively use the letter-sound strategy to read and learn new words. While Mike struggles with the letter-sound patterns in words, his classmates are using the multiletter chunk strategy to add words to their fluent reading vocabularies. Other fourth graders in his class are at the consolidated stage of movement toward word fluency (explained in chapter 6) and are transitional spellers. Nevertheless, the beginning sentence in Mike's story introduces readers to action and his thoughts flow logically. What's more, Mike is an enthusiastic learner when the load and the force are in balance.

What Mike Needs to Know to Move Toward Word Fluency: Mike needs to know more about the letter-sound patterns in words and he needs to be able to strategically use this knowledge when he reads and writes. As a fourth grader, Mike also needs to develop the knowledge of, and ability to use, the multiletter chunks in word structure to read and learn new words. Mike has to increase his awareness of the individual sounds in words and improve his ability to blend sounds together. And Mike must continue to be meaning focused, to use context cues along with letter-sound patterns and the multiletter chunks in word structure and to self-monitor, self-correct, and cross-check for meaning when reading new words.

Teaching Blending: It is critical that Mike's blending ability improve, for at present Mike typically adds, deletes, and rearranges sounds when he blends. Asked to blend /l/ + /a/ + /m/ + /p/, Mike may say something like /slamp/, /lap/, or /plam/. Arm blending, discussed in chapter 2, does not appeal to Mike because he does not want to use something so obvious in front of his fourth-grade friends. As an alternative, have Mike tap the side of a table (or desk) with his pencil for each sound to be blended. Many of the older children whom we teach find that this is an effective and acceptable technique to use while reading in school.

   Finger blending, explained in chapter 2, is another beneficial way for children like Mike to blend short words. The sliding sounds together activity is helpful, provided that it is modified to be appropriate for older children. Rather than drawing a slide on the board, as described in chapter 2, give Mike and other children sheets of paper with slides on them. Mike then writes letters on the slide himself (beginning at the top and ending near the bottom), blends the sounds represented by letters, and writes the whole word at the bottom of the slide. Writing letter-sound patterns or the multiletter chunks in word structure (the *-ing* in *jumping*) down the slide and writing the whole word at the bottom helps children like Mike develop phonemic awareness as well as knowledge of letter-sound and word structure cues. When writing the prefixes and suffixes—as well as other multiletter chunks in word structure—on the slide, have children write the entire group at once (*-ing*, *-ed*, or *re-*, for example). In so doing, children develop sensitivity to and an understanding of multiletter chunks that make up the structure of long words.

Teaching Letter-Sound Patterns and the Multiletter Chunks in Word Structure: If you have children like Mike in your classroom, they are likely to develop greater ability to segment words into sounds as a consequence of learning more about letter-sound patterns. Teach Mike to recognize and use the letter-sound patterns that he has not yet learned, and model for him how to apply this knowledge when reading new words. Additionally, teach fourth graders like Mike the high frequency prefixes and suffixes, and show children how to divide long words into affixes and base words (chapter 6).

You can expect the word building activity (chapter 5) to be effective and to shorten the time readers like Mike spend catching up with their classmates (Tunmer & Hoover, 1993). The use of modified cloze sentences (also described in chapter 5) focuses attention on letter-sound patterns while keeping words in context. Venn diagrams are a good way to demonstrate the way that a single letter-sound pattern represents more than one sound, and sorting will give Mike beneficial practice thinking about letter-sound patterns in words (chapter 5). Letter-sound compare and contrast charts, word puzzles, letter-sound bingo, word race, and block words also give children like Mike useful practice thinking about and using letter-sound patterns (chapter 5).

We like to use small white boards (or minichalkboards) to help children like Mike learn and use letter-sound patterns. Just ask children working in small groups to spell words that contain the letter-sound patterns you are teaching. For example, if you are helping children learn and use the *Vr* pattern, then you might ask them to spell words like *car, sir, mother,* and *store*. Ask children to explain why they put the *r* in words when spelling, and to listen for the /r/ in the words as they say them aloud. And when you have an opportunity to observe how children spell words, you see right away who uses letter-sound patterns correctly and who does not. Misspelled words are not penalized in any way, however. Children simply erase misspellings and fix words with minimal disruption to learning. As children spell, talk about letter-sound patterns, compare and contrast words, and discuss word meaning.

We know it is important for children like Mike to develop greater phonemic awareness and letter-sound knowledge. Yet we also know that the average fourth grader has moved well beyond letter-sound learning and the alphabetic stage of movement toward word fluency. So it is important to include Mike in the ongoing, grade-appropriate aspects of learning the multiletter chunks in word structure. Introduce Mike to fourth-grade prefixes and suffixes, as well as prefixes and suffixes from earlier grades that Mike has not yet learned. The affix graffiti activity, explained in chapter 6, is beneficial because the word finding and word writing focus is well within the competence of a child like Mike. So, too, is the complimenting classmates activity (described in detail in chapter 6). Children like Mike are quite capable of making the honor shield. An added benefit is that the honor shield may very well boost Mike's self-esteem when he reads the compliments of his friends. By having Mike participate in a small group, you can effectively balance the load and the force in using activities like creating words and word webs, both explained in chapter 6.

All things taken together, children benefit most when they have a great many experiences in reading and writing, and many opportunities to use the analogy, letter-sound, and multiletter chunk strategies when reading and spelling. As children use the letter-sound strategy, their awareness of the sound in words and knowledge of letter-sound relationships increases simultaneously. With greater phonemic awareness and greater knowledge of letter-sound patterns, children's ability to use the letter-sound strategy also improves. With greater phonemic awareness and letter-sound pattern knowledge, children notice and use the multiletter groups in word structure. As a consequence, the force that children like Shandra, Raymond, Melissa, and Mike bring to reading is greater and, by extension, the load these children are capable of lifting is heavier. By carefully and systematically adjusting the balance, children succeed, gain self-confidence, develop greater capacity to express themselves in writing, enjoy reading increasingly more difficult books, and eventually become independent readers who have a large fluent reading vocabulary.

Children Who Speak Languages Other Than English at Home

Many children whose families speak languages other than English benefit from extra help because the language spoken at home is different from the language of instruction at school and different from the language in which English-speaking authors write. These children bring to your classroom rich ethnic, cultural, and linguistic backgrounds and heritages. They also bring to reading a different complement of syntactic structures and vocabulary than children whose families speak English. As a consequence, children whose families speak languages other than English at home have three things to learn:

1. The structure of a new spoken language
2. A new vocabulary
3. A new written language

In contrast, native English speakers need only learn written English (Thonis, 1989). The challenge is even greater for older children who must not only learn English but also must master the technical information taught in content subject classes (Freeman & Freeman, 1993).

When teaching reading to children for whom English is a second language, we want to begin with spoken English. Your classroom reading program logically builds on children's ability to speak and understand English. Neither you nor I would consider attempting to learn to read a second language, say French, without any knowledge of French words and French sentence structure. We would first learn something about the words, sounds, and structure of the French language. Then we would begin to learn to read French. Likewise, children who do not speak English as their first language need to know something about English words, sounds, and structure before we teach them to read.

Children whose families speak languages other than English are most successful when they have opportunities to observe, infer, and grasp connections between spoken and written language (Verhoeven, 1990), and when they have opportunities to develop phonemic awareness, and to learn letter names and letter-sound patterns. After children have some understanding of spoken English, one way to balance the load and the force is to explore English words and sounds along with reading easy English stories (Crawford, 1993; Stuart, 1999).

In teaching phonemic awareness, you may observe that phonemic awareness in the first language may even transfer to the second language, at least for Spanish-speaking youngsters (Quiroga, Lemos-Britton, Mostafapour, Abbott, & Berninger, 2002). In other words, children in your classroom who have better phonemic awareness in Spanish are likely also to have better phonemic awareness in English and, additionally, to be better at reading English than children with low phonemic awareness of Spanish.

Of course, the mutually supportive relationship between developing phonemic awareness and learning letter-sound patterns is also beneficial for children who speak English as their second language (Muter & Diethelm, 2001). Children from multilingual backgrounds pay attention to the sounds in English as they learn English letter-sound patterns. In the opposite direction, as multilingual children develop better phonemic awareness in English they gain added knowledge of English letter-sound patterns.

There also appears to be a mutually supportive relationship among learning to speak, read, and write English, provided that children enter into reading instruction with some understanding of spoken English. When children understand how the English alphabet represents sounds, they become aware of syntactic structure (Dogger, 1981). Similarly, instruction in vocabulary not only increases children's reading comprehension (Bartley, 1993), but also extends their use of spoken English. This, in turn, enhances children's abilities to form thoughts in English when they write. Phonemic awareness and letter-sound pattern knowledge are important for the literacy learning of native English speakers and children who speak English as a second language (Chiappe, Siegel, & Wade-Woolley, 2002). Furthermore, the children in your classroom who speak English as a second language will learn to read English in the same manner as children for whom English is their second language, although second-language-English speakers may learn how letters represent sounds before they develop phonemic awareness. In other words, for some children who speak languages other than English at home, learning how letters represent sounds may come before phonemic awareness and support awareness of the sounds in English.

Native language literacy is important for balancing the load and the force, too. When the sounds in children's first language are also used in English, we see positive transfer from children's home language to English (Wade-Woolley & Geva, 2000). It stands to reason, then, that children who are literate in their home languages find it easier to learn to read and write English than children who are not literate in their native languages (Royer & Carlo, 1991). One reason for this is that children who can read and write their home languages understand the purpose of reading and writing. Children whose home languages are written in an alphabet have an even greater advantage because they understand the purpose and function of the alphabetic principle. They may bring to the English alphabetic code some, if not all, of the word identification strategies described in this book, albeit applied to reading new words in their home languages.

Sometimes you will observe the influence of children's home language as they read and write, as shown in Juana's story in Figure 7–7. When Juana writes,

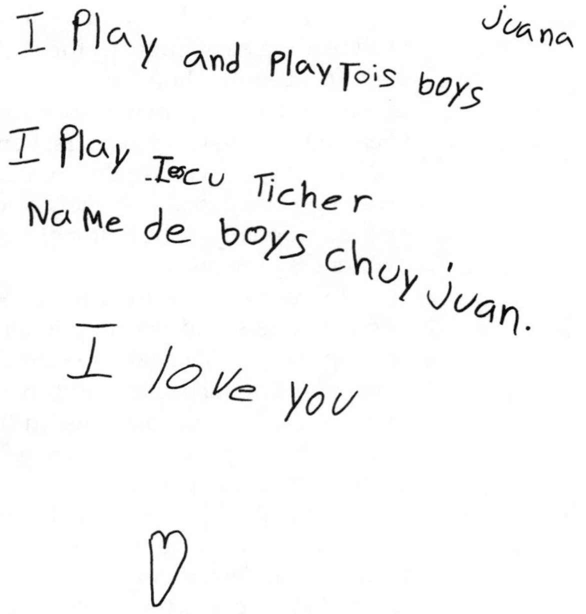

Figure 7–7 The written messages of children who speak languages other than English at home, such as Juana, whose family speaks Spanish, may reflect a combination of children's home language and English.

I Play and Play Tois boys Juana

I Play Iocu Ticher
Name de boys chuy Juan.

I love you

♡

she combines her knowledge of English with a rich knowledge of Spanish, her home language. Notice that Juana replaces *of* with *de*, the Spanish word that would ordinarily be used in this syntactic structure. Notice, too, that Juana writes *ticher* for *teacher*. The letter *i* in Spanish represents the sound heard in *routine*, not *line*, so Juana's spelling is consistent with her first language heritage. Juana also is aware of the way that the English alphabet represents sound, as you can see in her spelling of *tois* for *toys*. We can expect Juana to learn the rimes, letter-sound patterns, and multiletter chunks in word structure in basically the same order as children who speak English as their first language, although, depending on the child, at a somewhat slower pace (Rupley, Rodriquez, Mergen, Willson, & Nichols, 2000).

Chan, whose story is shown in Figure 7–8, has attended English-speaking schools longer than Juana. Hence, Chan brings greater knowledge of spoken and written English to reading and is therefore capable of lifting greater loads—he reads and understands more challenging materials than Juana. Even so, Chan's home language, Vietnamese, sometimes crosses over into written and spoken English. For instance, when Chan writes, he does not always include all function words such as prepositions and conjunctions. And when Chan reads aloud, he pronounces *mother* as /muder/ and leaves out most plurals, possessives, and many other word endings, thus reading *wanted* as /want/. This is so even though Chan's story is a retelling of a familiar book, *The Great Kapok Tree* (Cherry, 1990), which his teacher read several times in class, and the class discussed a good deal in relation to science.

The great kapot tree

The great kapot tree are The rainı forest.
The great kapot tree is larg.
The great kapot tree is where the animals live. The butterfly and The sasur live in The top loge. The monkey, the sloth live in The umbrella or canpy. The tree frog and the snak live in the understory. The Last is all the amimals can live There.

TOP

understory

umbrella

Last

Figure 7–8 The transfer of home languages to spoken and written English suggests that children are interacting with English text in meaningful ways.

Chan is learning English syntax, semantics, and vocabulary, as we see from his writing in Figure 7–8. Chan and Juana, like all readers of English, must automatically recognize the pronunciation and meaning of words, as explained in chapter 1. Interestingly, languages may overlap with English up to 20% (Graves, Juel, & Graves, 1998). The greater the overlap (the closer the match between children's home language and English) the more information children bring to learning to speak, read, and write English. Graves, et al. point out that Juana's home language, Spanish, has a good deal of overlap with English, while Chan's home language, Vietnamese, has relatively little overlap. Hence, depending on her home background and previous literacy experience in Spanish, Juana may bring more prior knowledge to English vocabulary than Chan. This means that, for some children whose home languages have less overlap with English, you may need to concentrate more time and attention on building the background needed to understand English vocabulary and syntax. In addition when children are gaining an understanding of English words, they need lots of support, including support from the reading context. So it is not surprising that children whose families do not speak English at home read words better in context than in lists (Wong & Underwood, 1996). According to Wong and Underwood's findings, you can expect children who do not speak English at home to benefit from the cues to words found in the reading context, while the native English speakers in your classroom may show no difference in their ability to read words in lists or in context.

The crossover, or transfer, of home languages to spoken and written English (substituting *de* for *of*, spelling *teacher* as *ticher*, omitting word endings and conjunctions, and using verbs inappropriately) suggests that children are interacting with English text in meaningful ways. Transfer is, indeed, an important sign of progress toward English literacy. Though the home languages Juana and Chan speak result in different types of transfer, you can expect children like these to learn to speak and read English equally well (Piper, 1993).

Nine Best Practices for Teaching Reading and Sharing Literacy With Second Language Learners

Both Juana and Chan are moving toward accomplished use of written English, each at a different point on a continuum. Given that children bring a wealth of understandings and insights to written English, what types of materials are most likely to help balance the load and the force; that is, to simultaneously support children's strategic use of our alphabetic writing system and enhance comprehension? For one thing, you can support children as they become literate in their home languages. For another thing, you can balance the load and the force so as to support developing the word identification strategies that are so important for literacy. To this end, we suggest that you consider achieving a point of balance by using these nine best practices:

1. Use culturally familiar reading materials. The children in your classroom who speak languages other than English at home will remember more information (Malik, 1990; Steffensen & Joag-dev, 1981) and make more elaborate connections when they read culturally familiar materials (Pritchard, 1990) than when they read materials that are far afield from their home cultures. Culturally unfamiliar materials require more background building and call for more explicit explanations than culturally familiar materials.

Establishing the right balance point depends to a considerable extent on whether materials are culturally familiar to children. This means that books, poems, articles, and plays that are culturally familiar to children who speak English at home may not be suitable matches for children whose families do not speak English. Furthermore, materials that are a good fit for Hispanic children may not be such a good fit for Arabic, Asian, or Native American children. This, of course, underscores the importance of being sensitive to children's cultural heritage and personal life experiences.

2. Use culturally familiar text when assessing children's reading ability. Culturally unfamiliar text is not a good measure of reading ability and, in fact, is likely to underestimate children's actual reading achievement (Garcia, 1991). From a practical point of view, you will find that children are better readers of the materials in your classroom—better at comprehending storybooks, novels, articles, and poems, and better at remembering information and concepts in content subject textbooks—when text is culturally relevant, worse readers when text is culturally unfamiliar. So, if you wish to get an informal assessment of children's reading abilities, use materials that correspond to children's prior knowledge and experience, and avoid materials that are detached from children's lives.

   3.   **Connect children's life experiences with your classroom reading program.**   It is important to connect children's everyday life experiences, concepts, and cultural values with classroom learning (Weaver, 1994). To do this, take frequent field trips and invite guest speakers whose home language is that spoken by the children whom you teach (in this case, Spanish for Juana and Vietnamese for Chan). Encourage children to talk about their life experiences and incorporate those experiences into your everyday classroom routine. Cook children's traditional foods; write signs in children's home languages; and make bulletin boards, wall charts, and labels in both English and the children's home languages. Use pictures and real objects (an orange, a fork, a toy car) to support classroom discussions whenever possible. Read books and traditional tales that embrace children's cultures; role-play, retell, and illustrate stories, folktales, and poems. Such activities build a strong context for learning, and provide ways to honor the cultures of children as well.

   4.   **Develop concepts before teaching English words.**   Children are bound to bring different prior experiences, native language vocabulary, and concepts to our classrooms. Consequently, some children already may have the concepts to connect with English words, while others may not. It is much easier for children to learn English words when they already understand the concepts that the words label. By extension, it is easier to learn English vocabulary reading and to use context cues to identify new words when children understand the concepts that the words label. There are three possible ways that spoken word meaning, concepts, and written word meaning may be connected:

   - Children may already know the concepts and have the words for these concepts in their home languages, but may not know the English labels for the familiar concepts. For example, Spanish-speaking children may know the spoken word /gato/ (tomcat) in their home language, and recognize tomcats when they see them. These children need to learn the English word (/cat/) for a familiar concept and native language word they already know. Once children recognize the English word /cat/ and understand that in English the word *cat* may refer to either a male or a female cat, they are then ready to learn the written word for cat.
   - A second possibility is that children already have a concept (*tomcat*) but have not learned the native language word (/gato/) for that concept. When words are common, as we see in the example of *gato*, it may be wise to enlist the assistance of a native language speaker to develop the native language word. In teaching the English word *cat* we want to link that word (/cat/) with the previously learned concept (*tomcat*). In this example we also would want to slightly adjust children's concept so as

to understand that in English /cat/ may refer to both male and female cats, while in Spanish *gato* only refers to tomcats.

- A third possibility is that children do not have the concept or word in their native language. Should an English word represent a concept that children do not understand, we will need to help children develop both the concept and the English word for that concept. Simply teaching the English word is not helpful because children do not understand the meaning of the English word they are learning.

So we see that it is important to find out whether children understand the concepts that English words label before teaching English vocabulary. If children do not yet understand the concepts, then we want to create learning opportunities to develop both the concepts and the vocabulary through such activities as viewing films, interacting with CD-ROMs, taking field trips, demonstrating word meaning, discussing pictures that represent concepts, and listening to stories that offer some explanation of the concepts.

5.   Use predictable books to practice and reinforce English language patterns and vocabulary.   Predictable books hold a special promise because they bring English syntax and English words within easy reach of young children who are beginning to read a language different from the one spoken at home. With pictures supporting comprehension and text that is patterned, predictable books open the door to literacy by presenting children with meaningful, enjoyable reading experiences that aid reading development (Burns, Roe, & Smith, 2002). Because the same English language patterns recur over and over, predictable books encourage young, beginning readers to anticipate sentence structure. Since the same words are read many times, children have many chances to remember them, thereby building their reading vocabularies. The same characteristics that make predictable books useful for younger children also make these books beneficial for older children who are novice readers of English (Arthur, 1991). So, do not hesitate to share predictable books with older children who are crossing the threshold of English literacy, provided, of course, that books are culturally and developmentally appropriate.

6.   Bring words and print from children's home languages into your classroom.   Find lots of books and magazines written in children's home languages, or use books and magazines that include words from children's home languages. Put these materials in your classroom library. Then create a classroom newspaper or magazine featuring articles written by children. Articles can be in children's home languages and in English, too. This way everyone has an opportunity to share in literacy experiences.

Also bring materials with words from children's home languages into your classroom reading program through the leisure reading children do during Sustained Silent Reading (SSR) or Drop Everything and Read (DARE)—two approaches to leisure reading that set aside time during the school day for reading for pleasure. As children read for pleasure, they use word identification strategies in context and have opportunities to develop a better understanding of English syntax and vocabulary. Intriguing storybooks, thrilling novels, touching poems, dramatic plays all offer gateways to literacy. Take advantage, too, of magazines published for beginning and advanced readers that are written in children's home languages.

7.   Read aloud to children.   When you read aloud, children have opportunities to develop a sense of the structure of stories, enjoy literature, and have experiences with English print that may not be available in their homes. Select from a wide variety of books, including books that are set in children's home countries and reflect children's cultural heritage. If you teach emergent and beginning readers, reread familiar books to give children multiple opportunities to hear the same English sentences and words. Older children enjoy chapter books, which are easily read one chapter at a time. Read to children often, and make reading aloud a normal part of your school day and an integral component in your balanced classroom reading program.

8.   Have children write often and for a variety of purposes.   Children whose families speak languages other than English at home express their thoughts in writing long before they speak English proficiently (Hudelson, 1984). Writing helps children reflect on meaningful messages in print, creates opportunities to use English syntax and vocabulary in meaningful ways, and supports insight into our English alphabetic writing system. Look for ways to combine read-aloud stories with writing activities, such as asking children to write about a memorable event or a fascinating character. If you teach young children, cut out the stories children write, fasten the stories to construction paper, and staple construction paper sheets together to make a giant accordion-style book. Accordion books link reading and writing directly and are wonderful resources to share with younger children. Then you might read aloud the accordion books, and ask children to read the books in chorus. Older children enjoy creating and publishing their own versions of favorite books and poems, not to mention rewriting the lyrics of songs, raps, and chants. This brings us to the use of writing to balance the load and the force.

Use the language experience approach with the less accomplished readers in your classroom and dialogue journals with more accomplished readers. Language experience is an approach whereby the stories that children read are stories written or dictated by them that are based on their own life experiences and reflect their own spoken language. Language experience stories make a special contribution because the messages children write are the same materials that they read, which directly links the text with the children's cultural background and daily experiences. Added to this, the words in language experience stories are a rich source of onsets, rimes, and letter-sound patterns to include in activities described in earlier chapters.

Dialogue journals are two-way communications between children and their teachers. These journals are particularly beneficial for children who read and write English with enough independence to put their thoughts on paper. When children like Chan write dialogue journals, they share their thoughts with their teachers. Their teachers, in turn, write reactions to children's messages, including personal comments and descriptions of relevant life experiences. This gives children opportunities to extend and refine their ability to use the alphabet to write, as well as opportunities to learn how to form their thoughts in such a way as to communicate with English-speaking readers. Should you choose to use dialogue journals with the children whom you teach, you can expect children's confidence with written language to improve and their command of spoken English to increase (Nurss & Hough, 1992).

9. Ask parents and others who are fluent in children's home languages to share their knowledge of language and culture. Welcome parents or adults who speak children's home languages into your classroom as resources for sharing language and culture. Ask parents and other adults to talk about their home culture and to volunteer in your class when possible. And when you do this, invite adults to help your class celebrate some of the holidays in children's home cultures. Ask resource persons to bring traditional dress and foods to your classroom and to demonstrate art and dance. Build a multicultural community in which all cultures and languages are celebrated, in which every child is honored, and in which every child is a reader and a writer.

All things considered, the greater the connection among everyday reading and writing activities, the more opportunities children have to use word identification strategies when reading and writing new words. The challenge is to balance the load and the force so as to foster the development of word identification strategies, nurture literacy, and ensure that all children become competent, meaning-driven readers. Balancing the load and the force creates a supportive learning environment; honors children's individual differences, needs, and preferences; and provides the basis on which children successfully read a variety of material for information and for pleasure.

REFERENCES

Armbruster, B. B., Lehr, F., & Osborn, J. (2001). *Put reading first: The research building blocks for teaching children to read kindergarten through grade 3.* Washington, DC: National Institute for Literacy.

Arthur, B. (1991). Working with new ESL students in a junior high school reading class. *The Journal of Reading, 34,* 628–631.

Bartley, N. (1993). Literature-based integrated language instruction and the language-deficient student. *Reading Research and Instruction, 32,* 31–37.

Burns, P. C., Roe, B. D., & Smith, S. H. (2002). *Teaching reading in today's elementary schools* (8th ed.). Boston: Houghton Mifflin.

Cardoso-Martins, C., Michalick, M. F., & Pollo, T. C. (2002). Is sensitivity to rhyme a developmental precursor to sensitivity to phoneme? Evidence from individuals with Down syndrome. *Reading and Writing: An Interdisciplinary Journal, 15,* 439–454.

Cherry, L. (1990). *The great kapok tree.* New York: Harcourt Brace.

Chiappe, P., Siegel, L. S., & Wade-Woolley, L. (2002). Linguistic diversity and the development of reading skills: A longitudinal study. *Scientific Studies in Reading, 6,* 369–400.

Crawford, L. W. (1993). Language and literacy learning in multicultural classrooms. Boston: Allyn & Bacon.

Dogger, B. (1981). Language-based reading theories, English orthography, and ESL pedagogy. In C. W. Twyford, W. Diehl, & K. Feathers (Eds.), Reading English as a second language: Moving from theory (pp. 21–28). *Monographs in Teaching and Learning, 4* (March).

Freeman, D. E., & Freeman, Y. S. (1993). Strategies for promoting the primary languages of all students. *The Reading Teacher, 46,* 552–558.

Garcia, G. E. (1991). Factors influencing the English reading test performance of Spanish-speaking Hispanic children. *Reading Research Quarterly, 26,* 371–392.

Graves, M. F., Juel, C., & Graves, B. (1998). Teaching reading in the 21st century. Boston: Allyn & Bacon.

Greaney, K. T., Tunmer, W. E., & Chapman, J. W. (1997). Effects of rime-based orthographic analogy training on the word recognition of children with reading disability. *Journal of Educational Psychology, 89,* 645–651.

Hudelson, S. (1984). Kan yu ret an rayt en ingles: Children become literate in English as a second language. *TESOL Quarterly, 18,* 221–238.

Juel, C., & Roper-Schneider, D. (1985). The influence of basal readers on first grade reading. *Reading Research Quarterly, 20,* 134–152.

Justice, L. M., & Ezell, H. K. (2002). Use of storybook reading to increase print awareness in at-risk children. *American Journal of Speech-Language Pathology, 11,* 17–29.

Malik, A. A. (1990). A psycholinguistic analysis of the reading behavior of ESL-proficient readers using culturally familiar and unfamiliar expository text. *American Educational Research Journal, 27,* 205–223.

Mesmer, H. A. E. (2001). Decodable text: A review of what we know. *Reading Research and Instruction, 40,* 121–142.

Muter, V., & Diethelm, K. (2001). The contribution of phonological skills and letter knowledge to early reading development in a multilingual population. *Language Learning, 51,* 187–219.

Nurss, J. R., & Hough, R. A. (1992). Reading and the ESL student. In S. J. Samuels & A. E. Farstrup (Eds.), *What research has to say about reading instruction* (2nd ed.). (pp. 277–313). Newark, DE: International Reading Association.

Piper, T. (1993). *And then there were two: Children and second language learning.* Markman, Ontario: Pippin.

Pritchard, R. (1990). The effects of cultural schemata on reading processing strategies. *Reading Research Quarterly, 25,* 273–295.

Quiroga, T., Lemon-Britton, Z., Mostafapour, E., Abbott, R. D., & Berninger, V. W. (2002). Phonological awareness and beginning reading in Spanish-speaking ESL first graders: Research into practice. *Journal of School Psychology, 40,* 85–111.

Royer, J. M., & Carlo, M. S. (1991). Transfer of comprehension skills from native to second language. *Journal of Reading, 34,* 450–455.

Rupley, W. H., Rodriquez, M., Mergen, S. L., Willson, V. L., & Nichols, W. D. (2000). *Reading and Writing: An Interdisciplinary Journal, 13,* 337–347.

Steffensen, M. S., & Joag-dev, C. (1981). Cultural knowledge and reading: Interference of facilitation. In C. W. Twyford, W. Diehl, & K. Feathers (Eds.), Reading English as a second language: Moving from theory (pp. 29–46). *Monographs in Teaching and Learning, 4* (March).

Stuart, M. (1999). Getting ready for reading: Early phoneme awareness and phonics teaching improves reading and spelling in inner-city second language learners. *British Journal of Educational Psychology, 69,* 587–605.

Thonis, E. W. (1989). Language minority students and reading. *The Reading Instruction Journal, 32,* 58–62.

Tunmer, W. E., & Hoover, W. A. (1993). Phonemic recoding skill and beginning reading. *Reading and Writing: An Interdisciplinary Journal, 5,* 161–179.

Verhoeven, L. T. (1990). Acquisition of reading in a second language. *Reading Research Quarterly, 15,* 90–114.

Wade-Woolley, L., & Geva, E. (2000). Processing novel phonemic contrasts in the acquisition of L2 word reading. *Scientific Studies in Reading, 4,* 261–266.

Weaver, C. (1994). *Reading process and practice: From socio-psycholinguistics to whole language* (2nd ed.). Portsmouth, NH: Heinemann.

Wong, M. Y., & Underwood, G. (1996). Do bilingual children read words better in lists or in context? *Journal of Research in Reading, 19,* 61–76.

APPENDIX A

Rimes for Word Reading and Spelling

Rime	Words
ab*	dab, fab, gab, jab, lab, nab, tab, blab, crab, drab, flab, grab, scab, slab, stab
ace	face, lace, pace, race, brace, grace, place, space, trace
ack*	back, hack, jack, lack, Mack, pack, rack, sack, tack, black, clack, crack, knack, quack, shack, slack, smack, snack, stack, track, whack, wrack
ad	bad, cad, dad, fad, gad, had, lad, mad, pad, sad, tad, brad, clad, glad
ade	fade, jade, made, wade, blade, glade, grade, shade, spade, trade
ag*	bag, gag, hag, jag, lag, nag, rag, sag, tag, wag, zag, brag, crag, drag, flag, shag, slag, snag, stag, swag
ail*	bail, fail, hail, jail, mail, nail, pail, rail, sail, tail, frail, quail, snail, trail
ain*	gain, main, pain, rain, vain, brain, chain, drain, plain, slain, Spain, sprain, stain, train

ake*	bake, cake, fake, Jake, lake, make, rake, sake, take, wake, awake, Blake, brake, drake, flake, quake, shake
ale*	bale, dale, gale, hale, kale, male, pale, sale, tale, vale, wale, scale, shale, stale, whale
all*	ball, call, fall, gall, hall, mall, pall, tall, wall, small, squall, stall
am*	dam, ham, jam, Pam, ram, Sam, tam, yam, clam, cram, gram, scam, sham, slam, swam, tram, scram
ame*	came, dame, fame, game, lame, name, same, tame, blame, flame, frame, shame
amp	damp, lamp, ramp, vamp, champ, clamp, cramp, scamp, stamp, tramp
an*	ban, can, Dan, fan, Jan, man, Nan, pan, ran, tan, van, bran, clan, plan, scan, span, Stan, than
and	band, hand, land, sand, bland, brand, gland, grand, stand, strand
ane	bane, cane, Jane, lane, mane, pane, sane, vane, wane, crane, plane
ang	bang, fang, gang, hang, pang, rang, sang, tang, clang, slang, sprang, twang
ank*	bank, dank, hank, lank, rank, sank, tank, yank, blank, clank, crank, drank, flank, frank, plank, prank, shank, shrank, spank, stank, swank, thank
ap*	cap, gap, lap, map, nap, rap, sap, tap, yap, zap, clap, flap, scrap, slap, snap, strap, trap, wrap
ash*	bash, cash, dash, gash, hash, lash, mash, rash, sash, brash, clash, crash, flash, gnash, slash, smash, stash, trash
at*	at, cat, fat, hat, mat, pat, rat, sat, tat, vat, brat, chat, drat, flat, gnat, scat, slat, spat, that
ate*	date, fate, gate, hate, Kate, late, mate, rate, crate, plate, skate, slate, state
aw*	caw, haw, jaw, law, maw, paw, raw, saw, claw, draw, flaw, gnaw, slaw, thaw
ay*	bay, day, gay, hay, jay, Kay, lay, may, nay, pay, ray, say, way, clay, flay, fray, gray, play, pray, quay, slay, spay, stay, stray, sway, tray
ear	dear, fear, gear, hear, near, rear, sear, tear, year, clear, shear, smear, spear
eam	beam, ream, seam, team, cream, dream, gleam, scream, steam
eat*	beat, feat, heat, meat, neat, peat, seat, bleat, cheat, cleat, pleat, treat, wheat
eck	deck, heck, neck, peck, check, fleck, speck, wreck

ed*	bed, fed, led, Ned, red, Ted, wed, bled, bred, fled, pled, shed, sled, sped
eed*	deed, feed, heed, need, reed, seed, weed, bleed, breed, creed, freed, greed, speed, steed, tweed
eep	beep, deep, Jeep, keep, peep, seep, bleep, cheep, creep, sheep, sleep, steep, sweep
eer	deer, jeer, leer, peer, veer, cheer, queer, sheer, sneer, steer
ell*	bell, cell, dell, fell, jell, sell, tell, well, yell, dwell, quell, shell, smell, spell, swell
en	Ben, den, hen, Len, men, pen, ten, yen, Zen, glen, Gwen, then, when, wren
end	bend, fend, lend, mend, rend, send, tend, vend, blend, spend, trend
est*	best, jest, lest, nest, pest, rest, test, vest, west, zest, chest, crest, guest, quest, wrest
et	bet, get, jet, let, met, net, pet, set, vet, wet, yet, fret, whet
ew*	dew, few, hew, mew, new, pew, blew, brew, crew, drew, flew, knew, screw, shrew, skew, slew, spew, stew
ice*	dice, lice, mice, nice, rice, vice, price, slice, spice, splice, thrice, trice, twice
ick*	Dick, hick, kick, lick, nick, pick, Rick, sick, tick, wick, brick, chick, click, crick, flick, prick, quick, slick, stick, thick, trick
ide*	bide, hide, ride, side, tide, wide, bride, chide, glide, guide, pride, slide, snide, stride
ig	big, dig, fig, gig, jig, pig, rig, brig, prig, sprig, swig, trig, twig
ight*	fight, light, might, night, right, sight, tight, bright, flight, fright, knight, plight, slight
ill*	bill, dill, fill, gill, hill, Jill, kill, mill, pill, sill, till, will, chill, drill, frill, grill, quill, shrill, spill, still, swill, thrill
im*	dim, him, Jim, Kim, rim, Tim, vim, brim, grim, prim, shim, skim, slim, swim, trim, whim
in*	bin, din, fin, gin, kin, pin, sin, tin, win, chin, grin, shin, skin, spin, thin, twin
ind	bind, find, hind, kind, mind, rind, wind, blind, grind
ine*	dine, fine, line, mine, nine, pine, vine, wine, brine, shine, spine, swine, twine, whine
ing*	ding, king, ping, ring, sing, wing, zing, bring, cling, fling, sling, sting, string, swing, thing
ink*	fink, kink, link, mink, pink, rink, sink, wink, blink, brink, chink, clink, drink, shrink, slink, stink, think

ip*	dip, hip, lip, nip, pip, rip, sip, tip, blip, chip, clip, drip, flip, grip, quip, ship, skip, slip, snip, strip, trip, whip
it*	it, fit, hit, kit, lit, pit, sit, wit, knit, quit, skit
ob*	Bob, cob, fob, gob, job, lob, mob, rob, sob, blob, glob, knob, slob, snob, throb
ock*	cock, dock, hock, jock, lock, mock, pock, rock, sock, block, chock, clock, crock, flock, frock, knock, shock, smock, stock
og	bog, cog, dog, fog, hog, jog, log, clog, flog, frog, grog, slog, smog
oil	boil, coil, foil, soil, toil, broil, spoil
oke*	coke, joke, poke, woke, yoke, broke, choke, smoke, spoke, stoke, stroke
old	bold, cold, fold, gold, hold, mold, sold, told, scold
ong	gong, long, song, tong, prong, strong, thong, wrong
op*	bop, hop, lop, mop, pop, sop, top, chop, clop, crop, drop, flop, plop, prop, shop, slop, stop
ore*	bore, core, fore, gore, lore, more, pore, sore, tore, chore, score, shore, snore, spore, store, swore
orn	born, corn, horn, morn, torn, worn, scorn, shorn, sworn, thorn
ot*	cot, dot, got, hot, jot, lot, not, pot, rot, sot, tot, blot, clot, knot, plot, Scot, shot, slot, spot, trot
ought	bought, fought, sought, brought, thought, wrought
out*	bout, gout, lout, pout, tout, clout, flout, grout, scout, shout, snout, spout, sprout, trout
ow*	(long o) bow, low, mow, row, tow, blow, crow, flow, glow, grow, know, show, slow, snow, stow, throw
ub	cub, dub, hub, nub, pub, rub, sub, tub, club, flub, grub, scrub, shrub, snub, stub
uck*	buck, duck, luck, muck, puck, suck, tuck, yuck, chuck, cluck, pluck, shuck, snuck, struck, stuck, truck
ug*	bug, dug, hug, jug, lug, mug, pug, rug, tug, chug, drug, plug, shrug, slug, smug, snug, thug
um*	bum, gum, hum, mum, rum, sum, chum, drum, glum, plum, scum, slum, swum
ump*	bump, dump, hump, jump, lump, pump, rump, chump, clump, frump, grump, plump, slump, stump, thump, trump
un	bun, fun, gun, nun, pun, run, sun, shun, spun, stun
ung	dung, hung, lung, rung, sung, clung, flung, slung, sprung, strung, stung, swung, wrung

unk*	bunk, dunk, funk, gunk, hunk, junk, punk, sunk, chunk, clunk, drunk, flunk, plunk, shrunk, skunk, slunk, spunk, stunk, trunk
ust	bust, dust, gust, just, lust, must, rust, crust, thrust, trust
ut	but, cut, gut, hut, jut, nut, rut, glut, shut, strut
y*	by, my, cry, dry, fly, fry, ply, pry, shy, sky, sly, spy, spry, sty, try, why, wry

---

Note: Pronunciation of /og/ may vary for children in different regions.

*Rimes with an asterisk are part of many different words, according to Cheek, Flippo, and Lindsey (1997) and/or Fry (1998).

**ow is pronounced with a long /o/ as in /know/.

Cheek, E. H., Flippo, R. F., & Lindsey, J. D. (1997). *Reading for success in elementary schools.* Dubuque, IA: Brown & Benchmark.

Fry, E. (1998). The most common phonograms. *The Reading Teacher, 52,* 620–622.

APPENDIX
B
Letter-Sound Patterns

Consonant Letter-Sound Patterns

Single Consonants

Single consonant letters represent the sounds heard in the following words:

B,b	boat	buffalo	K,k	kite	kangaroo	S,s	sun	daisy
C,c	cat	city	L,l	lion	lamp	T,t	turtle	table
D,d	dog	donkey	M,m	moon	monkey	V,v	van	valentine
F,f	fish	fox	N,n	nut	nest	W,w	wagon	wave
G,g	goat	gem	P,p	pig	popcorn	X,x	fox	exit
H,h	hat	hippopotamus	Q,q	queen	quack	Y,y	yo-yo	yellow
J,j	jet	jam	R,r	ring	rabbit	Z,z	zipper	zoo

- W,w and Y,y act as consonants when they are onsets, as in *wagon, wait, yellow,* and *barnyard.*
- Though Y,y represents the consonant sound heard in *yellow* when it is an onset, Y,y also acts as a vowel in many letter-sound patterns.
- X,x does not occur in many frequently used words and seldom represents the sound heard in *x-ray,* a favorite example in ABC books. Though X,x represents several sounds, the /ks/ in *fox* (particularly at the end of words) and the /gz/ in *exit* are most common.
- Consonants that represent more than one sound, such as *c, g,* and *s,* are explained later.

Qu

When Q,q is present in spelling, it almost always precedes U,u, which acts as a consonant.

Beginning qu /kw/ Sound		*Middle qu /kw/ Sound*		*Final que /k/ Sound*	
quack	quick	acquit	inquire	antique	physique
quaint	quiet	banquet	liquid	boutique	plaque
quarter	quit	conquest	request	critique	statuesque
queen	quote	eloquent	require	oblique	technique
question	quiz	frequent	sequin	opaque	unique

- Words spelled with *que* are borrowed from French and reflect the influence of French on our spelling system.
- Occasionally the *u* in *qu* is silent. Under this circumstance, *qu* represents the /k/ heard in *mosquito, quay, croquette,* and *quiche*. This occurs so seldom in English words that it does not merit specific attention.
- *Q, q* occurs without *u* in a few words, as in *Iraq,* but this is so rare in English that it does not warrant special consideration, either.

Double Consonants

Formed whenever the same consonants are side-by-side, the sound represented is usually that of a single consonant, as in *rabbit* and *cotton*.

- When there is a double consonant in a word, the consonant sound most often goes with the preceding vowel to form a pattern, as in *rabbit* (/rab/) and *mitten* (/mit/). The exception is when words are joined together to make compounds, in which case both sounds may be heard, as in *headdress* and *bookkeeper*. For the purpose of dividing words into syllables, the syllable division is between the double consonants (*rab - bit, mit - ten*), and the first syllable is most often the syllable that is accented.
- In some words spelled with a double *c,* the first *c* represents the sound of /k/ in *kite* and the second the /s/ in *save,* as in *accent, accept,* and *accident*.
- When suffixes are added to some words, such as *slam* and *wrap,* consonants are doubled, as in *slamming* and *wrapped*. Whereas it is relatively easy to infer the pronunciation of double consonants, it is much more challenging for children to learn when (and when not) to double consonants in writing suffixes.

Consonant Clusters (or Blends)

The sounds represented by letters in a consonant cluster are joined together during pronunciation. Some teachers' manuals refer to this pattern as a consonant blend.

Two-Letter Clusters

bl Cluster			*cl Cluster*			*fl Cluster*		
black	blew	bloom	claim	clay	clog	flag	fleet	flock
blade	blind	blouse	clam	clean	close	flake	flesh	flood
blame	blink	blow	clap	cliff	cloth	flame	flew	floor
blank	blip	blue	clash	clip	cloud	flare	flight	flop
blast	block	bluff	clasp	cloak	clown	flash	fling	flour
bleak	blond	blur	class	clock	club	flat	flip	flow
blend	blood	blush	claw	clod	clue	flea	float	flute

gl Cluster

glad	gleam	glory
glade	glen	gloss
gland	glide	glove
glance	gloat	glow
glare	glob	glue
glass	globe	glum
glaze	gloom	glut

pl Cluster

place	play	plug
plain	please	plum
plan	plod	plume
plane	plop	plump
plank	plot	plunge
plant	plow	plus
plate	pluck	plush

sl Cluster

slam	slid	slob
slant	slice	slop
slap	slick	slope
slave	slide	slot
sled	slim	slow
sleep	slip	slouch
sleet	slit	slump

br Cluster

brag	break	broil
brain	breeze	broke
brake	brick	brook
branch	bride	broom
brass	brim	brow
brave	bring	brown
bread	broad	brush

cr Cluster

crab	creek	cross
crack	creep	crow
craft	crew	crown
crash	crib	crumb
crate	crime	crush
crawl	crisp	crust
cream	crop	cry

dr Cluster

drag	drew	drool
drain	drift	droop
drank	drill	drove
drape	drink	drown
draw	drip	drug
dream	drive	drum
dress	drop	dry

fr Cluster

frame	friend	from
frank	Friday	front
Fred	fright	frost
free	frill	frown
freeze	frisky	frozen
French	frock	fruit
fresh	frog	fry

gr Cluster

grab	graph	grin
grade	grasp	grind
grain	graze	groom
grand	great	ground
grape	green	group
grass	greet	grow
grave	grew	growl

pr Cluster

prank	prim	proof
press	prime	prose
pretty	print	proud
prey	prize	prove
price	prod	prowl
prick	prom	prune
pride	prong	pry

tr Cluster

track	tray	troop
trade	treat	truck
trail	tree	true
train	trial	trunk
tramp	tribe	trust
trap	trick	truth
trash	trip	try

sc Cluster

scab	scarf	scorn
scald	scoff	scotch
scale	scold	scour
scalp	scone	scout
scan	scoop	scowl
scar	scope	scuff
scare	score	scum

sk Cluster

skate	skid	skipper
skeet	skiff	skirt
skein	skill	skit
skeleton	skim	skulk
sketch	skimp	skull
skew	skin	skunk
ski	skip	sky

sm Cluster

smack	smelter	smolder
small	smile	smooch
smart	smirk	smooth
smash	smite	smother
smear	smock	smudge
smell	smog	smug
smelt	smoke	smut

sn Cluster

snack	snatch	snob
snag	sneak	snoop
snail	sneer	snore
snake	sneeze	snort
snap	sniff	snout
snare	snip	snow
snarl	snipe	snub

sp Cluster

space	speed	spin
spade	spear	spit
span	spell	spoon
spank	spend	sport
spare	spice	spot
spark	spider	spun
speak	spill	spy

st Cluster

stack	star	stew
stag	start	stick
stage	state	still
stain	stay	stir
stair	steal	stone
stamp	stem	stop
stand	step	store

sw Cluster

swab	sway	swing
swam	sweep	swipe
swamp	sweet	swirl
swan	swell	swish
swap	swept	Swiss
swarm	swift	switch
swat	swim	swoop

tw Cluster

twain	twelve	twine
twang	twenty	twinge
tweak	twice	twinkle
tweed	twig	twirl
tweet	twilight	twist
tweeze	twill	twitch
twelfth	twin	twitter

- *sk, sm, sp,* and *st* occur at the beginning and the end of words, as in *mask, prism, clasp,* and *last.* All the other two-letter clusters occur at the beginning of words, not the end.
- The letters *wr* do not form a cluster. The *w* is silent, as in *wrap, write,* and *wreck.*
- Some letter combinations, such as *nd, mp, ld, nt, lk,* and *nk,* form a cluster at the end of words, as in *stand, jump, held, sent, talk,* and *sink.* In my experience, consonant clusters at the end of words are most easily learned as rimes (see appendix A).

Three-Letter Clusters

scr Cluster

scram	scream	scrod
scramble	screech	scroll
scrap	screen	scrooge
scrape	screw	scrub
scratch	scribe	scruffy
scrawl	scrimp	scrunch
scrawny	script	scruple

spl Cluster

splash	splice
splat	splint
splatter	splinter
splay	split
spleen	splotch
splendid	splurge
splendor	

spr Cluster

sprain	sprightly	spruce
sprang	spring	sprung
sprawl	sprinkle	spry
spray	sprint	
spread	sprite	
spree	sprocket	
sprig	sprout	

squ Cluster

squab	squash	squint
squabble	squat	squish
squad	squawk	squire
squall	squeak	squirm
squalor	squeal	squirrel
squander	square	squeeze
square	squash	squid

str Cluster

straight	streak	strip
strain	stream	stripe
strand	street	stroke
strange	strength	stroll
strap	stretch	strong
straw	strict	struck
stray	strike	strung

The following letters in these three-letter clusters represent only two sounds:

chr Cluster

christen	chronic
Christmas	chronicle
chrome	chronology
chromium	chrysalis
chromosome	chrysanthemum

sch Cluster

schedule	scholastic
schema	school
schematic	schooner
scheme	
scholar	

thr Cluster

thrash	thrift	throne
thread	thrill	throng
threat	thrive	throttle
three	throat	through
thresh	throb	throw

- Except for the frequently used words *Christmas, school,* and *schedule, chr* and *sch* are not often present in the words younger children are likely to read and spell.
- This is not the case for *thr*, which is part of many words. Generally speaking, through third grade, children read more words with two-letter clusters than three-letter clusters.
- Teach the three-letter clusters after readers know common two-letter clusters.

Consonant Digraphs

The letters in a consonant digraph represent one sound that is very different from the sounds the letters represent individually.

ch Digraph

chain	charm	chew
chair	chart	chimp
chalk	chat	chin
champ	chase	chip
chance	check	choose
change	cheer	chop
chant	cheese	churn

ph Digraph

phantom	philosopher	phosphorus
pharaoh	philosophy	photo
pharmacy	phobia	photograph
phase	phone	photosynthesis
pheasant	phoneme	phrase
phenomenon	phonics	physical
philodendron	phonograph	physics

sh Digraph

shade	she	short
shack	sheep	shot
shake	shell	should
shape	ship	shovel
shark	shirt	show
sharp	shoe	shut
shave	shop	shy

th Digraph (Voiceless)

thank	thief	thirteen
thatch	thigh	thirty
thaw	thin	thorn
theater	thing	thought
theft	think	thousand
theme	third	thumb
thick	thirst	thunder

th Digraph (Voiced)

than	there	though
that	these	thus
the	they	thy
thee	thine	
their	this	
them	those	
then	thou	

wh Digraph

what	which	whirl
whale	whiff	whisk
wheat	while	whisper
wheel	whim	whistle
when	whine	white
where	whip	whopper
whether	whir	why

tch Digraph

batch	glitch	patch
blotch	hatch	pitch
catch	hitch	scotch
clutch	hutch	sketch
ditch	itch	switch
Dutch	latch	watch
etch	match	witch

- Other sounds that the *ch* digraph represent are the /sh/ heard in *chivalay* and the /k/ heard in *choir*. Even though *ch* represents sounds other than that heard in *chirp*, this is the most frequent sound and so it is a good sound to try first.
- The digraph *ph* commonly represents the /f/ heard in *phone*. Every now and then *ph* represents the sound of /p/, and sometimes *ph* is silent.

- The digraphs *ch, ph, sh,* and *th* occur at the beginning of words, in the middle of words—such as *franchise, dolphin, bishop,* and *heathen*—and at the end of words, such as *perch, graph, fish,* and *teeth.*
- The letters *th* represent two sounds—the sound heard in *thank* (called voiceless) and that heard in *than* (called voiced). Advise readers to first try the voiceless /th/ in *thank* and, if that does not form a contextually meaningful word, to try the voiced /th/ in *than.*
- When *wh* precedes *o,* it represents the /h/ in *who.* The /hw/ sound in *white* is much more common, so encourage readers to first try the /hw/ sound and, if that does not form a meaningful word, to next try the /h/ sound. However, in some Americans' speech, the /h/ is not pronounced in a word such as *white;* just the /w/ is pronounced. This reflects readers' normal pronunciation and hence should not interfere with word identification.
- When the letter *e* follows the digraph *th* at the end of a word, such as in *bathe,* the *th* represents the voiced sound heard in *that.* This explains the difference in pronunciation between *cloth* and *clothe,* and *teeth* and *teethe.*
- *tch* occurs at the end of words, as in *catch, itch, match,* and *stretch.* Whereas readers should have no trouble inferring that the *t* in *tch* is silent, they must remember to include the *t* in spelling. Hence, *tch* may well be more problematic for spellers than for readers.
- The *ck* pattern (which represents the /k/ at the end of words such as *back*) and the *ng* pattern are not included here because they are quicker to learn as part of the rimes *ack, eck, ick, ock,* and *uck,* or the rimes *ang, ing, ong,* and *ung,* as shown in appendix A.
- *gh* also forms a digraph. As an onset, *gh* represents /g/, though few English words begin with *gh.* When *gh* is not an onset, there are two options: the *gh* is silent, as in *thigh,* or it represents /f/ as in *laugh.* When words include the sequence *ght,* the *gh* is silent, as in *bought* and *night.* Rimes with *gh* are a shortcut to word learning; look in appendix A for examples.

The Three Sounds of S, s

As an onset *S,s* represents the /s/ heard in *sack,* never /z/. Only two alternatives, /s/ or /z/, are possible when *s* is a middle or the last letter in a syllable. *S,s* is not troublesome for most readers and spellers. Encourage readers to form a mind-set to attempt pronunciation with the /s/ first and, if that fails, to try the /z/.

/s/ *Onset*			/s/ *Final Sound*			/z/ *Sound*		
sack	seed	sight	bass	grass	moose	amuse	ease	music
salt	self	sign	boss	goose	plus	arise	fuse	nose
save	sell	six	bus	horse	this	as	has	please
saw	send	soap	chase	house	toss	cause	his	rose
sea	set	sock	dress	kiss	us	closet	hose	those
seal	sick	soft	fuss	lease	verse	cousin	is	was
see	side	sun	gas	loss	yes	daisy	lose	wise

- *sure* and *sugar* are exceptions; the *s* in the beginning of these words represents the sound of /sh/.
- If *i* or *u* follows *s* in the middle of words, *s* may represent the sound heard in *mansion* and *erasure,* or the sound heard in *vision* and *pleasure.*
- When *-es* is a suffix as in *dishes* or *washes,* the *-es* represents /z/.

Ca, co, cu

When *c* precedes *a, o* and *u* (*ca, co, cu*), the *c* usually represents the /k/ heard in *kite* (called a hard sound).

ca Pattern			co Pattern			cu Pattern		
cab	camel	card	coal	comb	core	cub	cup	curl
cage	camp	cart	coat	come	cork	cube	cupid	curse
cake	can	case	coach	cone	corn	cuddle	cusp	curve
calf	cane	cast	cob	cook	cost	cue	cur	cusp
call	cap	cat	code	coop	cot	cuff	curb	custom
calm	cape	catch	cold	cop	cove	cull	curd	cut
came	car	cause	colt	cord	cow	cult	cure	cute

Ce, ci, cy

In the *ce, ci,* and *cy* patterns, the *c* usually represents the sound associated with the /s/ in *soap* (called a soft sound).

ce Pattern		ci Pattern		cy Pattern
cease	cent	cider	circumstance	cycle
cedar	center	cigar	circus	cyclone
ceiling	century	cinch	cirrus	cylinder
celery	ceramic	cinder	citizen	cymbal
cell	cereal	cinnamon	citrus	Cynthia
cellar	ceremony	circle	city	cypress
cement	certain	circuit	civil	cyst

- As an onset the *c* in *ci* represents /s/, but in the middle of words *ci* represents the /sh/ sound, as in *social*.

Ga, go, gu

When *g* precedes *a, o,* and *u* (*ga, go, gu*), the *g* usually represents the sound associated with the /g/ in *gate* (called the hard sound).

ga Pattern			go Pattern			gu Pattern		
gab	game	gate	go	gone	gore	guard	gulch	guppy
gag	gang	gather	gob	gong	gorge	guess	gulf	gurgle
gage	gap	gauge	goal	good	gorilla	guest	gull	gush
gain	gape	gave	goad	goof	gossip	guide	gulp	gust
gait	gas	gawk	goat	goon	got	guild	gum	gutter
gal	gash	gay	gold	goose	gourd	guilt	gun	guy
gale	gasp	gaze	golf	gopher	gown	guitar	gunk	guzzle

Ge, gi, gy

In the *ge, gi,* and *gy* patterns, the *g* usually represents the sound associated with the /j/ in *jelly* (called the soft sound).

ge Pattern		*gi Pattern*		*gy Pattern*	
gelatin	genius	giant	digit	gym	clergy
gem	gentle	gibe	engine	gypsy	ecology
gender	genuine	gigantic	fragile	gyroscope	energy
gene	geography	gin	legion	allergy	geology
general	gerbil	ginger	logic	analogy	lethargy
generic	germ	giraffe	magic	apology	strategy
generous	gesture	gist	margin	biology	zoology

- The combinations *ge* and *gi* are not as dependable as the others. Support readers as they learn to first try the sound of /j/ in *jelly* for *ge* and *gi* and, if that fails, try the sound of /g/ in *goat*.

Vowel Letter-Sound Patterns

Short Vowel Sounds and Short Vowel Patterns

a	in *apple*
e	in *edge*
i	in *igloo*
o	in *octopus*
u	in *umbrella*

CVC Short Vowel Pattern

The *CVC* pattern usually represents a short sound. This pattern consists of one vowel in a one-syllable word or in a single syllable. Short vowel sounds are often indicated by a breve (˘, căt). A single vowel preceding one or more consonants; as in *VC–at; CVC–cat; CCVC–chat* or *slat; CCVCC–black; CCVCCC–thatch; CCCVC–scrap; CCCVCCC–splotch.* The number of consonants following the vowel in this pattern does not affect the short vowel sound, although, of course, there are exceptions.

CVC Short Aa				*CVC Short Ee*			
bad	cat	mad	sat	bed	hem	men	red
bag	dad	man	tab	beg	hen	met	set
ban	fan	map	tag	bet	jet	net	shed
bat	fat	nap	tan	den	keg	peg	sled
cab	gas	pan	wag	fed	led	pen	ten
can	had	rag	van	fled	leg	pep	vet
cap	ham	sad	yam	gem	let	pet	web

CVC Short Ii

bib	dim	him	lit
bid	din	hip	mix
big	dip	his	pig
bin	fin	hit	pin
bit	fit	kid	rib
did	fix	kit	rim
dig	hid	lid	sit

CVC Short Oo

box	drop	job	mop
cob	fox	jot	nod
cod	frog	lob	not
cop	gob	lop	pod
cot	got	lot	pop
crop	hop	mob	pot
dot	hot	mom	top

CVC Short Uu

bud	cup	hum	pup
bug	cut	hut	rug
bum	dug	jug	run
bun	fun	lug	sub
bus	gum	mud	sun
but	gun	mug	tub
cub	hug	nut	tug

- Sometimes the vowel in a *CVC* pattern represents a long sound, as in *cold* (*old*), *colt* (*olt*), *find* (*ind*), *night* (*ight*), and *child* (*ild*). Considered within the context of rimes, combinations like these are quite predictable and, hence, best learned as rimes in word family words (see appendix A). Advise readers to try the short vowel sound first and, if that does not produce a meaningful word, to try a long vowel sound.

VCCe Short Vowel Pattern

In the *VCCe* pattern, the vowel generally represents a short sound and the *e* is silent. A consonant pattern before the vowel forms a *CVCCe* (*dance*) or *CCVCCe* (*chance*) sequence; it does not affect the sound the vowel in the *VCCe* pattern represents.

CVCCe

badge	rinse
dance	since
dense	bronze
fence	dodge
ledge	fudge
sense	judge
hinge	lunge

CCVCCe

blonde	prance
bridge	prince
bronze	sconce
chance	smudge
fringe	trance
glance	twinge
pledge	

- *dge* usually represents /j/ and the final *e* is silent. Never an onset, *dge* is included in the spelling of many different words and hence readers have ample opportunities to learn this pattern through reading and writing.

- Many, though not all, of the words in the above list end with *ge* or *ce*. In spellings, the final *e* signals readers that the sound of the *c* is /s/ and the sound of *g* is /j/, consistent with the *ce* and *ge* patterns. Without the final *e*, readers might pronounce the final *c* as /k/ (*epic*) and the final *g* as /g/ (*chug*). In this way, the final *e* in these *VCCe* patterns makes our writing system a more predictable and dependable representation of sound.
- The *VCCe* short vowel pattern is challenging to spellers inasmuch as the *e* is sometimes dropped when suffixes are added to words, as in *lodging* and *dancing*.
- If the short vowel sound does not result in a meaningful word with a *VCCe* pattern, advise readers to try the long sound.

Long Vowel Sounds and Long Vowel Patterns

Long Vowel Sounds

a	in *apron*
e	in *eraser*
i	in *ice*
o	in *overalls*
u	in *unicorn*

VCe Long Vowel Pattern

In the *VCe* pattern, the *e* is silent and the preceding vowel usually has a long sound, which is often indicated by a macron (ˇ). A consonant pattern before the vowel forms a *CVCe* (*save*) or a *CCVCE* (*shave*) sequence and does not affect the sound that the vowel in the *VCe* long vowel pattern represents.

aCe Pattern

bake	lace	safe
base	lane	sale
cake	made	same
came	make	shape
date	page	tape
face	pave	trade
game	rake	wade

eCe Pattern

cede
extreme
gene
scene
scheme
recede
theme

iCe Pattern

bike	hike	nice
dime	kite	nine
dine	life	price
drive	like	prize
file	line	side
fire	mile	smile
hide	mine	time

oCe Pattern

broke	nose	rope
close	note	rose
drove	phone	shone
froze	poke	smoke
globe	pole	stone
hole	robe	those
home	rode	throne

uCe Pattern

chute	flute	plume
cube	fume	prude
cute	fuse	prune
drupe	huge	rude
duke	June	rule
dune	mule	spruce
fluke	mute	tune

- There are some marked exceptions to the *VCe* long vowel pattern. For one thing, it is not conventional for English words to end in the letter *v*, so *e* is tacked on to avoid spelling *have* as *hav*, *love* as *lov*, and *live* as *liv*.
- Words spelled with *r* usually conform to the *r-controlled* (*Vr*) pattern, which explains the pronunciation of *care* and *more*.
- When the last syllable in a word is *ate* or *ite*, and when the syllable is not stressed in pronunciation, the *a* in *ate* and the *i* in *ite* do not represent a long sound, as in *climate*, *private*, and *granite*.
- Some borrowed words from French, such as *cafe*, are exceptions and are pronounced accordingly.

CV Long Vowel Pattern
In the *CV* pattern, the vowel usually represents a long sound.

Ca Pattern		*Ce Pattern*		*Ci Pattern*		*Co Pattern*	
basin	later	be	media	china	pilot	also	poem
canine	major	defer	meter	digest	rifle	banjo	polar
crazy	nation	feline	reform	giant	silent	locate	program
flavor	paper	female	regent	lion	spider	molar	rotate
haven	table	he	sequence	micro	tiger	moment	social
label	vapor	legal	we	migrant	title	no	total
labor	volcano	me	zebra	minus	tricycle	nomad	vocal

Cu Pattern

bugle	humid
cubic	menu
cucumber	museum
fuel	music
funeral	puny
future	pupil
human	tribunal

- There are many exceptions to the *CV* long vowel pattern, particularly if this pattern occurs in a syllable that is not accented; for example, the first syllable in *develop*.

The Letter *Y,y* as the Final Letter
The letter *y* at the end of word acts as a vowel. When *y* forms a separate final syllable, it generally represents the sound associated with long *e*, as in *bunny* and *silly*. *Y,y* at the end of a word with *no other vowels* represents the sound associated with long *i*, as in *by* and *try*.

Final Syllable (long e)		*Only Vowel (long i)*	
any	funny	by	shy
army	lady	cry	sky
baby	melody	dry	spy

body	silly	fly	spry
bunny	study	fry	sty
candy	taffy	my	try
city	tiny	pry	why

- Tell readers to try the sound of long *i* in very short words; the sound of long *e* in longer words. If one sound (long *i* or long *e*) does not work, the other one has a good chance of being correct.
- When the *ly* is a suffix as in *deeply* and *cheaply*, it represents long *e*. Advise readers to try long *e* if they think the *ly* is a suffix and long *i* if they think it is part of the base word. If one sound does not work, the other probably will.

VV Long Vowel Pattern

In the *VV* patterns of *ai, oa, ay, ee, ey,* and *ea*, the first vowel represents a long sound and the second is silent.

ai Pattern		*oa Pattern*		*ay Pattern*	
bait	main	boat	oak	bay	may
claim	nail	coast	oat	clay	pay
drain	paint	coat	poach	day	ray
fail	sail	foam	road	gay	stay
jail	train	loaf	throat	jay	tray
maid	waist	loan	toad	lay	way

ea Pattern		*ee Pattern*		*ey Pattern*	
beach	meat	beef	green	abbey	honey
dream	peak	creek	keep	alley	jersey
heat	real	creep	meet	barley	key
leaf	sea	deed	need	cagey	kidney
leap	sneak	deep	peel	donkey	medley
meal	treat	feel	queen	galley	money
mean	weak	feet	reef	hockey	valley

- Sometimes two adjacent vowels in the *VV* long vowel pattern are referred to as a vowel digraph because two letters represent one sound.
- Some teachers' manuals refer to the vowels in the *VV* long vowel pattern as a vowel team.
- *Y,y* is a vowel when it follows *a* and *e*, thereby creating the *VV* long vowel pattern of *ay* and *ey*.
- Most of the time, *ai* represents long *a*, but occasionally it represents the sound heard in *said* (seldom the sound in *plaid*). Tell readers to first try the long *a* sound and, should that fail to create a meaningful word, to try the sound heard in *said*.
- *ey* represents the sound of long *e* heard in *key* and the sound of long *a* heard in *they*. Advise readers to first try the sound of long *e* and, if that fails to produce a meaningful word, to try the sound of long *a*.

- *ea* sometimes represents the short *e* heard in *head*. Infrequently, *ea* represents a long *a* as in *great*. Advise readers to first try long *e* and, if that does not form a contextually meaningful word, to try short *e*.
- When two adjacent vowels are in different syllables, then both vowels represent a separate sound, as in *create*.

Other Vowel Patterns

Double oo

The double *oo* pattern usually represents the sound heard in *school* or the sound heard in *book*.

oo in school		*oo in book*	
boot	room	brook	look
cool	scoop	cook	nook
food	smooth	crook	shook
hoot	soon	foot	soot
moon	spoon	good	stood
pool	tooth	hood	took
proof	zoo	hook	wood

- Advise readers to try one sound and, if that does not result in a sensible word, to try the other sound.

Vowel Diphthongs

Ow, ou, oi, and *oy* often represent the following sounds in pronunciation: *ow* in *cow; oi* in *oil; ou* in *out; oy* in *boy.*

ow Pattern		*ou Pattern*	
brow	growl	cloud	noun
brown	how	flour	ouch
clown	now	grouch	pound
cow	plow	ground	proud
crowd	scowl	hour	scout
down	town	loud	shout
gown	wow	mouth	trout

oi Pattern		*oy Pattern*	
boil	moist	annoy	joy
broil	noise	boy	ploy
choice	point	coy	Roy
coin	soil	decoy	royal
coil	spoil	deploy	soy
foil	toil	employ	toy
join	voice	enjoy	troy

- *ow* also represents the long vowel sound /crow/, so readers have two sounds from which to choose—the /ow/ in /cow/ and the /o/ (long *o*) in /crow/. If one sound does not work, the other will.
- *oi* may be part of the multiletter groups *oise* (as in *noise*) and *oice* (as in *voice*). Encourage readers to draw these conclusions during the normal course of reading and writing.
- Though *ou* frequently represents the sounds heard in *out* and *cloud*, these two letters represent several other sounds in words; for example, *soul, tour, group, shoulder, encourage, could,* and *double. Your, pour,* and *four* are examples of other exceptions to the *ou* pattern. However, authors use words like *your, four, should, would,* and *could* so frequently that these words are added to children's fluent vocabulary early.

Vr or *r-Controlled* **Pattern**
The r affects pronunciation so that vowels cannot be classified as short or long.

ar Pattern		*er Pattern*		*ir Pattern*	
arm	hard	after	eager	bird	shirt
barn	jar	anger	enter	chirp	sir
car	mart	butter	ever	dirt	skirt
chart	park	cider	fever	fir	stir
dark	star	clerk	her	firm	third
far	tar	cover	over	flirt	twirl
farm	yard	diner	term	girl	whir

or Pattern		*ur Pattern*	
born	fort	blur	hurt
cord	horn	burn	nurse
corn	pork	burst	purr
cork	port	church	spurt
for	sort	curb	surf
fork	torn	curl	turf
form	worn	fur	turn

- The letters *ar* after *w* represent the sounds heard in *war* and *warm*, not the sound heard in *car*. This, however, is not overly difficult for observant readers to discover.

The *au* and *aw* **Patterns**
The *au* generally represents the sound heard in *fault*. The *aw* represent the sound heard in *straw*.

au Pattern		*aw Pattern*	
because	haul	awe	jaw
daunt	maul	brawl	lawn
exhaust	saucer	brawn	shawl
faun	staunch	claw	spawn
flaunt	taught	crawl	squaw

fraud	trauma	draw	thaw
fraught	vault	gawk	thrawl

- The *au* and *aw* patterns are fairly reliable. The *au* does not occur at the end of words. The *aw*, on the other hand, is used as an onset (*awe*), in the middle of words (*dawn*), and at the end of words (*draw*).

The *ew* and *ue* Patterns

The *ew* and *ue* patterns usually represent the sound in *blew* and *blue*.

ew Pattern		*ue* Pattern	
blew	jewel	argue	pursue
brew	screw	avenue	rescue
chew	shrew	blue	statue
crew	shrewd	due	sue
drew	slew	flue	tissue
flew	strewn	glue	true
grew	threw	issue	value
			virtue

- The *ue* pattern cannot be counted on to represent the sound heard in *blue* when the *ue* follows a *q* or a *g* in spelling, as in *antique* and *guess*. When children have lots of experience reading and writing words spelled with these sequences, they learn the sounds these letters represent.

APPENDIX
C
Generalizations for Adding Suffixes

-s, -ed, -ing, -ly, and -er to Words

The suffixes -s, -ed, -ing, -ly, and -er are the top five most frequently used word endings according to White, Sowell, and Yanagihara (1989). The following generalizations are helpful as guides when reading and spelling words with the suffixes of -s, -ed, -ing, -ly, and -er. When teaching children to recognize these common suffixes while reading and to spell words with these suffixes when writing, advise them that the suffixes themselves are always spelled the same. Sometimes, however, the spelling of the base word changes when a suffix is added. Of course, there are exceptions to these generalizations. Nevertheless, readers and writers will find them helpful because so many words are spelled with these six suffixes.

CVC Short Vowel Words
Add -s and -ly to one-syllable words with the CVC short vowel pattern:

	-s		-ly
bat	bats	glad	gladly
clap	claps	sad	sadly
stop	stops	dim	dimly
dog	dogs	low	lowly
hat	hats	bad	badly
win	wins	mad	madly

-ed, -ing, -er

Double the last consonant before adding *-ed, -ing,* and *-er* to words ending with the *CVC* short vowel pattern:

	-ed	*-ing*	*-er*
jog	jogged	jogging	jogger
drop	dropped	dropping	dropper
plan	planned	planning	planner
plot	plotted	plotting	plotter
slip	slipped	slipping	slipper
trap	trapped	trapping	trapper

Doubling the last consonant keeps *CVC* short vowel words with the *-ed, -ing,* and *-er* suffixes, such as *hop–hopping,* from being read as *VCe* long vowel words, like *hope–hoping.* Children need a lot of reading and spelling opportunities to successfully use this generalization when they write.

CVCC Short Vowel Words

Simply add *-s, -ed, -ing, -ly,* and *-er* to words ending in a *CVCC* short vowel pattern:

	-s	*-ed*	*-ing*
rest	rests	rested	resting
talk	talks	talked	talking
jump	jumps	jumped	jumping
call	calls	called	calling
help	helps	helped	helping
land	lands	landed	landing
	-ly	*-er*	
sick	sickly	sicker	
hard	hardly	harder	
cold	coldly	colder	
calm	calmly	calmer	
soft	softly	softer	
warm	warmly	warmer	

The reason we do not double the last consonant in the *CVCC* short vowel pattern is that there is no chance of confusing these short vowel words with long vowel *VCe* words, as explained previously.

VCe Long Vowel Pattern

Drop the final *e* and then add the *-ed, -ing,* and *-er* to words ending with the *VCe* long vowel pattern:

	-ed	*-ing*	*-er*
race	raced	racing	racer
joke	joked	joking	joker
bake	baked	baking	baker
dine	dined	dining	diner
hike	hiked	hiking	hiker
shave	shaved	shaving	shaver

Add *-s* and *-ly* to *VCe* long vowel words.

	-s		*-ly*
bike	bikes	nice	nicely
face	faces	home	homely

hope	hopes	late	lately
home	homes	huge	hugely
game	games	love	lovely
rule	rules	live	lively

VV Long Vowel Pattern

When words end with a *VV* long vowel pattern followed by a consonant, add the *-s, -ed, -ing, -ly*, and *-er* without changing the base word:

	-s	-ed	-ing
need	needs	needed	needing
load	loads	loaded	loading
peel	peels	peeled	peeling
roam	roams	roamed	roaming
fail	fails	failed	failing
soak	soaks	soaked	soaking
	-ly	-er	
cheap	cheaply	cheaper	
deep	deeply	deeper	
fair	fairly	fairer	
broad	broadly	broader	
plain	plainly	plainer	
sweet	sweetly	sweeter	

Words Ending in the *VV* Combinations of *ay, oy, ey*

Simply add *-s, -ed, -ing*, and *-er* to words ending in the *VV* combinations of *ay, oy*, and *ey*:

	-s	-ed	-ing
play	plays	played	playing
obey	obeys	obeyed	obeying
enjoy	enjoys	enjoyed	enjoying
spray	sprays	sprayed	spraying
stay	stays	stayed	staying
toy	toys	toyed	toying
	-er		
play	player		
gray	grayer		
gay	gayer		
spray	sprayer		
employ	employer		
buy	buyer		

Words Ending in *Y,y*

When a word ends in a *y*, change the *y* to an *i* before adding *-es, -ed*, and *-er:*

	-es	-ed	er
carry	carries	carried	carrier
worry	worries	worried	worrier
dry	dries	dried	drier
busy	busies	busied	busier
fancy	fancies	fancied	fancier
copy	copies	copied	copier

Adding *-es* to Words Ending in *s, ss, ch, sh, x, and z*
Add *-es* to words that end in *s, ss, ch, sh, x,* and *z* as in:

	-es		*-es*		*-es*		*-es*
bus	buses	beach	beaches	leash	leashes	fox	foxes
toss	tosses	porch	porches	crash	crashes	fix	fixes
pass	passes	branch	branches	bush	bushes	mix	mixes
class	classes	bench	benches	rush	rushes	tax	taxes
dress	dresses	catch	catches	fish	fishes	buzz	buzzes
boss	bosses	bunch	bunches	wish	wishes	waltz	waltzes

White, T. G., Sowell, J., & Yanagihara, A. (1989). Teaching elementary students to use word-part clues. *The Reading Teacher, 42,* 302–308.

APPENDIX D

Greek and Latin Roots

Roots	Meaning	Examples
aer(o) (Greek)	air, atmosphere	aerial, aerospace
ann (Latin)	year	annual, anniversary
anthr (opo) (Greek)	human	anthropology, philanthropist
art (Latin)	skill	artist, artifact
aqua (Latin)	water	aquatic, aquarium
ast(er) (Greek)	star	astrology, astronaut
aud (Latin)	hear	audience, auditory
aut(o) (Greek)	self	autobiography, automobile
biblio (Greek)	book	bibliography, bibliotherapy
bio (Greek)	life	biology, biodegradable
cap (Latin)	head	cap, capital
cardi (Greek)	heart	cardiology, cardiogram
chrom(at) (Greek)	color	chromatic, chromosome
cycl (Greek)	circle, wheel	cycle, bicycle
dem (Greek)	people	democracy, democratic
dyna (Greek)	power	dynamite, dynamic
fid (Latin)	faith, trust	fidelity, confidential

fin (Latin)	end, limit	final, finite, finish
firm (Latin)	strong, firm	confirm, affirm
ge(o) (Greek)	earth	geography, geology
gon (Greek)	angle	polygon, hexagon
grat (Latin)	pleasing, grateful	gratitude, gracious
hydr (Greek)	water	hydrant, dehydrate
loc (Latin)	place, put	locate, allocate
magn (Latin)	great, large	magnitude, magnificent
mal (Latin)	poor, inadequate	malnourished, maladjusted
misc (Latin)	mix, mingle	miscellaneous
mit (Latin)	send, soften	transmit, mitigate
neg (Latin)	deny	negative, renegade
ne(o) (Greek)	new	neonate, neophyte
omni (Latin)	all	omnivorous, omnipotent
ortho (Greek)	straight	orthodontics, orthodox
phon (Greek)	sound	phonics, phonograph
phot (Greek)	light	photograph, photo
port (Latin)	carry	export, portable
press (Latin)	press, force	pressure, repress
psych (Greek)	mind	psychology, psychosis
quest (Latin)	seek, ask	question, quest
rupt (Latin)	break	disrupt, interrupt
sci (Latin)	know	science, conscience
scribe (Latin)	write	inscribe, subscribe
sen (Latin)	old	senile, senior
sens (Latin)	feel, think	sensation, sensory
serv (Latin)	serve, save	servant, preserve
son (Latin)	sound	sonic, resonance
spec (Latin)	look, see	spectator, inspect
strict (Latin)	draw tight	constrict, restrict
tact (Latin)	touch	tactile, contact
tele (Greek)	far away, distant	telescope, telephone
ver (Latin)	true	verdict, verify
vid (Latin)	see	video, evident
voc (Latin)	voice	vocal, invoke

Key Vocabulary

accent The stress given to syllables. Accent affects the way we pronounce the vowels in long words.

accented syllables The vowels in accented syllables, also called primary accent, tend to follow the pronunciation we would expect from their placement in letter-sound patterns.

adding sounds Attaching a sound to a word, such as adding /p/ to /an/ to form /pan/ or /bee/ to /t/ to pronounce /beet/.

affixes The prefixes and suffixes attached to the beginning or end of words.

alphabetic principle The principle that, in writing, letters represent sounds and, therefore, readers can pronounce any word that is spelled the way it is pronounced.

alphabetic stage of movement toward word fluency Children are capable of reading new words by analyzing all the letter and sound patterns, and then using this information to pronounce the new words they see in text.

analogy-based phonics A phonics teaching approach in which children learn how vowels and consonants (*at, in, ap, up*) in words represent sounds (/at/ - /in/ - /ap/ - /up/) in familiar words and then use this information to read new words with the same patterns. Words that share the same pattern (*at*) belong to the same word family (*sat, hat, mat, pat, fat*).

analytic phonics Whole-to-part-to-whole phonics instruction in which children first learn a group of basic sight words with certain phonics patterns and then learn how the letter patterns in known words represent sound.

automatic stage of word reading Children instantly recognize all the words in everyday text.

base words The smallest real English words to which prefixes and suffixes are added (*play* or *elephant*, for example).

blending The ability to combine sounds into words. Children might combine onsets and rimes (/sh/ + /ip/ = /ship/) or individual phonemes (/p/ + /a/ + /n/ = /pan/).

breve (˘) A mark, ˘, placed over a vowel to show that the vowel represents a short sound, căt.

categorizing sounds Detecting the "odd" word to decide which of three or four words does not share a common sound, such as indicating that /bike/ does not belong in the sequence, /mile/ - /mop/ - /bike/.

compound words Words that are formed when two words—for example, *finger* and *print*—are glued together to create a third word—in this case, *fingerprint*.

configuration cue strategy Using word shape, word length, or unique letters to identify new words.

249

consolidated stage of movement toward word fluency   Children read new words by identifying and pronouncing meaningful and nonmeaningful multiletter chunks in words.

consonant clusters   Two or more consonants that appear together and form a consonant blend (*bl*, *tr*, *sm*, *scr*) when pronounced.

consonants   In teaching reading, we consider the consonant letters to be all the letters other than *a*, *e*, *i*, *o*, *u*, and *y* when *y* comes in the middle or at the end of a syllable.

contractions   Formed when one or more letters (and sounds) are deleted from words, with the deleted letter(s) replaced by an apostrophe—a visual clue telling readers that a word is abbreviated, as in *hasn't*, *he's*, *she'll*, and *let's*.

cross-checking strategy   Used whenever readers identify new words, this strategy involves making sure that identified words make sense in the reading context.

decodable books   Books that have an unusually high number of words that sound like they are spelled. Often these books consist of many words that represent a certain letter-sound pattern.

deleting sounds   Removing a sound from a word or syllable, such as taking the /b/ from /bit/ to pronounce /it/ or the /m/ from /seem/ to form /see/.

derivational suffixes   Word endings that change the part of speech, as in changing *read* (a verb) into *readable* (an adjective).

digraphs   Two letters that represent a sound that is different from the sounds the letters represent individually, such as *sh* (ship), *th* (thud), and *ch* (child).

diphthongs   The vowel-like sounds represented by *oy* and *oi* as heard in /boy/ and /oil/, and by *ou* and *ow* as heard in /out/ and cow/.

embedded phonics   Children learn only the phonics letter patterns they need to decode words in the books they are currently reading. Because embedded phonics uses a "teach as needed" stance, teachers and children do not follow a prescribed scope and sequence for learning phonics letter patterns.

environmental cue strategy   Associating meaning with the cues in logos, package designs, and labels in our everyday environment.

fluent reading vocabulary   The words readers recognize quickly, accurately, and effortlessly.

graphophonic cues   In this book, the letter-sound and word structure cues that help readers figure out how a word sounds and, when readers also consider the multiletter groups in word structure, perhaps word meaning.

identifying sounds   Recognizing the same sound in different words, such as indicating that /boy/ and /boat/ begin alike or that /book/ and /duck/ end alike.

incidental cues   Cues to reading new words that include word shape, length, or eye-catching letters. While these cues call for some attention to the features of written words, they do not involve using the alphabetic principle.

inflectional suffixes   Word endings that clarify word meaning or make meaning more specific, as the -*s* added to *cats* or the -*ed* added to *played*.

initial (or beginning) consonant substitution   Exchanging one beginning consonant (or onset) for another. For example, replacing the *sh* in *shade* with a *tr* to pronounce /trade/ or write *trade*.

interactive spelling   Spelling in which the teacher pronounces a word slowly, rubber bands the sounds, and encourages children to think of letters that represent each sound they hear.

invented spelling   A problem-solving stance in which words are spelled like they sound, such as *comin* for *common*.

isolating sounds   The ability to pronounce the beginning, ending, or middle sound in a word, such as saying that /man/ begins with /m/ or that /sun/ ends with /n/.

letter shape cues   Cues to word identity found in the unique shape of letters, such as the "tail" on the letter *j* in *jump* or the two "humps" in the letter *m* in *monkey*.

letter-sound patterns   Letters that routinely represent one or more sounds in words, such as the *ee* in *feet*, and *sh* and *or* in *short*.

linguistic approach   Reading materials consist of words that belong to the same word family, such as *Dan ran to the tan van to get the fan*. Children abstract their own generalizations about letter and sound relationships through reading words with the same spelling patterns, in this example the *an* pattern.

macron A mark, ‾, placed over a vowel to show that the vowel represents a long sound, lāke.

metacognitive awareness The self-awareness of what we know, how we know it, and how and when to use information. As it pertains to word identification, readers with metacognivitive awareness monitor their own reading, cross-check for meaning, and correct their own miscues.

onset The consonant(s) that comes before the vowel in a syllable or one-syllable word (the *s* in *sat* or the *ch* in *chat*).

partial alphabetic stage of movement toward word fluency The phase where children use one or two letter-sounds to recognize words.

phonemes The smallest sounds that differentiate one word from another. The /b/ in /bat/ is one phoneme, while the /h/ in /hat/ is another phoneme, as each sound differentiates one word (/bat/) from another (/hat/).

phonemic awareness The ability to think analytically about the sounds in words, and the ability to act on the basis of this analysis to separate words into sounds and to blend sounds into words.

phonetic cue strategy Recognizing words by remembering an association between a letter-sound (or a letter-name) and a written word.

phonetic spelling Spelling in which children represent all the sounds heard in words, although not always in a conventional manner.

phonetic stage of spelling Children correctly spell known words and spell new words the way they sound.

phonetically regular words Words that can be pronounced by associating sounds with letters.

phonics The systematic relationship between letters and sounds which is the principle that underpins all alphabetic languages, including English, Spanish, Arabic, French, and German, and a group of approaches to teaching these relationships.

phonogram The vowel and the consonants that come after it, such as the *an* in *man* and *can* or the *at* in *cat* and *mat*. Phonograms and rimes refer to the same letter groups inside short, one syllable words or syllables.

phonological awareness A broad term that refers to the awareness of and the ability to manipulate words, syllables, rhymes, and sounds.

picture cue strategy Inferring meaning from the illustrations in storybooks.

prealphabetic stage of movement toward word fluency Children use environmental print, pictures, and word configuration when reading. These children lack phonemic awareness, do not know letter-names (or know the names of only a few letters), and do not understand how letters represent sounds.

precommunicative stage of spelling Children whose writing shows no relationship between sounds and letters.

prefix A separate syllable attached to the beginning of words that either changes the meaning of the root word completely or makes meaning more specific.

rhyme awareness The ability to identify words that rhyme (/bad/ and /mad/), do not rhyme (bad/ and /dog/), and think of rhyming words (/bad/ - /sad/ - /had/).

rime The vowel and everything that follows it in a syllable or one-syllable word (the *at* in *sat* and *chat*).

root words Latin and Greek word parts borrowed from these two languages to form English words.

rubber banding Elongating sounds while pronouncing words, as in /mmmaaannn/. *Sound stretching* is another term for the same way of pronouncing words.

segmenting sounds Pronouncing each phoneme in the same order in which it occurs in a word, such as indicating that /mad/ consists of /m/ - /a/ - /d/.

self-correcting The process of rereading for accuracy so as to fix a previous miscue.

self-monitoring The ability to self-regulate one's own reading to be sure that it makes sense.

semantic cues Meaningful relationships among words in phrases, sentences, and paragraphs. Readers use these cues to determine whether an author's message is logical and represents real-world events and relationships.

semiphonetic stage of spelling Children spell known words conventionally, and use letters to represent some, but not all, of the important sounds in words, such as writing a *p* for *park* or *fs* for *friends*.

sight word vocabulary   Words that are recognized quickly, accurately, and effortlessly; also referred to as fluently recognized words.

sound awareness   The ability to isolate, identify, categorize, segment, add, delete, substitute, and blend sounds.

sound boxes   Connected boxes where each box represents a sound in a word.

sound stretching   Elongating sounds while pronouncing words, as in /fffiiinnn/. *Rubber banding* is another term for the same way of pronouncing words.

substituting sounds   Deleting a sound from a word, and then adding another in its place to make a different word. Examples include substituting the /n/ in /man/ for a /t/ to pronounce /mat/ or substituting the /sh/ in /ship/ for a /ch/ to pronounce /chip/.

syllable   The basic unit of pronunciation. Each syllable has one vowel sound and, perhaps, one or more consonant sounds (/o/ + /pen/ = /open/). The number of syllables in a word equals the number of vowels heard.

syntactic cues   Cues readers use to decide whether an author's word order is consistent with English grammar. Readers use these grammar-based cues to predict words in phrases and sentences.

synthetic phonics   Part-to-whole instruction where children associate sounds with letters to read, or "sound out," new words.

suffix   Usually a separate syllable attached to the end of words that changes grammatical function, makes meaning clearer, or adds information.

transitional stage of spelling   Children conventionally spell known words and, when spelling is not already memorized, children may represent sounds with incorrect letter-sound patterns or write letters in the wrong sequence.

unaccented syllables   Syllables that are not prominent in stress. Most vowels in unaccented syllables have a soft, or short, sound.

voice-print match   Connecting spoken words with written words, as demonstrated by pointing to each written word as it is read.

vowels   In teaching reading, we consider the vowel letters to be *a, e, i, o,* and *u,* and *y* when it comes in the middle (*cycle*) or at the end of a syllable or short word (*try*).

word family   A word group that shares the same rime or phonogram (*cat, rat, fat, sat, bat*).

word fluency   Fast, rapid, accurate, and effortless word recognition.

word length cues   Cues to a word's identity found in the length of words. Word length is useful only when words differ markedly in the number of letters (*hat - haircut*).

word shape cues   Cues to a word's identity found in the overall contour formed by letters that rise above, fall below, or stay on the line.

word tracking (or tracking)   Pointing to each written word as it is read aloud.

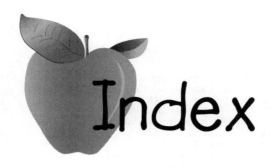

Index